Thebes in the Fifth Century

States and Cities of Ancient Greece

Edited by
R. F. WILLETTS

Argos and the Argolid   R. A. Tomlinson
The Foundations of Palatial Crete   K. Branigan
Mycenaean Greece   J. T. Hooker
The Dorian Aegean   Elizabeth M. Craik
Sparta and Lakonia   Paul Cartledge
The Ionians and Hellenism   C. J. Emlyn-Jones

Thebes in the Fifth Century
Heracles Resurgent

Nancy H. Demand

Departments of History and Classical Studies
Indiana University

Routledge & Kegan Paul
London, Boston, Melbourne and Henley

First published in 1982
by Routledge & Kegan Paul Plc
39 Store Street, London WC1E 7DD,
9 Park Street, Boston, Mass. 02108, USA,
296 Beaconsfield Parade, Middle Park,
Melbourne, 3206, Australia and
Broadway House, Newtown Road,
Henley-on-Thames, Oxon RG9 1EN
Printed in Great Britain by
The Thetford Press Ltd, Thetford, Norfolk
Copyright © Nancy Demand 1982

Library of Congress Cataloging in Publication Data

Demand, Nancy H.

Thebes in the fifth century.
(States and cities of ancient Greece)
Revision of thesis (Ph.D.)—Bryn Mawr, 1978.
Bibliography: p.
Includes index.
1. Thebes (Greece: Ancient city)   I. Title.
II. Series.
DF261.T3D45   1983   938   82-16702

ISBN 0-7100-9288-1

Contents

Plates

Preface

This book began as a doctoral dissertation, Boeotian Thebes in the Fifth Century (Bryn Mawr College, 1978). To my former supervisor, Professor Mabel Lang, I am principally indebted for its conception and early form. Professor Richard Hamilton also advised me, especially on the material about the poets, and made many helpful suggestions. The present book represents both a change in orientation and a considerable expansion of the material of the dissertation. Professors W. R. Connor, B. S. Ridgway, G. Pinney, and R. F. Willetts have read the manuscript, or portions of it, and made suggestions and comments which have led to these changes. Needless to say, they are not to be held responsible for the results, which are mine alone.

I am much indebted to Indiana University for a Summer Faculty Fellowship, which enabled me to visit Thebes and to complete my research, and to the Indiana University History Department for assistance with typing, and general support and encouragement throughout my work on revision and rewriting. Finally, I owe special thanks to my husband, Erhart, for his patience and encouragement through all the stages of this work.

Acknowledgments

The author and publishers gratefully acknowledge the assistance of the following institutions for the provision of illustrative material and for allowing it to be reproduced: Macmillan & Co., map of Boeotia; Bowdoin College Museum, plate 8; W. de Gruyter & Co., plate 9; Basel Historischen Museum, plate 2; British Museum, plate 1; Boston Museum of Fine Arts, plate 3; Athens National Museum, plate 4; Berlin Altes Museum, plate 7; Museo Archeologico, Reggio Calabria, plate 10; Thebes Museum, plate 6; Staatliche Museen, Berlin, plate 5; TAP Service, Publications, drawing of Saugenes stele; Bibliotheke Archaiologike Hetaireia, map of Thebes.

The author and publishers also wish to acknowledge the following for granting permission to quote from copyright sources: R. Lattimore's translation of Pindar, reprinted from The Odes of Pindar, by R. Lattimore by permission of the University of Chicago Press, Copyright 1947 by the University of Chicago; Sandys' translation of Pindar, reprinted from The Odes of Pindar, Sir John Sandys, tr., London, Heinemann, 1968.

1 Introduction

The fifth century in ancient Greece is familiar to us mostly through the great works of Athenian culture: the tragedies of Aeschylus, Sophocles, and Euripides; the comedies of Aristophanes; the fine Athenian vases; the Parthenon; the intellectual revolution brought about by the Sophists and Socrates; the historical works of Herodotus and Thucydides. Even Sparta, the city-state most often considered when our gaze lifts from Athens, usually is viewed as a unique and idiosyncratic opponent of Athenian virtue, rather than as one instance in a spectrum of widely varying Greek political and cultural forms. With material on Athens sufficient for more than a lifetime of enjoyment and study, and faced with the relative obscurity of the sources for other Greek cities, it is perhaps no wonder that we fall into the fallacy of equating ancient Greece with fifth-century Athens. But Greece was not only Athens, nor was all Greece, excluding Sparta, a 'cradle of democracy'. A multitude of city-states existed, in Greece itself, in Asia Minor, in southern Italy and Sicily, and on the Black Sea, all with widely varying cultures and political systems, and all just as much a part of Greek civilization as was the city of Athens.

Many of these other city-states had an oligarchic rather than a democratic form of government, and centered their lives upon the land and agriculture, as did the city of Thebes in Boeotia. While Thebes was no more representative of that non-existent entity, the typical Greek city-state of the classical period, than was Athens, nevertheless, as an agriculturally based, almost wholly self-sufficient oligarchy, it provides an interesting contrast to the naval-based democracy of Athens, with its dependence on external trade connections. The two cities perhaps represent the two poles of Greek experience, even though both were more powerful and more significant historically than most other Greek cities. In addition to its existence

as an oligarchic agricultural society, Thebes' place in
Greek history, as the power which would finally, in the
early fourth century, bring an end to Spartan military
supremacy in Greece, gives us good reason to look closely
at this particular city-state. And as we look, one
question is predominant: How was it that Thebes developed
the resources necessary to challenge Sparta with such
overwhelming success?

The fifth century in Thebes was an interim period, of
the sort not usually focused upon by traditional histories.
Its story is that of a society which was rebuilding itself
after having been defeated both materially and spiritually
in the Persian Wars - having been cast into the category
of traitor by its neighbors. In contrast, and to put the
Theban achievement into better perspective, we may consider
Athens, which had also suffered grievously from a material
point of view in the wars against the Persian invaders.
For Athens, the astounding fact of victory was the stimu-
lant which lightened the rebuilding process. Pride in
Marathon, the folklore of heroes, sparked an almost
unbounded optimism which carried the Athenian people not
only to recovery but beyond that to empire, daring
enterprise, and repeated recoveries from apparent disaster
throughout almost the entire Peloponnesian War. In
contrast, the Theban task after the Persian Wars was to
rebuild while bearing the mark of traitorous medism, to
repair and recover from both physical destruction and loss
of reputation and influence.

That the Thebans considered this task as Herculean
may be suggested by the mid-fifth-century coinage which
Thebes issued as it finally regained the hegemony over
its Boeotian neighbors. In creating their coins, Greek
states usually utilized meaningful symbols: perhaps an
ear of corn to indicate the importance of grain for an
agricultural community such as Metapontum or a dolphin
or a representation of harbor shape for sea-faring
cities, or a canting device which made an allusion,
perhaps punning, to the name of the city, or an image of
the most honored god in the city's cults. In the case of
Thebes, the device was traditionally a Boeotian shield,
a symbol shared by the cities of the Boeotian league and
representing both the league and Boeotian military
prowess. In the mid fifth century, however, the city
issued a series of coins featuring Heracles on the
reverse. (1) The hero is portrayed in a variety of
action poses: advancing into combat, stringing a bow,
triumphantly carrying off the Delphic tripod after a
victory, strangling the serpent as an infant. These coins
depicting the labors of Heracles seem especially appropri-

ate to evoke the labors which Thebes itself had recently
undergone, and to reflect the continuing determination of
the Thebans, a determination which was to lead to further
gains during the Peloponnesian War and to the eventual
broadening of its power beyond the borders of Boeotia, and,
in the fourth century, to all of Greece. Moreover, the
hero was himself an appropriate favorite for the Thebans
in another sense as well. He too had erred (even if in
madness), and had to carry out labors in recompense for
his mistake (his slavery to Omphale, in recompense for
the killing of his sons). Perhaps it is also not
irrelevant that most of his labors, including the most
famous series, resulted from the unjust jealousy and
persecution of Hera. Thus Thebes, too, labored, paying
for a mistake which it did not consider really its own
(Heracles acted in madness; Thebes came to see itself as
betrayed by a small group of unrepresentative men), and
suffering under the burden of unjust jealousy and persecution (of all the medizing cities, the onus seems to have
fallen most heavily on Thebes, placed there in large part
by the jealousy of Athens). (2)
    The qualities which made possible the recovery of Thebes
cannot be understood simply by recounting the political
and military moves which the Thebans made in the course
of this recovery. The reasons why one city, or one individual, laboriously climbs up from the abyss of failure,
while another passively succumbs, must be sought in
personality and character, rather than in outward actions
alone. A corollary of this, that even the stereotypical
image of a city, the distorted reflection of its personality in the eyes of others, exerts a powerful influence
upon actions and events, was recognized by the Athenians
in the fifth century. For Pindar, the old Attic reproach
of 'Boeotian pig' was still one worthy of lament. (3)
He was right, for it was not overcome even by his own
superb poetic abilities. Later in the century, Aristophanes' version of the stereotype was the dumb Theban of
the 'Acharnians', who is conned by the sharper-witted
Athenian into exchanging his valuable eels for a sycophant
packaged as an Athenian vase. (4) Alcibiades as a child,
rejecting the flute which prevented conversation, was
reported to have relegated it to the Thebans, on the
grounds that they could not talk anyway. (5) Even the
Theban hero Heracles appears to have undergone a meta-
morphosis during the Peloponnesian War as Athens grew
more anxious about Theban power, becoming the gluttonous
and buffoonish character of the 'Alcestis' and 'Frogs'.
(6)
    Recognizing with the Athenians the importance of image,

we must try to understand Thebes' fifth-century accomplishments in the light of a more accurate picture of its true
character, being especially concerned to correct the image
where it has been distorted. An initial jolt to the
Athenian picture of Thebes is provided by the presence of
two Thebans as Socrates' interlocutors in the 'Phaedo' of
Plato. It will be worth while to look more closely at
this apparent anomaly - philosophical Thebans - as well as
at other aspects of Theban culture. The city's poetry,
its crafts and its cults, all offer potential sources for
a clearer understanding of the spirit which was the basis
for its achievements.

The focus of this book will thus extend beyond the
usual material of political history to a broader consideration of the cultural and intellectual life of the city.
(7) We shall examine a wide range of somewhat disparate
material, including poetry, pottery, grave stelai, and
philosophical dialogues. From this material, we will
attempt to draw a coherent picture of Theban society in
the fifth century.

Working with this range of evidence, and attempting to
construct a picture of a society and to add depth to our
understanding of its history, is much like working on a
jigsaw puzzle: the hope is that the individual pieces,
which in themselves portray nothing recognizable, may,
when arranged together properly, reveal a coherent picture.
There are, of course, certain problems inherent in this
approach which must be mentioned at the outset. First of
all, there are many gaps in the available evidence, which
may distort the resultant picture, or even prevent it
from appearing. For instance, the physical city of the
fifth century is mostly buried beneath the living city
and has not been subjected to systematic excavation
(excavation has been understandably directed mainly
toward the Mycenaean remains, as well as being in the
nature of rescue operations). Literary evidence is also
fragmentary: for instance, the loss of most of the
'partheneia' of Pindar undoubtedly deprives us of much
information about Theban prosopography and cults, and
the life of Theban women. Still another problem is one
signalled by a defect in the analogy of the jigsaw puzzle.
This is the degree of imaginative interpretation necessary,
and the inevitably speculative nature of the results when
one goes beyond collecting the data and tries to make a
coherent picture out of it. Unlike the jigsaw puzzle, in
this enterprise an exact fit does not guarantee that the
piece really belongs where it has been put, nor is there
a picture on the box to verify these placements. The
problem is inevitable if one chooses to synthesize; the

question, then, is whether to synthesize. Given the
greatly increased significance and interest which the
material attains through being part of such a picture,
it seems worth while to run the risk that the picture
may be superseded by a more accurate one when (and if)
more evidence is obtained, especially since those who
reject the synthesis may still consider the data in and
for themselves.

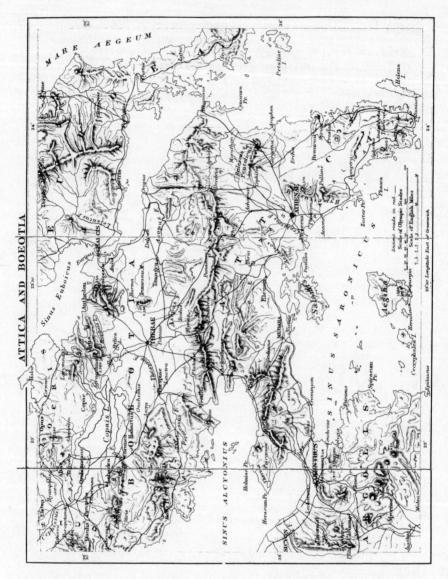

Fig.1 Map of Boeotia, with road system, from H.G. Dakyns,
Works of Xenophon, vol.1, courtesy Macmillan.

2 The city

It used to be believed that geography was destiny. This
is certainly true at least as far as the basic orientation
of a society is concerned: an inland city in an out of
the way place, poorly located for defense, will not
develop into a powerful sea - or even land - power. As
is now well recognized, however, geography is not an
inevitable determinant. Many other factors come into
play, and not least of these what one might call the
psychological aspects of character: even the best-located
city may fail to develop its full potential because of
poor leadership, poor choices, lack of a will to act, and
may squander its inherent advantages (or, as it is sometimes put, it may pursue other values). In the case of
Thebes, geographical location and the nature of the land
almost inevitably made the city into an agriculturally
based society, while its excellent strategic location
provided the promise of wider domination, a promise which
the Thebans constantly worked to bring to fruition.
These close ties between the city's situation and
character will repay a closer look at the very beginning
of our investigation of fifth-century Thebes.

Thebes is located well inland in central Boeotia, on a
low ridge of hills which separates the rich plains to the
north from the rolling but fertile land of the upper
Asopus basin to the south. (1) It thus commands fertile
farming land to both the north and the south. On all
sides the eastern Boeotian plain, in which the city is
centrally situated, is bounded by hills or mountains:
on the north, by Mt Hypatus and Ptoön, with its spur,
Sphinx Mountain (and by the lakes Iliki and Paralimni);
to the west, by the hills connecting Ptoön and Helicon;
to the east, by the Dritsa ridge; and to the south by
Mt Cithaeron and Pastra. The land enclosed in this ring
of mountains and hills is naturally isolated from its

7

neighbors beyond and lacks easy access to the sea. The
land far exceeded in ancient times what could be farmed
by the citizens of any one city, and a number of mostly
self-sufficient Boeotian communities shared in its bounty.
Perhaps because of their common Boeotian tribal origins,
and their individual self-sufficiency, none had ever
fallen into the subordinate position of perioikioi, or
'dwellers round about', as had Sparta's near neighbors
(although the smaller cities seem constantly to have
been on guard against the ambitions of Thebes), nor had
the earliest Boeotian settlers made helots of those whom
they encountered already settled upon the land, as had
Sparta with other of her neighbors. Furthermore, unlike
Attica, Boeotia as a whole never submitted to a synoikism,
or a political unification with a central capital; rather,
the cities eventually developed their early tribal and
religious ties and relationships into a federal league
while retaining their own individual character and
independence.
     The city of Thebes itself centers around a low hill
or acropolis, called the Kadmeia, which is part of the
low ridge of hills which runs east-west from the hill of
Soros (ancient Teumessus) to the foot of Mt Helicon. It
is not the highest of these hills, but it is the best
watered spot in the ridge, being surrounded by springs
and streams, from which water was carried to the Kadmeia
by underground water channel. (2) The Kadmeia itself is
pear shaped, about 750 yards long and half that in width,
and about 200 feet in elevation at the southern end and
150 at the northern. (3)
     Although the Kadmeian hill is not high, its defensive
capabilities are enhanced by the presence on the west of
the stream of the Dirke and on the east by the gully
called the 'Hollow Way'. The natural defensive features
of the site had been augmented in Mycenaean times by the
walling of the Kadmeia; the famous Seven Gates of Thebes
were situated in this wall, probably at the points of
natural access. (4) Late in the sixth century, the lower
walls were added, (5) signalling both the growth of the
city and the conflicts in which it was involved in the
consolidation of its hegemony in this period. A large
area was enclosed, extending well beyond the rivers
Dirke and Ismenos to deep defensible gullies to the east
and west. The new walls gave protection to the homes of
the Thebans, (6) who no longer lived on the Kadmeia:
that ancient citadel was now given over to the ancient
shrines of Theban history and cult, and to official
buildings. (7)
     The outer walls survived the Persian Wars and withstood

the twenty-day siege of the Greeks bent on punishing the
medism of the city. (8) At the beginning of the
Peloponnesian War they attracted the inhabitants of smaller
unwalled towns (Skolos, Erythrae, Skaphae, Aulis, Schoinos,
Potniae, and others), who moved into the city, doubling its
population. (9) During the course of the fifth century
other Boeotian cities lost their walls, sometimes thanks
to Thebes. Tanagra's wall was destroyed in 457 by the
Athenians, just before the Spartans helped the Thebans to
increase their own walls. (10) Plataea's wall was
destroyed by the Thebans after its surrender in 427 (Thuc.
3.68), and Thespiae's was destroyed by Thebes in 423
(Thuc. 4.133). It is also possible that the walls of
Orchomenos suffered damage in the earthquake of 426
(Thuc. 3.87). As these walls fell and Theban walls were
improved, the relative power of the Seven-Gated city grew
among its Boeotian neighbors.

   The flatness of the plain north of Thebes lent itself
well to the use of cavalry, and the relatively easy access
through the mountains to the north early forced upon Thebes
the development of this type of warfare, since the city
was subject to the incursions of Thessalian cavalry forces
by this route. Aristotle pointed out the political
implications of such a situation:

>   When the country is adapted for cavalry, then a strong
>   oligarchy is likely to be established. For the
>   security of the inhabitants depends upon a force of
>   this sort, and only rich men can afford to keep horses.
>   (Aristotle, 'Pol.' 1321a9-12, tr. Jowett)

   The Theban oligarchy was relatively stable - for Greece,
one might say that it was exceptionally stable. There is
little to suggest the sort of internal conflict, or stasis,
which often led the citizens of other Greek cities to
conspire with outsiders. It may be the case that Athens
gained control of the city in 457 through the exploitation
of stasis, although there is no real evidence for this,
aside from the unlikelihood that they could have gained
control of the strongly fortified city otherwise, without
a major siege. After the fact, an extreme faction was
credited with forcing a policy of medism upon the city
during the Persian Wars; and following the Peloponnesian
War (and possibly for a considerable time earlier) there
was political division between pro- and anti-Lacedaemonian
parties, which may have more or less paralyzed effective
action in either direction, but which did not go so far as
conspiracy with outsiders. (11) This amounts to very
little evidence for stasis in comparison with the active
factionalism which dominated the politics of so many Greek
cities in the fifth century. The only real threat to

Theban political stability in the fifth century very likely
occurred during the period of Athenian domination of
Boeotia, when Athens probably supported its own sympathizers
for positions of political importance in the city. The law,
reported by Aristotle, (12) which limited the holding of
office to those who had not sold in the agora for ten years
may have been passed in order to remove political power from
such 'new men' after the expulsion of the Athenians.

The reason for the unusual political stability of Thebes
was undoubtedly its economic stability. The economy of
Thebes was predominantly agricultural, and the agricultural
production was abundant. That Thebans ate well was the
essence of the Theban stereotype fostered by its less well-
endowed neighbors and epitomized in the charge, 'Boeotian
pig'. (13) In the fifth century, this agricultural bounty
was used primarily for home consumption. Some Boeotian
delicacies did find their way to the Athenian gourmet, (14)
but the provision of eels and wild birds and game to the
Athenian market was probably only a casual and occasional
occupation. Some Theban chariots may have been made for
export, (15) and a few pieces of Theban pottery turn up
here and there, although these were probably carried by
casual travellers, and not by traders. Reed mats, wicks
and flutes are other possibilities as minor items of
trade, (16) but on the whole fifth-century Thebes was not
actively involved in trade on a scale which affected its
fundamental outlook on life or its basic social structure.
There apparently was an abundance of food for all, and thus
little need to look elsewhere.

Much has been written on both sides of the question of
the suitability for trade of the geographical situation
of Thebes. (17) The city's inland location led to
considerable skepticism about its potential as a trading
site; it seems clear now, however, that the geographical
difficulties have at times been overstated. (18) Although
its geographical situation did not push Thebes in the
direction of trade, it obviously was not an unsurmountable
obstacle. Hence the explanation for the lack of activity
on the part of fifth-century Thebans in trade must lie
elsewhere. Relative abundance of food supply, combined
with the predominance of well-to-do landed families within
the political and social structure, offers the best
explanation. It was not the case that wealthy Thebans
were adverse to travelling: some of them must have
travelled much of the time in order to participate in as
many games and contests as they did. (19) It was, rather,
that the wealthy (the major candidates for travel)
disdained travel for trade, with a sure instinct for the
inevitable social and political changes that extensive

trade would bring about. Hesiod, although only a first-
generation Boeotian and seemingly not a wealthy man
(although certainly not a poor man), offers a good
example of the Boeotian attitude toward sailing and trade:
if his brother is so foolish as to want to gain a quick
profit by trade, Hesiod can offer him the traditional
lore about seamanship, passed down through the poet's
craft, but he himself wants as little as possible to do
with boats, sailing, or trade (he stresses that his only
sea voyage was for the proper aristocratic purpose of
participating in a contest at funeral games for a king).
(20)
    Not only the Boeotians, but landed aristocrats everywhere
in Greece, saw the ideal life as one of self-sufficient
farming. Even in Athens, where the sea became the first
line of supply and defense in the fifth-century, and where
the resulting richness of life was clearly apparent, strong
opposition to naval and trading interests continued to
thrive among conservatives (whose actions may not have
matched their words in every case) throughout the fifth
century. (21)
    Although Thebes enjoyed a position of self-sufficiency
in its economy, and evidently felt no economic or political
need to go beyond the borders of Boeotia, within the
Boeotian sphere the situation was entirely different. The
first impression which one receives on looking at a map of
ancient Boeotia is that Thebes was the center of a network
of roads radiating outward in all directions. This central
location and the ease of movement within Boeotia itself
created by this ancient road network (basically an
enhancement of natural routes) were vital factors in
continually fostering Theban ambitions for hegemony among
the Boeotian cities. The central location gave the
advantage of protection against unexpected attack by
outsiders, and it also made it possible for Thebes to
give swift aid to the other Boeotian cities against both
external and internal threats. The ability to offer
protection was a major factor in attracting the allegiance
of smaller cities (as Herodotus makes clear in his account
of the origins of Plataea's alliance with Athens, Hdt.
6.108). (22) That Thebes exploited this potential and
often played the role of protector and champion was
demonstrated several times during the Peloponnesian War.
In 426 the Thebans went to the assistance of the Tanagrans
when they were attacked by Athens (Thuc. 3.91); in 414
they moved to suppress a democratic uprising in Thespiae
(Thuc. 6.95); and in 413 they drove off the Thracians who
had attacked and massacred the inhabitants of Mycalessos,
recovering the plunder and killing at least some of the

attackers (Thuc. 7.29). Each time Thebes succeeded in
protecting or avenging its neighbors, its value as an ally
was enhanced. Neither of Thebes' potential rivals for
Boeotian ascendancy could boast a similar central position
and potential: Orchomenos was virtually a border city,
and Tanagra lacked the central position within an extensive
road network which Thebes possessed.

The fifth-century city of Thebes in its physical makeup
was rather typical of classical Greek cities. The city
centered upon an ancient walled acropolis, whose defensive
functions had been shifted to new outer walls, and which
now served as a ceremonial center, given up to shrines,
especially those reflecting the earliest traditions of the
city. Thus the Kadmeia contained the ruins of the old
Mycenaean palace, interpreted as the 'House of Kadmos',
the shrines and temples of Aphrodite, Demeter Thesmophoria,
Zeus Ammon, Zeus Hypsistos, and the bird observatory of
Teiresias the prophet. Certain important governmental
functions also kept their home on the Kadmeia; thus we
find that the Theban Council met on the Kadmeia (much as
the Council of the Areopagus at Athens met on the Areopagus
rock adjacent to the Acropolis). (23)

The residential quarters in the fifth-century were
located in the lower city, which today also is primarily
residential. The population appears to have been dispersed
throughout the area encompassed by the outer walls, even
spilling out into the unwalled area to the south (which
may have been the location of the Spartan-assisted effort
to extend the lower walls in 457). (24) The archaeological
finds give no signs of large concentrations of people, and
some clusters of burials suggest individual family
cemeteries, probably located on ancestral plots. (25)
This fits in well with evidence from other sources: the
ability of Thebes to sustain a doubled population after
the influx of refugees during the Peloponnesian War also
suggests thinly dispersed homesteads, (26) while Herodotus
9.41 implies that the area within the outer walls was
also used for cultivation early in the century.

In the midst of these residential areas (as well as on
the Kadmeia, in the agora, and associated with the
gymnasia) were numerous shrines, temples, and holy spots
mostly dedicated to local deities and heroes. (27) On
the east side of the lower city stood the temple of
Dionysos, the House of Lykos, the memorial of Semele, the
stone of Alkmene, and the tombs of Melanippos, Tydaeus,
Hector, Asphodikos, and the children of Oedipus. On the
west side of the lower city were located the temples of
Themis, the Muses, and Zeus Agoraios, as well as numerous
other shrines and holy spots, including the spring of

Dirke. It was in this western area that Pindar lived,
near the shrine of the Mother of the Gods. The small
hill to the north of the Kadmeia was considered to be the
tomb of the founders, Amphion and Zethos. Outside the
lower walls there were many more holy spots, as well as
two major shrines: to the south, the temple of Heracles
with its stadium and gymnasium, and to the southeast, the
temple of Apollo Ismenos.

Two major institutions of a classical Greek city - its
agora and its gymnasium - were located on the east side
of the lower city (a second gymnasium, that of Heracles,
was outside the walls to the south). It is these institutions which reveal most clearly the differences between
classical and modern culture, and for this reason, perhaps
it will be useful to consider them in a comparative
context. (28)

The ancient Greek agora was a large open space which
served as a meeting place, market place, and civic center.
It was physically defined by its stoas, offering shelter
and shade, temples, and other civic buildings, and adorned
with statues and shrines. The Theban agora contained the
shrines of Artemis Eukleia, Apollo Rescuer, Athena Girder,
and Hermes Agoraios (Paus. 9.17.2-3). (29) After the
battle of Delion, the city of Thebes celebrated by adding
a great new stoa to its agora, embellishing it with bronze
statues and with the spoils of victory (Diod. 12.70). In
the agora men could while away their time, engage in
conversations ranging from gossip to philosophical
discussion, learn the news, eat a snack, shop, pay
reverence to a favorite deity, carry on the business of
the city, all in surroundings which intermingled civic,
religious, and commercial elements.

What is it that fulfils the function of the agora in
Thebes today? As in many small Greek towns, it is the
coffee-house, with adjoining street. A recent 'New York
Times' article, speaking of the coffee-house as an
endangered species, called it 'a den of male chauvinism,
political debate and petty gambling.... It is at the
village kafeneion that patrons would debate their problems,
listen to an announcement by the mayor or receive the
civil servant sent from Athens. For the illiterate, it
would be the place where newspapers could be read aloud
or a television provided before sets became common house-
hold property'. (30) While serving many of the same
purposes as the agora, unlike the agora, the coffee-house
is a small, private, and confined space. It is true that
it opens out into the public street, but the modern street
is mainly a passageway through commercial establishments,
for the convenience of vehicles first and foremost. The

street does provide pedestrians with a way to move from
one shop or business appointment to another, but it does
not offer shelter or inviting spaces for relaxation and
conversation, as did the agora. In the evenings, however,
especially on the weekend, the Thebans turn their main
street into a promenade, and then it serves, in some
manner, one of the functions of the ancient agora. Both
the coffee-house and the street are, however, basically
commercial; neither offers the aesthetic interests, nor
the civic and religious aspects, which were the major
components of the ancient agora. Neither defines a
comfortable space, with shade and shelter, open to all.

A second basic institution of the classical Greek city
was the gymnasium and its complex of related spaces and
buildings. Thebes had two gymnasia, that of Iolaos,
within the walls of the lower city (probably dating from
before these walls), and that of Heracles, outside the
walls to the south. The ancient gymnasium offered males
of all ages a place to gather and talk while enjoying
exercise and bathing. It also served important educational
functions, both informally and formally. On the informal
level, it was a place where youths and adults naturally
mingled with each other in sports, offering ample opportunity for the formation of those pederastic friendships
by which boys were initiated into the values of the adult
culture (traditionally, such lovers took vows at the altar
of Iolaos, whose friendship with Heracles provided a role
model for young Thebans). (31) On the formal level,
gymnasia and their adjacent grounds were used for military
training and drill, and teachers offered lectures within
the gymnasium colonnades. We can imagine Plato's
Pythagorean Thebans learning their philosophy in such a
setting. All this took place in pleasant, green
surroundings, offering fresh water and shade (only in
Hellenistic times did Greek gymnasia move into the city
center and lose their rural attributes).

In Thebes today, nothing seems to have replaced the
gymnasium as a place of exercise (the city has a modern
stadium, which offers spectators the chance to watch
others exercise). In larger cities, there are of course
private clubs and YMCAs and YWCAs. Some of the educational
functions have been taken over by the secondary school -
although such schools segregate the age groups rather
than integrating them. For military training, there is
the army, which again separates and segregates a certain
age group from the general society.

This comparison between the ancient city, with its agora
and gymnasia, and the modern city, highlights some of the
values of Greek civilization which have long been praised

by modern cities. It is true that in many ways life must
have been pleasanter for Theban males in the fifth century
that it is today, and that real human needs were perhaps
better met, for this group at least. But we should not
forget a factor which has in fact often been overlooked:
these advantages were extended only to males and not to
their female counterparts. Women did not enjoy the
benefits of the agora or the gymnasium - and, since they
were the caretakers of the home, they also suffered more
than did men from the inconveniences in domestic arrange-
ments which existed.

In summary, the fifth-century city of Thebes was centrally
located within the fertile plains of Boeotia, in a position
of natural strength which was enhanced by notable walls.
Its agriculturally based economy provided ample supplies
of food for its people, and it engaged in little trade.
In its inland position and isolated self-sufficiency it
could have served as a prototype of the oligarchic ideal,
as expressed by Plato in the 'Laws' (704Bff.). Plato's
city would be set inland also - the presence of good
harbors eighty stadia away is distressing to Plato, but
at least there is some protective distance:
> Had it to be on the coast, well furnished with harbors
> and ill off for many of its necessaries, not productive
> of all, we should need a mighty protector and lawgivers
> who were more than men to prevent the development of
> much refined vice.... ('Laws', 704D, tr. A.E. Taylor)
(Fortunately, Plato's site also lacked pine and cypress,
the materials of boat building, a further protection
against the contamination of commerce. Today Thebes is
not possessed of such assets either, and probably was not
in antiquity either.) The internal government of Thebes
was indeed an oligarchy, which was joined to its Boeotian
neighbors in a loose federation, over which it continually
sought to extend its control. Its public buildings and
institutions (agora, gymnasia, shrines, and temples) were
those of a typical Greek city.
  Nothing in this brief background sketch, however,
reveals the unique characteristics of the city. To see
these, and to appreciate its personality and the use it
made of its physical assets, we need to consider in detail
its history and its cults, its music and the products of
its craftsmen.

3 Theban political and military history during the fifth century

THEBAN POLITICAL STRUCTURE

The political structure of Thebes was oligarchic, requiring
a property qualification for full citizenship. We have
some evidence for a fairly broadly based oligarchy in the
late fifth century in a speech of the Thebans at Plataea
as reported by Thucydides. In this speech, the Thebans
argue that the city itself was not responsible for its
medism, since it was in the hands of a small clique of men
at the time, and did not enjoy its usual isonomic
oligarchy:

> Our city happened then to be neither an oligarchy giving
> equal rights before the law (an 'oligarchia isonomos'),
> nor a democracy; it was rather what is farthest from
> law and moderation, a small group of men holding control
> of affairs (a 'dynasteia'). (Thuc. 3.62)

Isonomia was a political principle implying equality of
political rights for full citizens. (2) In Thebes, it
seems most probable that property sufficient to qualify
one as a hoplite warrior was the minimum required also to
qualify as a full citizen. (3) This meant that about one
third of the total number of male citizens enjoyed the
benefits of full citizenship, which included eligibility
for office; whether those who failed to meet the property
qualification had the right to vote for the election of
their officials is not known. (4) Any full citizen was,
however, eligible for membership in one of the four
councils, each of which acted in turn as the executive
body, preparing matters which would be discussed by all
four councils (all four councils had to approve before
any action could be taken). (5) Isonomia refers then to
the equal opportunity of every full citizen to be a member
of a council and thus to participate in official decision-
making, as well as to serve in office if elected.

As an oligarchic state, Thebes was one among a large
group of Greek states which had varying forms of
oligarchic constitution; some of the others were Corinth,
Megara (after 424), Elis, Chios, Lesbos, Opuntian Locri,
Epizephyrian Locri, Croton, Rhegium, Acragas, Colophon,
Cyme, Massalia, and Epidauros. States of course sometimes
changed their constitutions, going from democratic to
oligarchic, or vice versa; often this occurred as the
result of changes in political loyalties, as when states
which allied themselves - or were conquered by - democratic
Athens themselves became democracies (as Thebes itself
was to do once for a short period when under Athenian
domination). Such changes and developments in constitution
and political form as occurred in Thebes can, however, best
be viewed in the context of a consideration of the political
and military history of the city.

EARLY HISTORY AND THE ORIGINS OF THE BOEOTIAN LEAGUE

Thebes was among the palace sites of Mycenaean Greece, a
city whose past is reflected in the ivories, seals, linear
B inscriptions and jewelry of the museum in Thebes, as
well as in the mythological traditions which were given new
life in the plays of the Athenian tragedians. We do not
know what befell the city during the collapse of Mycenaean
civilization and in the dark period which followed, but
the insignificance of Thebes in the Homeric 'Catalogue of
Ships' suggests that the city underwent a fairly extensive
eclipse (Boeotia is, however, well represented in the
epic tradition, as well as in the 'Catalogue'). By the
sixth century, however, Thebes appears to have become the
predominent power in a loose federation of Boeotian cities,
and to have also become involved in political maneuverings
beyond the borders of Boeotia. (6)
    The nature of this early Boeotian federation is by no
means clear. The best evidence for the league at any
period consists in an account of its form in 395 BC, which
is contained in a papyrus fragment of the work of an
unknown historian, called by the uninspiring name P. (7)
P tells us that in 395 Boeotia was divided into eleven
districts according to population. Each of these districts
supplied one Boeotarch, 60 Bouleutai for a federal council
(which was divided into four sections, as were the councils
of the cities, each section taking a turn at acting as
Probouloi), (8) and a corps of approximately 1,000 hoplites
and 100 horsemen. The citizens of each district were in
turn divided into four divisions or councils for local
administration, as we have noted in Thebes. Thebes,

Orchomenos (with Hyettos), (9) and Thespiae (with Eutresis
and Thisbae) each comprised two districts; Tanagra formed
one district; while Haliartos, Lebadea and Coronea formed
another, as did Acraephium, Copai and Chaeronea.   In 395
Plataea, Scolos, Erythrae, Scaphae, and some unidentified
other towns were allotted two districts which were under
Theban control.

There is general agreement among scholars that this
same constitution, with variations in the assignments of
districts, (10) was in effect from about 447 BC. (11)
Recently, however, R.J. Buck has claimed that this formal
organization went back to the period of the early federation in the sixth century. (12) Before we can evaluate
this new theory, however, we should consider the other
possible evidence for the early league.

There are passages in both Herodotus and Thucydides
which suggest the existence of some sort of league before
the fifth century, with Thebes in a predominant position,
or at least asserting a claim to such a position.   Thus
Herodotus reports that in 519 (or 509) the Corinthians
assisted the Plataeans against the Thebans when the
Plataeans wanted to escape from Boeotian ties; (13) he
also tells us that in 507 the Thebans asserted that the
peoples closest to them - the men of Tanagra, Coronea,
and Thespiae - had always fought on their side (5.79).
The problem which exists in evaluating this Herodotean
evidence is brought out, however, by the probability
that Herodotus in this passage is anachronistic, reflecting
conditions in Greece after the outbreak of the Peloponnesian War: it was only at this .time that Tanagra could
have been said to have been 'closest' to Thebes; before
447, Haliartos would have been among the three closest.
Similarly, Herodotus' casual interchanging of the terms
'Boeotian' and 'Theban', and his references to
Boeotarchs, appear to be anachronistic reflections of
his own times. (14)

Unfortunately, the evidence from Thucydides is no more
secure. At 3.61ff. the Thebans are portrayed making the
claim that they were the ones who settled the land of
Boeotia, founded Plataea, and held early supremacy. This
claim, however, occurs in the context of a highly
rhetorical speech, and cannot be taken at face value
(although it may none the less have had a certain foundation at least in accepted belief, or it would not have
been thought persuasive).

Both Herodotus and Thucydides reflect fifth-century
views and political positions, and must, therefore, be
used with caution. The existence of a 'federal' coinage
may seem to offer a firmer foundation. (15) The earliest

such league coinage is Head's Type I: Aeginetic drachmas and smaller divisions issued by Thebes, Haliartos and Tanagra, all bearing the shield of Heracles and now dated 550-525. (16) Head's Type II, which bear the shield and an initial of the issuing or sponsoring city on the mill-sail reverse (Acraephium, Coronea, Haliartos, Mycalessus, Pharae, Tanagra, and Thebes are represented) is now dated 'perhaps well after' 519, because of the absence of coins from Plataea. (17) Unfortunately, we cannot really fathom the significance of these coins: does the shield indicate a formal league, (18) and if so, what are the details of its organization? What does the difference between Type I and Type II signify in terms of league structure (if anything)? Which (if any) is the predominant city, and what does this predominance amount to?

The ancient evidence thus leaves us with an inadequate foundation upon which to construct a picture of the Boeotian league before the fifth century, and the creation of such a picture involves an inevitable resort to many probabilities. This brings us back to Buck's proposal to extend the formal league structure evidenced in 395 back to the sixth century. Arguing that the league was created by a deliberate act of formal constitution in 520/519, perhaps in response to the threat of a Thessalian invasion, Buck relies upon an a priori assumption to project the formal structure of the fourth century back into the sixth: the proportion of 60 councillors to each Boeotarch is odd enough to date back to the beginning of the league, as is the quadripartite division found later in the fifth century, and into the fourth century. (19) This, however, is a matter of probability, and it is just as probable (in fact, as I will argue below, it is more probable) that the oddness of the number 60 and the quadripartite division are marks of sophisticated rather than primitive thinking. Thus Buck's reconstruction fails to be convincing.

Most scholars are in fact agreed in holding the view that the early league was not created by fiat at some definite date, but grew up gradually and naturally from early local, ethnic, and religious ties. (20) According to this view of the league, its various member states held varying statuses according to their own particular situations and relationships at any given time, with Thebes often asserting a claim to ascendancy, an ascendancy which (if it was more than a mere claim), probably amounted at best to a position of first among equals. (21) Since such a league would not have been a formally constituted body with a complex system of representation, but a loose and informal grouping developed out of long-standing ties and relationships determined mainly by the resources and

character of the land itself and by ethnic and religious
ties, it would not have been the sort of political
grouping which would have been formally dissolved even by
such a catastrophe as defeat in the Persian Wars of its
principal members. And, in fact, the continued minting
of 'federal' coinage (Head's Type III, with coins struck
at Tanagra in the name of the Boeotians, dated 480-457)
demonstrates that at least some Boeotians did continue
to think of themselves as a group with common interests
after the war, and that this grouping survived and adapted
itself to the temporary eclipse of its natural leader.
(22) (This interim period, during which some sort of
league apparently continued to exist, is another argument
against the theory that the fourth-century structure went
back to the sixth century: it seems highly unlikely that
an elaborate structure such as characterized this later
league could have been preserved intact throughout the
period of upheaval in Boeotia following the war, as a
looser 'natural' grouping might.)

THE PERSIAN WARS

The problems which Thebes had with Plataea, and possibly
with other recalcitrant Boeotian communities, at the end
of the sixth century as that city tried to establish its
leadership of Boeotia were soon completely overshadowed
by the threat and the reality of the Persian invasion in
the early fifth century. Thebes' decision to medize had
long-range consequences for the city, and therefore it
is worth while to consider the period and its events
closely.
     The decision of Thebes to medize, and the fact of its
actual support of the Persian cause, have never been in
question, but the timing of the Theban decision, the
actual role played by Thebes in various aspects of the
war, and the responsibility for the policy of medism,
have all been subject to dispute, even in antiquity. A
good example of such dispute involves the earliest Theban
action connected with the war which is recorded by our
sources: the participation of 500 Thebans under the
command of Mnamias in the abortive Thessalian expedition
of 480. (23) The very existence of this expedition has
been called into question by modern scholars, (24) mainly
because the reasons given by Herodotus for the abrupt
abandonment of a major expedition - that Alexander of
Macedon sent word to them about the size of Xerxes'
expedition, or (in Herodotus' own judgment) informed them
about the existence of other routes south by which Tempe

could be turned - have never seemed adequate or convincing.
Yet to believe that the report of an expedition of this
size would have been completely fabricated (or even
elaborated from a minor mission) as early as Herodotus,
who lived within the lifetime of those who would have taken
part or known participants, is hardly reasonable. It seems
that we must accept the fact of the Thessalian expedition
more or less as Herodotus describes it, although we need
not accept the reasons he offers for its termination (he
himself was apparently not satisfied with the information
which he had received on this point, and offers his own
hypothesis). (25) As for the participation of 500 Thebans
in this expedition, our only source is Plutarch in 'De
Herodoti malignitate' 31 (864D). Plutarch does not name
his source, but since he gives the name of the commander,
he may here have been citing Aristophanes of Boeotia, whom
he elsewhere cites (866F) as having used an official list
of magistrates. While no other source mentions this
contingent, Ephorus does tell us that the Boeotians medized
only after the expedition had left Tempe; (26) for the
Thebans, with the decision to medize not yet taken, interest
in stopping the Persians in Thessaly would have been great.
Thus, given the citing of the leader's name, (27) possibly
from official records, and the degree to which Theban
interests were involved, it seems best to accept the
existence of a Theban contingent.

The Theban decision to medize in fact seems to have been
made at some time during the turmoil which accompanied the
battle of Thermopylae. When the Greek forces were being
called out to take a stand at Thermopylae, the Thebans were
divided among themselves about participation and sent only
a relatively small group of 400 from among the 'opposition
party', presumably the party which opposed medism. This,
at least, is how Diodorus describes the situation (11.4.7).
Herodotus has a somewhat different version (7.205). He
says that Leonidas asked the Thebans for troops in order
to test them, since accusations of medism had been brought
against them. The Thebans sent men, but, Herodotus adds
somewhat ominously, they had other things in mind. I
think that here we can fairly dismiss Herodotus' insight
into the minds of the Thebans as an unwarrented editorial
inference. Even the motive attributed to Leonidas in
asking Theban help seems questionable; the man did not
need a special motive to cause him to ask for troops from
Thebes, and in levying his forces he undoubtedly faced the
task of convincing many dubious and reluctant people
besides those in Thebes. Perhaps the important point is
that in this account Herodotus contradicts his later claim
that the men were present at Thermopylae as hostages, for

it is part of his story here that they *seemed* to go
willingly, keeping to themselves their other thoughts.
(Leonidas could have converted them into hostages later
when he saw that their hearts were not with him, but why
would he have treated them differently from the other
Greeks who were also wavering in spirit and whom he sent
away (8.220)?) (28)

The Thebans evidently fought until the situation was in
fact hopeless. Herodotus portrays with some relish their
disgraceful surrender, after they had deserted the
Lacedaemonians and Thespians as these took up their suicide
stand (8.225). He moralized that even so, the Thebans did
not all fare well, for some were killed as they tried to
surrender, and some others, including Leontiades, suffered
branding with the mark of the Great King. Plutarch
questions the branding, on the grounds that it was never
mentioned before Herodotus; does he then have access to a
fifth-century source earlier than Herodotus? Other later
sources available to us also do not mention the branding,
or even the presence of the Thebans in the final encounter.
Diodorus says nothing about the Thebans being detained for
the battle; he reports only that the Thespians remained
with the Spartans (11.9.2). Pausanias adds 80 Mycenaeans
to the Greek force, but says nothing of the presence of
Thebans. (29) Finally, Herodotus' account is thrown into
doubt by the report of Plutarch, resting on the evidence
of Aristophanes, who had here used the archon lists, and
Nicander of Colophon, that the leader of the Theban
contingent was not Leontiades but Anaxandros, (30) Perhaps
a conjecture would not be out of order here. Herodotus
singles out Leontiades not only as the leader but as among
those who were branded. The family of Leontiades was one
of the most important in Thebes, if we can judge from
Thucydides' comment about his son in the later fifth
century (2.2); we may, therefore, suppose that Leontiades
had been a fairly visible person in Thebes. It is possible
that he bore a scar from this battle (in which he was
probably too young to hold command), and that this scar
was referred to as a mark of the Great King. Such talk
could account for Herodotus' assumption that he had led
the Theban troops, as well as for the story of the
branding.

With the decisive Greek defeat at Thermopylae, the city
of Thebes set itself upon a clear path of support for the
Persian cause. It is hard to imagine what other path they
could choose, short of mass suicide. According to
Herodotus, the Thebans offered a conspicuous welcome to
the Macedonian commanders as a visible signal to Xerxes
of their medism. Did they also bring about the destruction

of Thespiae and Plataea by denouncing these cities to the
Persians, as Herodotus says (8.50)? We cannot be sure of
the actual role played by the Thebans in this, but the
Persians themselves surely already knew of the hostility
of these two cities, whose men they had faced at Marathon
and at Thermopylae, and there was no need of Theban
denunciations to spark the idea of punishment in their
minds. It is therefore difficult to accept Herodotus'
claim that the Thebans caused these destructions, although
we can assume, I think, that few dissenting voices would
have been raised, and even that some of the Thebans might
not have been above offering encouragement.

After the Persian defeat at Salamis and the departure
of Xerxes, the remaining Persian forces under Mardonius
withdrew to winter in Thessaly. At this time Mardonius
sent out a Carian by the name of Mys to consult the
oracles in the Boeotian region, among them the Theban
oracles of Amphiarios and the Ismenian Apollo, as well as
the oracle of Apollo at Ptoion, which Herodotus tells us
was then under Theban control (8.133-5). Mardonius'
motive may have been to test the extent to which the pro-
Persian sentiments of the Boeotians had survived the
Persian defeat and the exodus of the Great King.
(Herodotus does not know the information which Mardonius
sought, but suggests that it was about the current state
of affairs and not about future events.) In the course
of these consultations, the oracle of Apollo at Ptoion
created a sensation by speaking to Mys in his own Carian
tongue, (31) baffling the Thebans. Since, shortly after
Mys' return, Mardonius sent Alexander of Macedon as an
ambassador to Athens, Herodotus surmises that the message
which Ptoion had deliberately concealed from the Thebans
had directed Mardonius to seek to gain the alliance of
the Athenians. The message could as well have been a
gloomy prognosis for the Persian military effort, leading
Mardonius to shift to negotiations: Plutarch's version
of the consultations included not only the Carian Mys,
but also a Lydian who received an unpromising response
from the oracle of Amphiarios. (32)

When the attempt at negotiations with the Athenians
failed, Mardonius set out again with his army to retake
that city, gathering troops as he went. When he reached
Thebes, Herodotus reports that the Thebans tried to
persuade him to station his forces there, and to abandon
the policy of open warfare for subversion of the Greeks
by gold, exploiting the political divisions and animosi-
ties within the cities (9.3). This suggestion has an
anachronistic air about it; (33) one wonders what
Herodotus' source could have been, since Mardonius rejected

the idea. There might be some element of truth behind it,
however, since Herodotus attributes a similar idea to
Artabazos (9.4), and Diodorus (11.28) says that Mardonius
actually sent money to men in some Peloponnesian cities,
although he does not name Thebes as an instigator. The
actual receipt of money by individuals would have been
noticed quickly in these small cities, and the accusation
passed down in local gossip; Diodorus does here appear
to have different sources from Herodotus. Nevertheless,
Herodotus says nothing about any such actual subversion,
but only reports a rejected suggestion. His account thus
looks suspiciously like an attempt to cast aspersions upon
the name of Thebes.

Some Thebans probably took part in Mardonius' expedition
to Athens, during which he seized the abandoned city and
further devastated it. The Persians soon withdrew again
to Boeotia, however, having received a message from the
Argives that the Lacedaemonians were on the march. When
Mardonius reached Theban territory again, he set out to
build a fortification for his camp which could also serve
as a place of refuge in case of defeat (Hdt. 9.15, 65).
To obtain material for this stockade, he cut down the
trees, including fruit trees, thus beginning the destruction
of Theban property with which the war was to end. Herodotus
stresses that Mardonius did this from necessity, and not
because of any anti-Persian activities on the part of the
Thebans, thus forestalling any danger that his audience
might suspect that the Thebans were less than 100 per cent
behind the Persian cause. Ironically, in doing this he
also focuses attention upon the uneven nature of an
alliance between a small city and a great power, and its
uncertain value for the weaker party. It is interesting,
though perhaps not intentional, that the same point is
implicit in the very next section of Herodotus' narrative,
in which he recounts the story told him by Thersander of
Orchomenos (9.16). This story is interesting for several
reasons, but especially in this context because it does
so closely echo the idea of the helpless subjection of
those living under a despotic power and the price which
was paid for the acceptance of Persian overlordship.
Thersander's dinner companion, one among 50 Persians
invited to this dinner by the Thebans and thus presumably
a high ranking figure, foresees the defeat of the Persian
army, yet he can do nothing to prevent it: 'Whatever is
to come from the god, man cannot prevent, for no one is
willing to listen to reason. Knowing full well what will
happen, we Persians follow along, bound by necessity.
The worst anguish for a man is to know what is going to
happen, and yet to be unable to do anything about it'. In

part, the Persian attributes his helplessness to the
inevitability of the decrees of the gods, yet in this
case, the instrument of that destiny is the leader who is
unwilling to listen, which the Persian also realizes.
Herodotus makes much of this story, undoubtedly seeing in
it some of his own favorite convictions; in particular,
it is a form of the Tragic Warner pattern, (34) and fore-
shadows the more explicit Warner played by Artabazus at
9.41. Herodotus stresses the reliability of Thersander's
story by naming his informant twice, and adding the
information that Thersander had told the story to others
before the battle of Plataea. Thus he emphasizes the
importance he lays upon the story as a well-attested
instance of precognition (part of the Warner pattern).
The story is also interesting for the more pedestrian
information which it conveys: for its portrayal of social
relations between the Boeotians and the Persians (with the
possible moral slur cast upon Thebans who lolled about in
eastern luxury while the loyal Greeks fought and died for
their freedom), and for the number of high ranking Boeotian
collaborators which it attests (although here the numbers
are suspiciously round); for its demonstration of Herodotus'
loose use of the term 'Theban' (not all the 50 Thebans were
in fact from that city - at least one was an Orchomenian);
and, finally, for its demonstration that not all the main
Boeotian collaborators suffered execution after the war.
    The Thebans fought vigorously on the side of the Persians
at Plataea, losing 300 men (Hdt. 9.67, 69), but it must not
be overlooked that they were in effect fighting on their own
territory and for their own survival. It was no longer a
matter of sending a representative contingent. In the final
rout, the Thebans took refuge within their own walls while
most of the Persians sought the protection of their camp and
stockade; Artabazus (the Warner) headed toward Phokis and
from there escaped to the Hellespont with his men. The
Greeks succeeded in breaking into the Persian defenses, and
a great slaughter followed.
    Once the Persians were disposed of, the Greeks turned to
the punishment of the Thebans (Hdt. 9.86-88). They marched
upon the city, demanding the surrender of the leaders, and
especially those foremost among them, Attiginos and
Timagenides. When the Thebans refused, the allied Greeks
replied that they would then take the city, and they laid
siege and began ravaging the land. On the twentieth day
the Theban leaders offered to give themselves up, expecting,
as Herodotus says, to be put on trial, and trusting that
they would be able to bribe their way out. Herodotus puts
the rationale behind the surrender into the mouth of
Timagenides, into whose speech he has carefully worked a

refutation of the argument (seen from Thucydides 3.62 to
have been current among the Thebans in the later fifth
century) that only the leaders, and not the Theban people
as a whole, had been responsible for the medizing. An
unspecified number of men were delivered up to the Greeks
as leaders of the medizing; Pausanias spirited them off
to Corinth and an irregular and apparently illegal
execution, without benefit of trial. Attaginos somehow
had managed to escape, and so his sons were offered in his
place, but Pausanias refused to extend the punishment to
children who were innocent of the guilt of medizing. This
does seem to suggest that the great majority of the Theban
adults, who also escaped punishment, were considered in
some sense as innocent victims as well, but probably the
realities of Greek maneuverings for balance of power
provided the real basis for the escape of the ordinary
Thebans from destruction or enslavement.

Thus ended Thebes' medizing role in the Persian Wars.
The city was left with its defenses intact, its territory
cut down and ravaged, an unknown number of its leading
citizens dead, probably the best part of its fighting
force wiped out, and with a reputation for shameful
behavior which was to be more lasting than any of these
other disabilities. Since Herodotus' history appears to
have been a major factor in perpetuating this reputation,
a word about his handling of the Theban role in the war
is in order. Plutarch of course long ago charged Herodotus
with malice in his 'De Herodotis malignitate'. Although
Plutarch was not always himself fair or justified in his
charges, (35) yet a certain bias on the part of Herodotus
does seem to creep through in those passages in which he
imputes the worst possible motives to the Thebans'
actions, reads their inner thoughts, or reports private
conversations whose content he would have had no way to
learn. For instance, prejudice seems inherent in his
report of the hidden intentions of the Thebans who went
to Thermopylae, and their status as hostages; in his
attribution to the Thebans of the suggestion to subvert
disaffected Greek factions with gold; in his emphasis on
the necessity of the Persian destruction of Theban
property; and in his insight into the expectations of
the Theban leaders as they gave themselves up to the
Greeks. Of course, these need not all be inventions of
Herodotus. The Plataeans and Thespians may well have
believed in a Theban denunciation, and Pausanias might
very well have defended the speedy execution of the Thebans
on the grounds that they would otherwise have succeeded
in their plans to foil justice. None the less, it does
seem to be the case that Herodotus sees these events through

a strong haze of anti-Theban feeling, generated by the
Athenian situation in the late fifth century.

479-457 BC: THE POST-WAR PERIOD

Upon its defeat, Thebes disappears almost entirely from
the pages of extant history for over twenty years, re-
appearing only briefly in 470 when the Thebans restored
to Delion a statue which had been stolen by Persian
soldiers in 490, and left with the Delians by the Persian
Datis on his way home, with orders to restore it to
Delion. The Delians had never carried out the orders,
and in 470 the Thebans, in response to an oracle, undertook to take it back (Hdt. 6.118). A brief and tantalizing
report, this probably should be taken as recording a
mythico-political move on the part of the Thebans. Delion
is said to be within Theban territory by Herodotus
(speaking for his own day), but within Tanagran territory
by Pausanias (9.20.1). In this post-war period, the
coinage suggests that Tanagra was making a bid for control
of the Boeotians. Theban coins from the period are few,
(36) suggesting a period of economic slowdown as well as
a slackening of Theban predominance in Boeotia. Tanagran
coins are more plentiful, and some bear a 'B', 'B-O', or
'B-O-I', which has been interpreted to imply that Tanagra
made a counter-claim to Boeotian leadership during the
relative eclipse of Thebes. (37) If this was the case,
in 470 we may get a glimpse of Thebes trying to whittle
away the influence of Tanagra by this service to the
people of Delion. (As another possibility, Larsen believes
that Orchomenos for a time filled the leadership gap, but
there is less evidence for this.) (38)
     Another sort of witness to the situation of the city
at war's end is found in Pindar's 'Isthmian' 8: (39)
                    Slipped free of great sorrows,
  let us not fall into desolation of garlands;
  cherish not your grief; we have ceased from evils
      above our strength,
  Let us communicate some sweetness even after the
      hardship, since from above our heads
  some god has turned aside that stone of Tantalus,
  a weight Hellas could never dare. But now
  the terror has gone by and taken
  away the strong brooding in my heart; it is better
      always to watch what is close at hand
  in everything. A treacherous age hangs over men's heads;
  it makes crooked the way of life. But even this can
      be healed

in man, with freedom. We must be of good hope. (lines
   5-16, tr. Lattimore)
Despite the loss of life, property, and status which befell
Thebes as a result of its part in the war, there is in
'Isthmian' 8 a predominant note of relief and hope. The
prospect of life after a Persian victory can never have
been very bright for most Thebans: living among their
fellow Greeks as puppets of the Great King, even in the
favored position which collaborators might hope to achieve,
may indeed have appeared to be no more appealing than
living under the great stone of Tantalus, at least to the
majority who nourished no tempting visions of special
favor and profits. Once that stone had been lifted away,
the Thebans could get back to their old pursuits, to the
winning of honors in the games, and to the regaining of
their lost predominance among their Boeotian neighbors.
No matter that new and formidable difficulties were
involved; given freedom to act, and determination, recovery
would be only a matter of time.
    The poems of Pindar, many of which date from this
otherwise poorly documented period and contain apparent
historical allusions, are on the whole more frustrating
than rewarding as sources for Theban history, despite
this valuable glimpse into Pindar's own reactions. In
most of the odes, what at first sight appear to be clear
references to known historical events dissolve into
uncertainty in the light of the disputes of scholars
offering widely differing identifications for these
events. Two examples will illustrate the elusive quality
of this material.
    In 'Isthmian' 1 Pindar speaks of the father of the
recipient of the poem, a man by the name of Asopodoros,
who was welcomed by Orchomenos when he suffered shipwreck,
but who is now back home again in Thebes. Was this
Asopodoros the Asopodoros who commanded the Theban
cavalry at Plataea? The identification, so tempting, has
been strongly challenged. (40) Whoever he may have been,
depending upon whether we interpret his shipwreck and
recovery at Orchomenos literally or metaphorically, we
can add to our fund of 'historical knowledge' one of the
following:
1 the exile or escape of Asopodoros to Orchomenos in the
   aftermath of the defeat at Plataea, or
2 the personal participation of a member of a wealthy
   Theban family in trade, as well as his earlier stay in
   Orchomenos while recovering from the financial
   misfortune of an (actual?) shipwreck, and his family's
   return to affluent life in Thebes.
Unfortunately, in this as in many cases, we cannot be

certain whether the meaning is literal or metaphorical -
scholars have been divided on the question from antiquity
(41) - and so we cannot choose between these two
interesting alternatives.

Another ode which should throw light on the post-war
period is 'Isthmian' 4, composed for Melissus of Thebes,
whose victory is said to have reawakened his family's
honor after its long sleep following the deaths of four
of its members in one battle. Was Melissus' Isthmian
victory in 474, and was the battle then Plataea? (42)
Or was this an earlier battle, which took place between
Thebes and Athens following the expulsion of the
Peisistratids? (43) Or is the battle simple unidentifi-
able? (44) Perhaps the most that can be drawn from this
ode, and its accompanying 'Isthmian' 3, is that in the
late 470s an aristocratic house has survived the Persian
defeat (in which it may not even have been militarily
involved, if all male members old enough to participate
had been lost earlier), and has enough wealth to
commission Pindar. If so, this wealth may be marginal,
for 'I'.3, composed for the same Melissus, celebrates a
victory in the following year, and its employment of the
same meter as 'I'.4 has been attributed to economy, in
that it makes possible the use of the chorus already
trained for the earlier ode. (45)

'Isthmian' 8, which we considered earlier for its
portrayal of the poet's relief at the ending of the
war, and which seems to be securely dated to this period,
raises the possibility of another type of historical
relevance which must be considered. It was composed for
Cleandros of Aegina, and it plays upon the relationship
of Thebe and Aegina as twin daughters of Asopus. In the
context of the poem, this relationship is used to
justify a Theban poet in dedicating his song to a son of
Aegina. In doing this, was Pindar asserting a purely
personal tie between himself and the Aeginetans (one
quarter of the epinician odes were written for Aeginetans;
the two cities had recently been fighting on opposite
sides in the Persian Wars, and some Aeginetans might not
approve of Cleandros' choice of a Theban poet to celebrate
his victory), or can it be concluded that he also speaks
for the city of Thebes as it seeks to re-establish
political relationships damaged by the war? The latter
view has been suggested; (46) any decision about its
validity must, however, be postponed until we consider
another major area of Pindar's poetic activity and other
examples of such mythological relationships.

Prior to the medism of Thebes, Pindar had received two
commissions from Akragas in Sicily. He composed

'Pythian' 12 for the flute player Midas, and 'Pythian' 6
for Xenokrates, brother and colleague of Theron, ruler of
Akragas. In 476 the connection was renewed when Pindar
received no fewer than five commissions to celebrate
Olympic victories won by Hieron of Syracuse, Theron of
Akragas, and Hagesidamus of Epizephyrian Lokri, a
dependency of Hieron. Thus began a long and fruitful
association between the poet and the Sicilian rulers,
their friends and dependants. In the fall of 476 the
poet left for Sicily, in part to carry out these
commissions; he remained until spring, composing other
works as well during his stay. On his return to Thebes,
he continued to produce works for this western market.

     In one of the earliest among the Sicilian odes,
'Olympian' 2, Pindar traces the descent of the family of
Theron from Kadmus, thus revealing a mythological kinship
between Theron and himself as a Theban, similar to the
kinship which he revealed between the Aeginetans and
himself in 'Isthmian' 8. Similar links are later
asserted for Cyrene and Thebes ('P'.5.73ff.), and for
Stymphalus in Arcadia and Thebes ('O'.6.82ff.). (47)
Were these links meant only to relate poet and patron,
or did they also have implications for Theban foreign
policy? Within the Greek tradition, mythology was
frequently used for purposes of political persuasion and
propaganda; consider, for instance, the Spartan theft
of the bones of Orestes from Tegea, related by Herodotus
(1.67-8), or the retrieval of the bones of Theseus from
Skyros by Cimon, related by Plutarch ('Cimon' 8.5-6).
The poet, it would seem, must have been sensitive to the
possibility of producing political overtones by the use
of mythology - unless, of course, he was employing a
poetic convention which was generally understood to be
without political significance. That these instances of
mythological kinship do in fact fall into the category
of poetic convention seems assured when we consider them
more closely. While Aegina was a good candidate for
Theban political overtures, and it would be most significant to discover that Thebes was carrying out a formal
diplomatic campaign in Sicily in the post-war years,
what are we to make of Stymphalus in Arcadia? The
relationship in this case appears clearly to have been
dictated by the accidental fact that Pindar's Syracusan
patron also had a home there, and not by any Theban
endeavors to cultivate this obscure Arcadian town.
Attention to all the instances thus should lead us to the
conclusion that these cases of mythological kinship were
introduced simply as instances of a poetic convention by
which the poet drew attention away from the commercial

relationship between himself and his patron, and sought to elevate the relationship even beyond 'xenia' to kinship. Political implications were not intended, and would not have been read into the passages by the ancient audience. There is one inference, however, which it does seem safe to draw from the abundance of material composed by Pindar during these post-war years for the western Greek world. That inference is that the Thebans and the western Greeks were by no means unknown to each other. Nor was it only Pindar who had direct contact with the west. Poems and commissions were sent back and forth, and these required messengers. Pindar names some of his own couriers and representatives: Nicasippus took 'Isthmian' 2 to Akragas, while Aeneas took 'Olympian' 6 to Stymphalus. Pindar also mentions sending 'Pythian' 2 and 'Pythian' 3 to Syracuse ('P'.2.67f.; 'P'.3.63ff.), as well as 'Olympian' 7 to Rhodes ('O'.7.8). Just as the presence of imported pots is used to postulate commercial connections between importing and exporting cities, so the existence of a market in poetry should be taken seriously as a sign of cultural contact between the two areas. As Pindar himself said:

This song, like Phoenician merchandise, is sent over the grey sea. ('P'.2.67-8)

457-447: TANAGRA, OENOPHYTA, AND THE ATHENIAN HEGEMONY

In 457 Thebes again reappears in the pages of history, and, in fact, we are suddenly faced with an embarrassment of riches: not one, but two sources, Thucydides and Diodorus. Unfortunately, however, these two sources conflict with each other quite frequently. For example, in 457, (48) when the Spartans were in central Greece to aid the people of Doris against an attack by the Phocians (Thuc. 1.107; Diod. 11.79), and after the battle of Tanagra, Diodorus reports that the Thebans saw their opportunity and asked for Spartan help in regaining leadership in Boeotia (11.81). The Spartans agreed to assist them, persuaded by the Theban offer to fight the Athenians, and hoping to provide a counterweight to the increasing power of Athens; as part of this assistance they extended the lower wall of the city. (49) In Thucydides' account of the same events, however, nothing is said about a Theban request for assistance, or about such assistance being given to them by the Spartans. The discrepancies between these two accounts have occasioned serious problems for modern scholars: some reject Diodorus completely, (50) while others find Thucydides'

account wanting and consider Diodorus to be a valuable
supplement. (51) Since the matter involves the question
of the degree and timing of Theban recovery and political
ambition after the Persian Wars, it is worth considering
in some detail.
    The account of Diodorus (11.79.4-83.4) clearly appears
to be a conflation of (at least) two sources: there are
two battles of Tanagra (11.80.2-3 and 11.80.6), both
ending inconclusively with nightfall, and two battles of
Oenophyta (11.81.6-82.5 and 11.83.1). Between the two
pairs of battles there is a passage (possibly misplaced)
which recounts the Theban-Lacedaemonian plan to win back
the hegemony over the Boeotians for the Thebans (11.81.1-4);
at some point between these plans and the Athenian attack
(Oenophyta), the Lacedaemonians disappear from the scene,
so that the battle(s) of Oenophyta are fought only between
the Athenians and the Boeotians. The account of Thucydides,
on the other hand, is highly compressed, but clearly
reflects some of the same material which we find in
Diodorus: the Lacedaemonians begin by coming to the aid
of Doris, their return is cut off at Ceraneia, the
Athenians raise 14,000 men, including a Thessalian
contingent which goes over to the enemy, and the battle
of Tanagra results. Later the Athenians defeat the
Boeotians at the battle of Oenophyta. On the other hand,
there are serious discrepancies between the two accounts.
Thucydides does not mention a Theban-Lacedaemonian plan
to restore the hegemony of Thebes; since the plan, if it
did exist, failed, and Thucydides is presenting only a
capsule account of a fifty-year period in this part of
his work, this is perhaps understandable, but it does
leave puzzling problems. Why did the Lacedaemonians come
with so many troops if their sole aim in the beginning
was to aid the Dorians? The answer to this problem,
suggested by Reece, (52) seems to be that they did not,
contrary to both Thucydides and Diodorus (only Diodorus,
probably misreading Thucydides, specifically states that
the allies were Peloponnesians); rather, the number of
10,000 was made up in Boeotia, when the Lacedaemonians
found themselves faced with the prospect of Athenian
opposition to their return home. A bargain was probably
struck: in return for Theban assistance against the
Athenians, Sparta would help Thebes regain hegemony.
Diodorus tells of this bargain, but, along with much else
in his account, the report seems to be out of chronological
order. Part of the Spartan assistance was help in
extending the walls of Thebes, part the joint stand at
Tanagra and the later Boeotian battle at Oenophyta. Why
did the battle take place at Tanagra? Tanagra seems to

have been making an attempt to obtain the hegemony of
the Boeotians, (53) possibly with the backing of the
Athenians. Thus a battle there, which would presumably
strike a blow not only at Athens, but at Tanagra as well
(since it was fought on Tanagran territory, which would
suffer damage), makes more sense if the Lacedaemonians
are interested in rearranging the power structure of the
Boeotian cities, as Diodorus reports. In addition to the
fact that Diodorus' account provides information which
makes sense out of the events (although he himself does
not make sense out of the battle sequences, and thus need
not be suspected of rationalizing), he is also supported
in his picture of a Sparta interested in reviving Theban
hegemony by Plato in the 'Menexenus' (242A).

Other troubling discrepancies occur between the accounts
of Diodorus and Thucydides. For Diodorus, the battle(s)
of Tanagra end inconclusively and a four-month truce is
arranged. He does not mention the return home of the
Lacedaemonians, who, on the contrary, seem to spend some
time helping Thebes, if this section is not misplaced
(but they do return, for they do not participate in the
battle of Oenophyta). Moreover, in his account the
chronology of the battle of Oenophyta is not clear (are
we to assume that the Athenians waited to attack until
after the expiration of the truce?). In the account of
Thucydides, the Lacedaemonians win a victory and then
return home (but the timing is not defined), and in 62
days the Athenians return to win the battle of Oenophyta.

In at least the report of an indecisive battle at
Tanagra, Diodorus is again supported by Plato's
'Menexenus'. The accounts of Diodorus and Thucydides
can be reconciled if we assume that, following an
indecisive battle, a treaty was agreed to which gave the
Lacedaemonians the right to an unmolested evacuation of
their troops, and that this treaty, because it gave the
Lacedaemonians this concession, would perhaps have been
interpreted as a Lacedaemonian victory; if the treaty did
not bind the Athenians in their relations with the
Boeotians (which it may not have done, since some
concession would have been necessary to their side as
well), there would be no need to mention it in a
condensed account, since it was irrelevant to the
Athenian attack at Oenophyta.

What are we to conclude about the relative merits of
Diodorus in this instance? Thucydides' report is reasonable and self-consistent, except for its attaching the
10,000 allied troops to Sparta from the outset of the
operation against Phocis, but it clearly omits much in the
way of detail which is reported in Diodorus. Diodorus is

confused in the way in which he puts together his sources,
but the points of confusion are evident: they occur in the
seams of his story, but the raw material which he incorporated seems untouched by this confusion. His basic building
blocks are a brief and a more detailed account of Tanagra,
an account of Theban and Lacedaemonian motivation, a long
and a short version of Oenophyta (the long version
containing a moralizing tale which may be a separate
element), and an editorial section of his own on Myronides'
victory. In the case of both battles, the short version
could have been a condensation of the longer version by one
of his sources, (54) although he evidently failed to
recognize this. Plato in the 'Menexenus' knows Diodorus'
versions of the battles and the motivation, but he perhaps
knew them not from Diodorus' source, Ephorus, but from
Ephorus' source. (55) Thus we can postulate a longer
version of both battles, including the motivation section,
going back to the fourth century at least, from which
Diodorus drew indirectly through Ephorus (the doubling
would have occurred when either Ephorus or Diodorus used
both the original and an epitomized form of this source,
failing to recognize that they were the same; Diodorus is
probably the guilty one, to judge from his general
propensity for doublets). (56) It thus seems reasonable
to view the account of Diodorus as a helpful supplement
to Thucydides' abridged account, and to accept its picture
of a Thebes eager for a renewal of former authority and
playing at politics with Sparta in 457.

The aftermath of the Boeotian defeat at Oenophyta was
a decade of Athenian dominance in Boeotia. Whether this
dominance extended to Thebes as well as to the other
Boeotian communities is another historical puzzle.
Diodorus says that Myronides took all the Boeotian towns
except Thebes. Thucydides says that the Athenians were
masters of the Boeotian country (1.108). Since Aristotle
tells us that the bad administration of democracy in
Thebes after Oenophyta led to the fall of the democratic
government ('Pol.' 1302b29), we would perhaps do best to
conclude that there was a brief period of democratic
government in Thebes after Oenophyta, brought about
under the direction of Athens which had gained its way
by taking advantage of stasis rather than by conquest
(it seems unlikely that Thebes with its walls could have
been taken by anything less than a major battle, and we
have no account of such an event). This allows us to
reconcile Diodorus (Myronides did not capture Thebes in
the same way as he did many other Boeotian cities, by
warfare) and Thucydides (Athens did in fact become master
of Boeotia, but in the case of Thebes this mastery came

about by means of stasis rather than by conquest).

The Athenians probably maintained control over Thebes during the entire decade between Oenophyta and Coronea, although during most of this time they supported a moderate oligarchy (following the failure of an attempt to impose democratic government). (57) During this decade Thebans must have taken part in the Athenian expedition against Thessaly along with men from other Boeotian cities (Thuc. 1.111); some Thebans may also have been involved in the Athenian expedition which restored the temple at Delphi to the Phokians after the Lacedaemonians had given it to the Delphians in the Second Sacred War (Thuc. 1.112). From the success of the Boeotians in the battle of Coronea, we may assume that dissatisfaction with Athenian domination grew during these years among the citizens of the Boeotian cities as well as among those exiled from these cities; it seems that this dissatisfaction with the outsider was also effective in muting inter-Boeotian disputes and laying the foundation for a renewal of the Boeotian league.

447-431: CORONEA AND THE RENEWED BOEOTIAN LEAGUE

In 447 Athens was suffering from widespread unrest within its empire. This is reflected in the tribute list for that year, which is the shortest list of the series except for the first year, and which records that many states made only partial payments. (58) In that situation the seizure of power by Boeotian exiles in Chaeronea, Orchomenos and other unspecified Boeotian cities brought as an Athenian response the sending of 1,000 Athenian heavy infantry to Boeotia, with allied contingents, under Tolmides. This force, after it succeeded in taking Chaeronea, was ambushed and decisively defeated; its leader died in the fighting. Athens was forced to evacuate Boeotia in order to regain the prisoners taken in that encounter. The main source for these events is Thucydides 1.113 (an even briefer account, evidently from the same source, is found in Diodorus 12.6). Plutarch adds information, portraying Pericles as trying to dissuade Tolmides from an expedition with such an in-adequate force ('Pericles' 18), and gives us the name of the Boeotian commander, Sparton ('Agesilaus' 19.2).

In 427, in the speech at the trial of the Plataeans (Thuc. 3.62), the Thebans refer to Coronea as a Theban victory, and so it was long considered, at least in its immediate effect. (59) Larsen has suggested, however, that the Boeotian attack was instigated primarily by Orchomenos,

and that that city was the prime beneficiary, obtaining
the hegemony of the Boeotians. (60) This theory has
attracted support, (61) but it does not seem tenable. It
is a complex construction resting at bottom upon Larsen's
reading of Thucydides 1.113. According to this reading,
Orchomenos was the leader of the revolt against Athens.
But Thucydides does not say this; he speaks only of the
actions of exiles who had gained control of Orchomenos,
Chaeronea, and other Boeotian places. As Dull has pointed
out, if exiles were in control of Orchomenos, it could not
be said to be acting on its own behalf, nor does Thucydides
single out Orchomenos as the leader (the Athenians attacked
Chaeronea; Larsen's explanation of this – that this was a
border fort of Orchomenos – does not seem convincing).
Moreoever, it is Thebes, and only Thebes, which issues
coinage after 447, a fact which alone seems to rule out
the thesis that Orchomenos held the hegemony between 447
and 431.

   With the return of the Theban exiles after the withdrawal
of the Athenians, changes must certainly have been made in
the structure of the Theban government, even if (as seems
to have been the case) a moderate oligarchy had been in
power during the later years of Athenian control. The
returning exiles, as the authors of Boeotian freedom, would
certainly have claimed a right to a major role in Theban
political life, while those who had ruled during the
period of Athenian dominance, some of whom were probably
'new men' created by the Athenians, would have been
reluctant to retire from public life. Müller suggested
that at this time the prohibition was instituted against
participation in trade for ten years prior to holding
office; (62) this would have provided a means of incor-
porating some few of the 'new men' into the government
while probably excluding many more (the entire period
of Athenian rule was only ten years, and of those who
were able to rise into the group of office holders under
the more lenient requirements which we may assume to have
been in effect then, few would have spent the entire ten
years in their new position). Those excluded may have
been satisfied with the prospect of becoming eligible
within a relatively brief period of time. This seems to
be a reasonable reconstruction of events (although one
does wonder about the source of these 'new men' in a city
which shows little evidence of trade), especially since
we know that the oligarchy in 427 was considered to be
much more open than that of the Persian War period (Thuc.
3.62). This suggests that a mechanism existed for
introducing a wider group into the power structure in the
later fifth century (perhaps the lowering of the property

37 Chapter 3

qualification would have been enough to account for the 'new men').

It was not only the internal affairs of Thebes which required reorganization after Coronea; an even greater need was for a reconstitution of the Boeotian league in a form which would be acceptable to the other Boeotian cities. It had been many years since the league had functioned in an effective way, (63) and it was hardly possible at this point to return to the 'natural' relationships which had been in force prior to the Persian War. Nor had the other Boeotian cities been particularly happy with the Theban domination which at times marked the archaic league. None the less, the need to protect against further outside interference in Boeotian affairs demanded some sort of effective means of co-operation. This was accomplished by the creation of a highly sophisticated political organization which was theoretically representational (Bruce says of it that it seemed to amount to 'little more than the principle of proportional representation'), (64) but which was none the less tilted toward Theban control in practical application. What tilted it in Thebes' favor were certain practical aspects of the organization. The first was the fact that the meetings of the Federal Council were held in Thebes. From a naive point of view this could be seen as perfectly reasonable: the city was centrally located, and, because it was the largest Boeotian city, had more capacity than any of the others to supply the needs of visiting council members. None the less, being the seat of the governing council gave Thebes a considerable advantage, since the Theban councillors would be more likely to be present at any given meeting, and could be present with much less inconvenience and financial outlay to themselves (or to their city, if the cities helped defray individual expenses). (65) Secondly, Thebes was the only city to mint coins between 447 and 387. (66) Thirdly, Thebes also appears to have been the seat of the federal treasury, (67) which would also have appeared reasonable, considering the strength of the Theban defences; nevertheless, the actual physical presence of the treasury funds in Thebes would have added considerably to Theban power and options, as we can see by considering the uses made by Athens of the treasury of the Athenian Confederacy after its transfer from Delos to Athens.

It thus appears that in 447 someone in Thebes was exercising considerable political ingenuity in creating a federal structure which would appear scrupulously fair to all its members, and thus would be acceptable to the other Boeotian communities, but which would still give

the balance of power to Thebes. Allied to this political
sophistication is a similar sophistication in the
political application of number. Glotz has argued that
the number of members in the federal council, 660, was
the smallest number which would have allowed all the
communities to have been proportionally represented. (68)
Given any number of membership units (whether it was
eleven or ten, or whatever, really does not matter at this
point), each itself composed of from one to five autonomous
city-states, the problem of the equal representation of
these individual city-states arises. Clearly neither 50
nor 100 would be a manageable number for units with three
city-state members; 60 would be the most useful number,
since it is divisible by 5, 4, 3, 2, and 1, and would thus
allow membership units composed in a variety of ways to
achieve equal representation within their own unit.
Starting from this basis of 60, the council would be
composed of 60 x X, or 660, if the membership units
numbered eleven.

The practical use of number manipulation for political
purposes can be seen as early as Cleisthenes, who divided
the Athenian state into three districts, then divided each
of these into ten; this yielded thirty units or trityes,
which were then regrouped into ten triads, with one tritye
from each district; thus ten new tribes were formed with
mixed membership from all three districts. Each tribe
then contributed 50 members toward the council of 500, and
also provided the basis for constituting other political
entities, such as army units. Pythagorean influence has
been suspected in this use of numbers; (69) however, it
is not necessary to look far for Cleisthenes' primary
motivation: to replace a closed tribal system, break up
three existing locally based spheres of political
influence (plain, shore, and hills), and to give each
of these three areas representation within the council
even when its own people could not, for practical reasons,
be present. That the choice of the number 10 for the
tribes and 50/500 for the council would be convenient in
a society with an acrophonic number system based on 10
and 5 does not require any complex calculation. (70) The
case of the Boeotian league is somewhat more complex,
however, since there was such variety possible within
the single units, and the possibility of expansion or
retraction was evidently foreseen. The choice of a basis
of 60 aimed at providing a number which would allow equal
representation for districts varying from one to five
member cities. A similar line of reasoning underlies
Plato's choice of the number of households in the ideal
state in the 'Laws' (737E-738A): the number 5,040 is

selected because it is divisible by all the integers up to ten and thus can be the basis for many different groupings of households for different purposes. In the case of the Boeotian league, Larsen has also recognized a high degree of sophistication in the quadripartite division of the citizen bodies of the cities and of the federal council, which he believes shows that 'the constitution must be the conscious work of someone with a theory and plan of government.' (71) The choice of 60 as a basis for representation reinforces this conclusion.

This sophisticated use of political arithmetic, and the existence in Plato of similar motivations in the choice of a number base, does bring to mind the Pythagoreans, who were interested in both politics and number, and whose influence on Plato was strong. It may not be a pure coincidence that tradition brings the Pythagorean Lysis to Thebes at just about this time. He had gone first to Achaea at about mid-century, and then, after an unspecified time, he went on to settle in Thebes. (72) The political changes in Boeotia with the expulsion of the Athenians may well have made Thebes an attractive place in which to settle, for there would have been need for political reorganization along oligarchic lines, and the Pythagoreans generally were interested in political theory and committed to oligarchical government. It is interesting to note as well that an expedition was sent from Achaea to Italy at about this same time to mediate political difficulties there which had arisen as a result of the persecution of the Pythagoreans, and to establish a constitution on the Achaean model (which was, however, democratic). (73) It looks as though the Achaeans had special interest in political theory, and that at just about the time of Lysis' arrival (perhaps as a result of his arrival with a request for assistance, although since he was an expelled Pythagorean, this may be rather unlikely) discussion must have centered on finding a constitutional solution to the political difficulties in Italy. Lysis would surely have participated in this discussion, if only because he would have been a valuable source of information about one of the disputing sides in the Italian situation. Thus upon his arrival in Thebes he would have been awake to the possible utility of constitutional manipulations as a means of achieving political aims. The advice of a Pythagorean could account for the sudden appearance in Boeotia of a rather complex and sophisticated federal organization which had some similarities to Plato's ideal state, and which shows its affinities with political theorizing in the additional fact that it seems to have served as the model for the constitution proposed by the Athenian oligarchs in 411. (74)

The influence of Lysis is of course conjectural, and it is all too easy to raise the spectre of Pythagorean influence whenever number enters the picture, as Lévêque and Vidal-Naquet have demonstrated so well in the case of Cleisthenes. The important point is the apparent existence of political theorizing at this time in Thebes, a city from which Socrates drew followers: if, after all, the theorizing is a purely native product, its reappearance in Plato is perhaps all the more interesting.

THE PELOPONNESIAN WAR (75)

Thebes played an active and important role in this war from the very beginning. The opening action of the war was the Theban/Boeotian attack on Plataea. (76) According to Thucydides, the Thebans approached Plataea expecting a relatively easy success, since they had been invited in by a Plataean party, and it was still peacetime. Consequently, they went in with a very small force (somewhat over 300 men), and, once inside and apparently successful, they simply issued an invitation to the Plataeans to join the Boeotian league. They had clearly miscalculated the depth of Plataean animosity and will to resist, as events showed.

The Plataeans, discovering the actual size of the Theban force, co-ordinated a surprise counter-attack and fell upon the Thebans with great ferocity, killing many and capturing a large number. According to the Theban account, those Thebans who had escaped, joining reinforcements which had arrived too late, withdrew from the vicinity of the city upon a promise and an oath that the prisoners would be returned in exchange for this withdrawal. The Plataeans, however, put the prisoners to death, claiming that their promise had been contingent not upon Theban withdrawal but upon the result of negotiations, and that there had been no oath.

As it turned out, the affair at Plataea proved to be the beginning of hostilities in the war, but it seems unlikely that Thebes intended this, or that it viewed the action against Plataea as anything more than a local effort to secure its situation before the storm of actual war broke. On the other hand, co-ordination of efforts between Thebes and Sparta may have been involved in Archidamos' assault on Oropus in the first Lacedaemonian invasion of Attica: loss of control of Oropus would have been a serious obstacle to the Athenian maintenance of the garrison which it had established at Plataea. The Boeotians provided their own contingent as well as cavalry for the main force in this first invasion, sending

their other forces to ravage the territory of Plataea,
and it seems likely that their interests had an influence
upon the strategy of the invasion (Thuc. 2.12, 22).

In 430 Thebes probably took part in the second invasion
of Attica (Thuc. 2.47). The very first years of the war
also seem to have been the time of the immigration of the
populations of the smaller unwalled Boeotian cities into
Thebes, mentioned by the anonymous historian P ('Hell. Ox.'
12.3).

In 429, perhaps motivated in part by fear of the plague,
the Lacedaemonian forces marched to Plataea rather than
invading Attica. After the failure of their initial
efforts to take the city, they built a wall of circum-
vallation and withdrew, leaving behind enough troops to
guard half the wall, with the Boeotians providing the rest
of the garrison. After two years of siege, the Plataeans
finally were forced by lack of supplies to surrender. The
besiegers were under the command of a Spartan, and the
decisions about the method of surrender and the fate of
the defenders were taken by the Spartans, but, in fact,
as Thucydides portrays it, Thebes was the decisive factor
in these decisions. A technically voluntary surrender
was obtained by the offer of a fair trial; however, the
trial which ensued involved only the question, 'Have you
done anything to help the Spartans and their allies?'
Despite Plataean objections, the Spartans carried out
this 'trial', motivated mainly if not entirely by their
desire to please the Thebans. The surviving male
prisoners were executed as a result, and in 426 the city
was razed and an inn and a temple of Hera were constructed
on the site, while the land was given on ten-year leases
to Theban citizens (Thuc. 3.52-68).

In the same year in which Plataea was razed, 426,
earthquakes occurred throughout Boeotia, especially
affecting Orchomenos (Thuc. 3.87). This could well have
been a stroke of luck for Thebes, since extensive or
serious damage to Orchomenos and its defenses would have
enhanced Thebes' position in relation to its ancient
rival. (77) Thebes found yet another opportunity to
enhance its standing in Boeotia in this same year when
it went to the assistance of the Tanagrans who were
attacked by Athens (Thuc. 3.91). (78)

In 424 the Boeotians carried out their first independent
action outside of Boeotia when they anticipated Brasidas'
actions against the threat of an Athenian takeover of
Megara. The Megarid was, of course, a vital area for
communications between the Peloponnesus and central
Greece, and Theban interests were closely involved.
Upon the arrival of Brasidas, the Boeotians turned over a

force of 2,200 hoplites and 600 horse to his command
(Thuc. 4.72).

In this same year the Theban exile Ptoiodoros made
overtures to the Athenians, and the result was an Athenian
plan for a triple thrust into Boeotia. This rather
complex operation, undermined by Athenian miscalculations
and a betrayal of the plot, ended in the battle of Delion,
in which Thebes played a decisive role in one of the major
Athenian defeats of the war. (79) Nor were the Thebans
particularly humble and restrained about this achievement.
With the spoils of the battle they triumphantly built a
great stoa in their agora, embellishing it with bronze
statues. Possibly among them were one or both of the
bronze horse and chariot figures of the artist Aristeides
mentioned by Pliny ('HN' 34.72). They covered the walls
of the other stoas and temples with so much loot from
their fallen enemies that, as Diodorus says, they appeared
to be made of bronze. They even instituted a special
festival to mark the occasion in future days, according
to Diodoros; it was called the Delia and was held not at
Thebes but at the battle site at Delion (Diod. 12.70).
Some individual families also joined in the conspicuous
celebration, memorializing their own fallen heroes with
the engraved stelai attributed to Aristeides as well,
which are among the most important surviving works of
Theban art today (see below, Chapter 7).   .

In 423 the Thebans saw a further opportunity to gain
from the battle of Delion. The city of Thespiae had been
weakened by the loss of the best of its young men (Thuc.
4.133). An extant casualty list for some of these
Thespians, as well as one listing 61 Tanagrans and 2
Eretrians who fell, bears witness today to these losses.
(80) Like Plataea, Thespiae had a long record of
opposition to Thebes, reflected in its support of the
Greek cause in the Persian Wars, for which it suffered
the destruction attributed to Theban instigation by
Herodotus. Evidence of on-going friendly relations with
the Athenians comes to light in a decree of 447/6 (the
time of the reconstruction of the confederacy of the
Boeotians, and thus a politically sensitive moment) in
which the Athenians awarded proxenia to four Thespians.
(81) In 423 the Thebans, seeing their opportunity,
charged the city with being pro-Athenian and dismantled
its walls. The benefits of this for Thebes were twofold.
In a purely military sense, the dismantlement of the wall
left Thebes as the only fortified place in the Asopos
valley, and thus in a far stronger position than formerly.
In political terms, Theban control of Thespiae gave it
political control of two new districts within the

confederacy. With its two original districts, and the
two which had come under its power when Plataea fell, this
gave Thebes six districts out of the eleven in the league,
an absolute majority which was effective in all three
areas of league affairs: the executive, legislative, and
judiciary. At the same time, Thebes itself furnished only
two-elevenths of the troops and paid for only two-elevenths
of the league's expenditures. (82)

In the negotiations for the Peace of Nicias in 421,
Thebes (along with Corinth, Elis and Megara) rejected the
treaty (Thuc. 5.17, 22), and throughout the 'peace', the
Boeotians maintained only a series of ten-day truces
(Thuc. 5.26). The rejection by the Boeotians of the peace
soon became the basis for a Spartan alliance with Athens.
This alliance in turn caused anti-Spartan agitation among
Sparta's former allies, including the Thebans. (83)
Reflections of these bad feelings can be found in the
Theban response to requests for aid from Herakleia in
Trachis in 418: Thebes sent 1,000 picked hoplites, who
dismissed the Lacedaemonian governor Agesippidas on a
charge of misgovernment (Thuc. 5.51; Diod.12.77.4).
Nevertheless, the Spartan connection was not abandoned,
for in 418 the Boeotians assisted the Lacedaemonians
against Argive pressure on Epidauros (Thuc. 5.53-61).

With the resumption of active warfare, internal
bickerings were overcome and Thebes played a major role
in weakening Athens. Thebans assisted in the fortification
of Decelea, and Theban plundering of Attica from this
stronghold was one of the principal causes of the defeat
of Athens, according to Thucydides. (84) In the meantime,
the city did not forget its own Boeotian interests,
stepping in to suppress a democratic uprising in Thespiae
in 414 (Thuc. 6.95).

In 413 a Boeotian contingent was sent to Sicily under
the command of two Thebans and a Thespian (Thuc.7.19, 43;
Diod. 13.7.7). This was the first real venture of the
Boeotians far beyond their borders. In the same year
Thebans also went to the rescue of Mycalessos when it was
attacked by a group of Thracian mercenaries being escorted
back to Thrace by the Athenians. This attack was actually
an indirect effect of Boeotian raids on Attica from
Decelea, for Athens was so hard pressed in both the Attic
countryside and in Sicily that it could not afford to
keep these troops, who had arrived too late to serve with
the reinforcements sent to Sicily under Demosthenes.

In 411 the enemy control of Decelea took on new
significance for Athens, for it provided a refuge for some
of the more extreme Athenian oligarchs after the overthrow
of their coup. Another of the oligarchs, Aristarchus, who

was also one of the Athenian generals for the year, did the
Boeotians a signal favor when he went not to Decelea but
to Oenoe. Taking advantage of his position as general,
he ordered the unsuspecting garrison to surrender to the
Corinthians and Boeotians who had been besieging it.
Boeotia thus gained control of this fort, which had
been serving the Athenians as a base for harassment of
the raiders from Decelea (Thuc. 8.98).

In 410 all the Boeotian cities joined in assisting the
Euboeans in the task of building a causeway and bridge
across the Euripus at Chalcis. (85) In 408, the Thebans
again went far afield when a corps of Boeotians, under
the command of the Theban Koeratadas, served with the
Lacedaemonian forces at Byzantium; Koeratadas was
captured and taken to Athens, but he managed to escape.
(86) In the same year, the Boeotians contributed 900
cavalry to Agis' attack on Athens (Diod. 13.72.3-9).
Finally, the last recorded Theban involvement in the war
occurred in 406, when a Boeotian contingent under the
command of the Theban Trasondas held the left wing in
the sea battle at Arginusae. (87)

The war clearly enhanced Thebes' position within
Boeotia, while also bringing the city to the fore as a
major contender for power beyond Boeotian borders
(clearly these two were not unconnected). This new
Theban international weight was to have immediate and
important effects in the post-war period.

POST-WAR PERIOD, 404-399

At the close of the war the Thebans were in the forefront
of those who favored the destruction of Athens. The
Spartans, however, rejected this extreme action, already
seeing the need for a counterbalance to the rising power
of Thebes. (88) Thebes' own recognition of its enhanced
place in the Greek scene is reflected in the Theban
claim of the tithe belonging to Apollo at Decelea, (89)
an action by which Thebes made an independent claim to
victory in the war. (90) Such a claim was clearly not
without justification in the light of the Theban
contribution to the defeat of Athens, but the claim
nevertheless angered the Spartans. It was a sign of
things to come. Thebes had already shown a potential for
independent and even anti-Lacedaemonian action during
the Peace of Nicias, and this potential was to become
actualized in the years immediately following the
conclusion of the war.

In 404 the Thebans voted aid to the Athenian exiles,

and they gave refuge to a large number of these men,
including Thrasybulos. Although the city apparently
stopped short of official support of these Athenian
exiles in the form of troops, assistance was given 'in
secret', although it is not known whether this was given
by individuals acting privately, or by the city itself.
(91) The Thebans also refused a Spartan request for aid
against the exiles when they had succeeded in establishing
themselves in the Piraeus (Xen. 'Hell.' 2.4.30). They
also refused a Spartan request for assistance against
Elis (Xen. 'Hell.' 3.2.21ff.; Diod. 14.17.4ff.). The
Boeotians did supply troops to the Lacedaemonian contingent
sent to aid Cyrus (Diod. 14.6.1); in this case, however,
the Thebans may have been more interested in repaying debts
due to the Persians (in the hope of future help?) than
they were in co-operating with their former ally, and this
should not necessarily be seen as a pro-Laconian act.

On the other hand, Theban behavior could not be classified as consistently pro-Athenian either, in view of their
annexation of Oropus in 402/1, an action which must have
been very annoying to the Athenians. Cloché is undoubtedly
right in his assessment of the situation during this
period: there were two parties competing for power in
Thebes, the pro-Lacedaemonian and the anti-Lacedaemonian
parties which we learn of from the author of the 'Hellenica
Oxyrhynchia' (12.1), and neither party was strong enough
to have its own way entirely. (92) Thus aid was denied to
the Spartans, but no positive action was taken against
them. Nor, as we have seen, was the city pro-Athenian,
although such charges were leveled against Ismenias, the
leader of the anti-Lacedaemonian party by Leontiades, the
leader of the pro-Lacedaemonians ('Hell. Ox.' 12.1). It
was a period of flux and readjustment, with the pro-
Lacedaemonian party, which had great power during the
Decelean phase of the war ('Hell. Ox.' 12.3), gradually
losing this power to the other party as Theban anger at
Sparta's unwillingness to share the booty of the war was
enhanced by repeated instances of Spartan highhandedness.

The war brought Thebes many blessings: a more
confident mastery of Boeotia, new resources of wealth,
and a new daring to venture beyond Boeotian borders.
None of the other participants had gained so much, and
by 404 the stage was being set for the fourth century,
when Thebes would put an effective end to Spartan power
and spend its own brief moment in the spotlight as
hegemon of Greece.

THEBES*

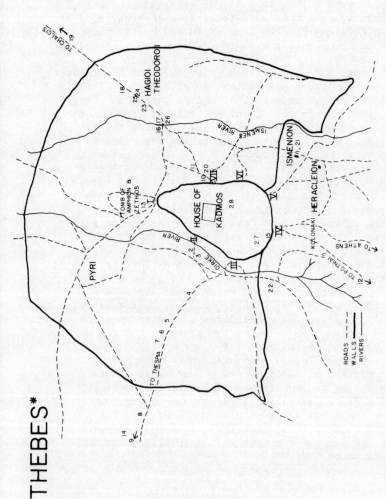

Fig. 2 Map of Thebes, adapted from the map of Keramopoullos, 'Archaiologikon Deltion', vol.3, 1917, with the line of the outer wall changed in accordance with the map of Pharaklas in 'Archaiologikon Deltion', vol.22, 1967. The numbered locations are only approximations, derived from Pausanias

Cults and Sacred Places

1 Ares fountain
2 Tomb of Menoikeus
3 Dragging of Antigone
4 House of Pindar
  Shrine of the Mother
5 Themis
6 Moirai
7 Zeus Agoraios
8 Heracles Rhinokoloustes
9 Kabeirion
10 Dionysos Lysios
   Image of Semele
   Tomb of Semele
   Stone of Alkmene
   Tombs of children of Amphion
   Ruins of house of Lykos
11 Artemis Eukleia
   Statue of lion dedicated by
     Heracles
   Tombs of Androkleia and
     Alkis
   Apollo Rescuer
   Hermes Agoraios
12 Amphiarios' chasm
13 Athena Zosterias
14 Heracles Hippodetos
15 Zeus Hypsistos

16 Tomb of Hector
17 Fountain of Odysseus
18 Teiresias' cenotaph
19 Snake's Head
20 Iolaos
21 Tomb of Kaänthos
22 Athena Onca
23 Grave of Melanippos
24 Tydeus
25 Eteokles and Polyneikes
26 Asphodikos
27 Teiresias' bird observatory
28 Harmonia's wedding song by
     the Muses

House of Kadmos

   Dionysos Kadmeios
   Demeter Thesmophoria
   Chamber of Harmonia
   Chamber of Semele

Heracleion

   Tomb of Amphitryon
   House of Amphitryon
   Chamber of Alkmene
   Tomb of children of Heracles
   Chastiser Stone

   Pharmakides
   Apollo Spondios

Ismenion

   Henioche and Pyrrha
   Manto's seat
   Athena Pronaia
   Hermes Pronaios

Gates

I   Ogygian
II   Neistan
III Krenaian
IV   Hypsistean
V   Electran
VI   Homoloid
VII Proitidian

4 The cults of fifth-century Thebes

Perhaps the clearest and most accessible evidence for the
personality of a Greek city lies in its cults, the peculiar
and idiosyncratic way in which it assimilated Olympian and
local divinities and honored and celebrated them. In the
case of Thebes, the very landscape itself seems to have
been pervaded by divinity - rocks and stones, caves and
crevices, mounds and ancient ruins, grassy spots and ash
piles, all shared in harboring divinity in a way which
probably reflected the most ancient religious impulses of
the people. And when this divinity achieved a degree of
personality, it usually did so as a part of a complex set
of interrelated extended families, linked by blood ties
and marriage relationships, in much the same way as any
human being achieved a recognized place in the community.
(1)
    Neither these ties to the landscape nor the genealogical
systematization were especially unusual for a Greek city;
what was perhaps somewhat unusual was the fact that at
Thebes it was not the Olympians who predominated in this
community of gods, and when they did appear, it was often
in a form of assimilation to a local god in which it was
by no means certain that the Olympian became the dominant
element. Thus worship was offered in the Ismenion to
Apollo Ismenios - or to Ismenos himself, the son of Apollo
and the local nymph Melia. Sometimes the subordination
took place by means of a cult foundation: an Olympian
god was installed in the local scene by means of a cult
foundation by a more important native divinity. Thus
Amphitryon dedicated the images of Athena at the sanctuary
of Athena Zosterias, Kadmos founded the shrine of Athena
Onca, and Harmonia dedicated images of Aphrodite (who was
also her mother). Sometimes assimilation took place by
intermarriage, with the newcomer gaining status and
position as an in-law, as in the case of Heracles, who

joined the family of Kadmos by marrying his daughter Megara.
    This interconnected network of divinities linked by
family or story connections served to validate and clarify
the place of the individual in the system. It also seems
to reflect a love of system and order for its own sake, a
concern for systematization which interestingly enough
showed itself much earlier in this same area of the Greek
world, in the 'Theogony' of Hesiod (the farmer's concern
for everything in its proper time and place, which we find
in the 'Works and Days', may perhaps offer a clue to this
concern for order). Using this interconnected network as
a working framework, we will now turn to a more detailed
consideration of the Theban cult system, beginning with
the Theban favorite, Heracles.

HERACLES

We have seen that Heracles held a special place in the
affections of the Theban people, that they identified
themselves with him through the symbolism of their
coinage, and that their jealous neighbors, the Athenians,
played upon this special relationship, portraying the
hero-god as a glutton and buffoon as a way of expressing
a similar opinion about the Thebans themselves. (2) Yet
despite Heracles' fifth-century popularity at Thebes, and
his adoption as the alter ego of the city, he appears to
have been a late-comer among the family of Theban
divinities. (3) Although he was said to have been born
in Thebes, in the Theban mythological family he was only
an in-law, the hero who married Megara, the king's
daughter.
    The marriage between Heracles and Megara did not even
last: after he had killed their children in a fit of
madness, he gave her to his nephew and friend, Iolaos
(according to another version of the story, he killed
her as well as the children in his madness). The
marriage/mistress/rape connection was commonly used by
the Greeks to provide various cities with family
connections for their favorite local heroes or deities,
and the brevity of these relationships was evidently of
little concern as long as offspring ensued; usually a son
resulted who could provide the desired ancestral link
with the divinity. In the case of Heracles, no son of
Megara and Heracles survived, but the tenuousness of the
connection (Heracles was, after all, only the ex-husband
of Megara) did not seem to bother the Thebans, who
appeared to compensate for it by the multiplicity of holy
spots associated with the hero-god's life and actions which
they honored in the city and its vicinity.

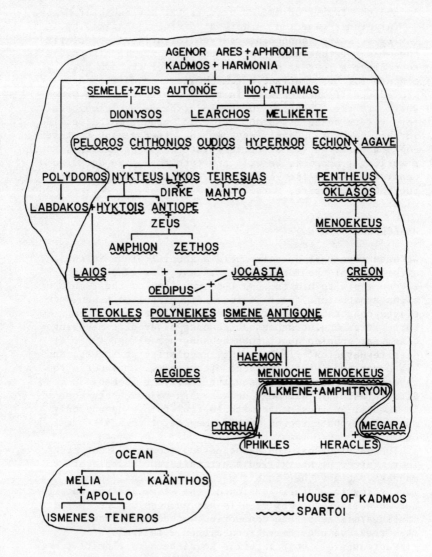

Fig. 3 Mythological families in Theban cults

Heracles' birthplace was located at Thebes at least from
the time of Homer ('Il.' 19.99). Associated with this
event were the tomb of Amphitryon, Heracles' foster father,
and his house (Pindar, 'Pythian' 9.84; 'Nemean' 4.20), and
the chamber of Alkmene, his mother, said to have been
built by Trophonius and Agamedes (Paus. 9.11.1). Also
revered were the indistinct images of the Pharmakides,
sent by Hera to hinder the birth of Heracles (Paus. 9.11.3),
as well as Galanthias, who helped Alkmene give birth.
Sacrifices were offered to Galanthias before the festival
of Heracles; (4) as a punishment for helping Alkmene, she
was turned into a weasel, but Hecate took pity on her and
made her her minister. Aelian reports the story of the
weasel's assistance to Alkmene, and says that for this
reason the Thebans worshipped weasels. On the other hand,
Pausanias reports that it was Historis, the daughter of
Teiresias, who helped Alkmene. (5) Also associated with
Heracles' family were the two stone images of Athena at
the sanctuary of Athena Zosterias, said to have been
dedicated by Amphitryon, and the stone of Alkmene, which
stood in place of a tomb in the precinct of the temple of
Dionysos Lysios. (6)

Places associated with Heracles' later life and
activities include the tomb of his children by Megara, and
the Chastiser stone, thrown by Athena to prevent him from
killing his foster father Amphitryon also in his madness.
Both of these were within his temple precinct. Other holy
spots associated with his activities were located apart
from his temple complex, and mainly marked 'historical'
events in his assistance to the city. Thus there were
three shrines associated with his deliverance of Thebes
from the control of Orchomenos: near the sanctuary of
the Kabeiroi there was a large shrine of Heracles
Hippodetos - when the Orchomenians came with an army,
Heracles bound their chariot horses at night at this
spot (Paus. 9.26.1); on the road from the Neistan gate
there was a sanctuary of Heracles Rhinokoloustes, which
celebrated the spot where Heracles cut off the noses of
the heralds sent from Orchomenos to demand the tribute
(Paus. 9.25.4); and there was a statue of a lion in front
of the temple of Artemis Eukleia, said to have been
dedicated by Heracles after his defeat of King Erginos of
Orchomenos (Paus. 9.17.1). This cult of Artemis appears
to have had a further connection with Heracles: Ziehen
argues that it was a cult dedicated to a previously
independent goddess, Eukleia, daughter of Heracles and
Myrto (Plut. 'Arist.' 20.6). Its precinct also contained
the tombs of Androkleia and Alkis, daughters of Antipoenos
who sacrificed themselves to secure Heracles' victory over
Orchomenos (Paus. 9.17.1).

In addition to these holy places associated with his
life and activities, Heracles also possessed an impressive
temple complex, situated outside the walls of the city,
which contained a temple, gymnasium, and race course. (7)
The carvings on the temple pediments, and perhaps the
temple which Pausanias saw, dated to the fourth century
(the work of Praxiteles), (8) but the colossal figures of
Athena and Heracles carved by Alcamenes were dedicated by
Thrasybulos and his associates after they put down the
tyranny of the Thirty with assistance from Thebans, thus
in the late fifth century.

Iolaos, Heracles' nephew, companion, lover, and
successor as husband of Megara, also had a hero-shrine,
which stood outside the Proitidian gate (Paus. 9.23.1).
It too had a gymnasium and racecourse. Iolaos figures
fairly prominently in the odes of Pindar, (9) which
suggests that his popularity and importance were considerable among the aristocratic class for which Pindar wrote.
Heracles and Iolaos were patron divinities and role-models
for the aristocratic practice of male homosexual relationships, and young Theban lovers took vows at the tomb of
Iolaos. (10)

Finally, Pollux (1.30) reports a festival of Heracles
Melon, but it is uncertain whether this referred to a
children's game, a dedication (of sheep or apples?), a
placing of the flocks (and possibly the fruit trees)
under the protection of Heracles, or a confusion with a
parallel story about Heracles in the Attic deme Melite.
(11)

THE HOUSE OF KADMOS

Actually, according to the mythological tradition, the
founder of Thebes, Kadmos, was himself an immigrant with
no earlier family connections in the city. His right to
a role in the city's history was guaranteed not by family
connections, but by an oracle. While searching for his
sister Europe (who had been abducted by Zeus) the
Phoenician Kadmos had inquired at Delphi, and was directed
to follow a guiding cow until she sank to the ground, and
there to found a city, which was, of course, Thebes. (12)

The question of Kadmos' traditional Phoenician origins
has been much debated, and the subject of much skepticism.
(13) Recently, however, it has been shown to be much more
plausible than had earlier been thought, on the basis of
new finds from Thebes itself (in particular, a cache of
about 100 cylinder seals, thirty of them of undisputed
oriental origin), as well as discoveries at Ugarit in North

Syria. (14)   At least a small settlement, perhaps of
refugees, from this area now seems to be a distinct
possibility.

Whether or not the Phoenician origin of Kadmos was a
true folk memory or the result of some other process of
folk-reasoning, it appears to have been given new significance in Athens after the defeat of the Athenians by the
Boeotians at Coroneia in 447 by just that person who first
brings it out clearly even to us - Herodotus. We perhaps
tend to overlook the extent to which the Persian Wars, as
we know them, are a creation of Herodotus. Equally, we
tend to overlook the formative power his writing must have
exerted upon its first audiences and readers, shaping
their conception of that conflict and, in fact, creating
the bipolar world view - Greek vs. Barbarian, East vs.
West, Freedom vs. Slavery - which dominated their thinking.
Thus the contribution he made to the Kadmos myth was to
reveal its deeper significance, and to allow Athenians to
see the medism of the Thebans as the act of a 'venomous'
people, a people who were barbarian by their very origins.
This must have been a welcome notion after the Athenians'
defeat by these earth-born men (after all, the Athenians
claimed the virtue of autochthony for themselves, but
clearly the snakey autochthonous origin of the Thebans
was of a quite different order of things, hardly a virtue,
when it was intertwined with the story of the Phoenician
Kadmos).

In the fifth century, Kadmos appears to have been still
an important character in the mythical history of Thebes.
He did not have an active cult or receive worship, but
he must have impinged heavily upon the consciousness of
the Thebans whose acropolis was named after him and who
were frequently confronted by his house, which was the
site of active cults (Dionysos, Demeter Thesmophoria),
and by other sacred spots connected with his story.

Harmonia, the wife of Kadmos, also seems to have lacked
an active cult in the fifth century, but she too had her
place in Thebes: the ruins of her chamber served as a
memorial of her role in Theban history, while the spot in
the Agora where the Muses sang at her wedding was still
pointed out in Pausanias' day (9.12.3-4). Moreover, there
were sacred places associated with her parents, Ares and
Aphrodite.

Pausanias mentions a fountain sacred to Ares on the
Ismenian hill (9.10.5). His cult seems to have faded in
historical times, (15) but its earlier importance is
attested not only in legend (it is from the teeth of Ares'
dragon-protector that the Spartoi sprung), but also by
the existence of a double shrine to Ares and Aphrodite with

images which were said to have been dedicated by Polyneikes
on the road from Argos to Mantinea (Paus. 2.25.1). Ares
is also invoked as one of the gods of the city in
Aeschylus' 'Seven against Thebes', (16) although this may
be due at least in part to the dramatic situation of the
play.
    The mother of Harmonia, Aphrodite, seems to have played
a very minor role in the cult-life of the city. Pausanias
reports three wooden images, said to have been the figure-
heads from the ships of Kadmos, which were dedicated by
Harmonia to Aphrodite, under the names Ourania, Pandemos,
and Apostrophia (9.16.3-4).
    An important Theban cult which was connected with the
family of Kadmos at least topographically was that of
Demeter Thesmophoria: her shrine was in the house of
Kadmos, and her cult may have been thought of as a Kadmeian
foundation. Her festival, the Thesmophoria, was celebrated
by the women of Thebes; during the celebration, which was
held on the Kadmeia, the men of the council could not
confer on the Kadmeia in their usual spot, but had to meet
in the lower city. (17) Ziehen assumes rites similar to
those known from Athens and from Potniae (Paus. 9.8.1).
    Another Kadmeian foundation was that of Athena Onca
(Paus. 9.12.2). Her image and altar were located at the
spot where the cow which Delphi had directed Kadmos to
follow sank down exhausted, providing Kadmos with a sign
indicating the proper site for the new city. The cult
figures three times in the 'Seven' of Aeschylus (lines
164, 487, and 501), and was located by Hesychius at the
Ogygian gate; (18) some modern scholars locate it at the
modern chapel of Hagia Trias. (19)
    Of the children of Kadmos - Agave, Autonoë, Ino, Semele
and Polydamos - only Ino and Semele appear to have had
cults in the fifth century. (20) Ino was not only the
aunt of Dionysos, but she and her husband Athamas were
chosen by Zeus to be his foster parents, which so angered
Hera that she drove the couple mad. Athamas consequently
killed one of their sons, Learchos, and Ino, having killed
the other, Melikertes, in a boiling cauldron, leaped into
the sea with his body; she was transformed into the sea-
goddess Ino Leucothea and the child into the deity
Palaimon. (21) She may have provided the archetype of a
primitive Maenad, and been a manifestation of pre-
Dionysiac feminine mysteries in central Greece. (22)
    Semele was the most famous of the children of Kadmos;
her chamber was a holy spot in the house of Kadmos, and
the cult of her son Dionysos was, along with that of
Apollo Ismenios, one of the two chief cults in the city.
His shrine, in which he was called Dionysos Kadmeios, was

in the house of Kadmos (Paus. 9.12.3-4). The cult object
was a log which was said to have been hurled from heaven
along with the thunderbolt which killed Semele; it was
adorned with bronze by Polydorus. At the festival of
Dionysos, which was held every third year, the Agrionia,
a sacred drama of pursuit and counterpursuit was carried
out by the women of the city and the priest of Dionysos
on Mt Kithairon (Farnell believes that this rite, in which
women chased a male priest, gave rise to the legend of
Pentheus, celebrated in the 'Bacchae' of Euripides).
The ritual took place at night and was orgiastic in
character. (23) An inscription of the first century AD
(but considered by the editors to be a renewal of an
earlier inscription), (24) records that the Magnesians
sent for Theban cult personnel, the Maenads, to establish
Dionysiac rites in Magnesia. This suggests that Thebes
was traditionally considered to be the center of Dionysiac
worship, and the place from which authentic rites could
be obtained.

Dionysos had another shrine near the Proitidian gate,
the temple of Dionysos Lysios (Paus. 9.16.6-7). The
interpretation of the epithet given by Pausanias
(Deliverer) is a political one: when some Theban prisoners
in the hands of the Thracians had reached Haliartos, they
had been delivered by the god (we see a similar deliverance
from imprisonment by a god in the 'Bacchae' of Euripides).
In antiquity the epithet was, however, interpreted as
deliverance from care (Plut. 'Qu. Symp.' 716B), and
possession by the god was seen as the means of deliverance.
(25) Some modern scholars, such as Farnell, have suggested
that the deliverance was rather *from* the possession by
the god (and thus a form of psychotherapy?); (26) the
tradition, however, which is recorded by Pausanias ties in
well with the Theban propensity to interpret landmarks in
historical (or mythological-historical) rather than
psychological terms. A number of related cult places
were located within the precinct of the temple: the
image of Semele and her tomb, the stone of Alcmene, the
tombs of the children of Amphion, and the ruins of the
house of Lykos.

AMPHION AND ZETHOS

A second major family group in the Theban cult system is
that of Chthonios the Spartos, which included Amphion and
Zethos. One of the puzzles of Theban mythical history is
the duplication of foundation legends, the one involving
Kadmos and the other involving this pair of brothers. In

the Catalogue of Women in the 'Odyssey' we first find the
non-Kadmeian foundation story:

> After her I saw Antiope, who was the daughter
> of Asopos, who claimed she had also lain in the embraces
> of Zeus, and borne two sons to him, Amphion and Zethus.
> These first established the foundations of seven-gated
> Thebes, and built the bulwarks, since without bulwarks
> they could not
> have lived, for all their strength, in Thebes of wide
> spaces. ('Od.' 11.260-5, tr. Lattimore)

Attempts to rationalize or eliminate the conflicting
legends were made even in antiquity. Thus a possible
reconciliation of the two foundation legends is offered
by Euripides in the 'Antiope': (27) the city of Amphion
and Zethos was to be built on the river Ismenos, apart
from the Kadmeia (lines 80-2). Pausanias records the
same rationalizing tradition: Amphion and Zethos founded
the lower city, while Kadmos established the city on the
Kadmeian hill (2.6.4). (28) In Book 9, however, Pausanias
recounts the story in a way which suggests rivalry between
the Kadmeian line and the descendants of Chthonios, one of
the Spartoi or earth-born men (9.5.3-9). Members of the
latter family, the brothers Nykteus and Lykos, served
loyally as regents for young members of the former family,
first for Labdakos, then for his son Laios; during the
regency of Lykos for Laios, however, the grandsons of
Nykteus, Amphion and Zethos, arrived with an army and,
defeating Lykos, managed to take over the royal power.
When they died without issue, the sovereign power returned
to Laios. In this version the rule of Amphion and Zethos
bears the mark of an illegitimate interregnum (a tyranny)
and they are punished by loss of descendants. In the
version (or versions) recorded by Euripides (in the
'Antiope', and in the 'Hercules', 25-34); however, Lykos
is portrayed as an outsider, and his ouster by Amphion
and Zethos is accomplished with the intervention of
Hermes and the blessing of Zeus ('Antiope' 64ff., 104f.).
These variant versions may have been invented in a
propaganda battle between those who saw themselves as
descendants of an original population (the Spartoi) and
those who traced their descent back to incoming settlers
(Kadmos and his group). (29) There is also the possibility
that propaganda efforts were made on behalf of Theban unity
at some time: it may be that the alternative paternity
accorded to Antiope in the 'Odyssey' (where she is the
daughter of Asopos rather than of Nykteus) marks an effort
to give Amphion and Zethos an autochthonous origin which
transcended narrow clan lines.

Both Pausanias and Euripides are rationalizing, and

some of their material may have been drawn from later
propagandistic use of myth; in addition, Euripides has
also incorporated late fifth-century ideas into the story
(for instance, according to Page, the editor of the
papyrus fragments of the 'Antiope', Amphion and Zethos
are opposed as representatives of the active and the
contemplative lives). All of these uncertainties and
possibilities make it rather hopeless to try to discover
the origins of the story, or its original form, from our
later sources, or to attempt a modern reconciliation
which reflects history. (30)

Amphion and Zethos had a tomb, a small mound of earth,
according to Pausanias, from which the inhabitants of
the village of Tithorea in Phokis tried to steal earth
during a specific time of the year, believing in an
oracle of Bakis which promised better crops for them and
worse for Thebes if they transferred earth from this
tomb to that of Phokos and Antiope at this time. To
prevent the theft, the Thebans watched the tomb carefully
during the dangerous period (9.17.4). This tomb has been
identified as the hill north of the Kadmeia. It consists
of a mound in the shape of a step pyramid, which has
added to speculation about possible foreign origins for
Theban culture. (31) The tombs of the children of
Amphion (Niobe's children), who died of the plague
(Paus. 9.5.9), were in the sanctuary of Dionysos Lysios,
while their funeral pyre was about a half stade away,
with ashes still present in the time of Pausanias
(9.17.2).

Plutarch tells of the tomb of Dirke, wife of Lykos,
who was killed by Amphion and Zethos because she
tormented Antiope (Euripides, 'Antiope',Apollod. 3.5.5).
The location of this tomb was known only to the Theban
officials called hipparchs (cavalry commanders). The
hipparch completing his term of office took the incoming
hipparch to the tomb alone at night, and together they
performed fireless sacrifices in secret, then removed all
traces of the ritual and went away separately (Plut.
'De gen.' 578B). The house of Lykos, Dirke's husband,
was within the sanctuary of Dionysos Lysios.

HOUSE OF LAIOS AND THE STORY OF THE SEVEN

According to Pausanias' version of the Theban foundation
legend in his Book 9, after the death of Amphion and
Zethos, sovereign power returned to Laios. Laios was a
compromise figure, in the sense that myth represented him
as a child of an intermarriage between the immigrant house

of Kadmos and the autochthonous Spartos Chthonios (whose
father, Labdakos, married Nykteis, daughter of Nykteus,
according to Apollodorus, 3.5.5). It is uncertain
whether or not there was a cult of Laios in Thebes;
Pausanias mentions none. There is no suggestion of a
cult of his son Oedipus either, but there are the landmarks
associated with his story: the mountain of the Sphinx
(Paus. 9.26.2), the fountain of Oedipus (Paus. 9.17.5-6),
and the place called the Dragging of Antigone (Paus.
9.25.2). Cult interest centered rather upon the story
of Oedipus' sons, Eteokles and Polyneikes, and the war
which their quarrel brought on. A number of cults were
associated with the various participants in this story,
all minor in importance yet perhaps gaining in significance
from their number. Sacrifices were offered at the tombs
of Eteokles and Polyneikes in Pausanias' day (Paus. 9.18.3).
Farnell suggests that the worship was ancestral rather
than heroic; (32) Ziehen even doubts the antiquity of the
cult, as there is no other evidence for it. The cult of
Melanippos, one of the defenders of Thebes, is of particular interest since it was the one which Cleisthenes of
Sicyon took to Sicyon in order to drive out Adrastos, who
was the leader of the attack against Thebes and therefore
Melanippos' mortal enemy (Hdt. 5.67). It seems unlikely
that the Thebans actually gave up the bones to Cleisthenes;
Ziehen is probably right in suggesting that they merely
gave a copy of the cult figure. The grave of Asphodikos,
one of the Theban fighters, was shown in Pausanias' day
(9.18.6), but no evidence exists that he received worship.
The burial spot of Tydeus was marked by three unwrought
stones (Paus. 9.18.2), and there was a tomb of Menoikeus,
sone of Kreon, near the Neistan gate (but Wilamowitz
believed that he was an invention of Euripides). (33)
The spot where the Argive seer Amphiaraos, who was tricked
into participating in the expedition, was swallowed up by
the earth was shown to Pausanias. (34) He reports that
it consisted of a small enclosure with pillars, adding
that birds would not sit on the pillars, nor would
animals graze on the nearby grass. Herodotus gives more
information about the oracle of Amphiaraos: consultation
was by incubation, and the Thebans themselves could not
consult the oracle because, when given the choice, they
had adopted Amphiaraos as ally rather than prophet. (35)
   Finally, there were several spots associated with the
seer Teiresias, who was closely involved with the story
of the Seven, as well as with a number of other Greek
stories. His cenotaph was on the road to Chalcis (Paus.
9.18.4), and his bird observatory was on the Kadmeia
(Paus. 9.16.1). On the road to Glisas a place surrounded

by unwrought stones was identified as the Snake's Head,
celebrating the place where Teiresias cut off the head
of a snake, although Pausanias does not know exactly what
distinguished this particular snake (9.19.3). Pindar
connects Teiresias with the cult of Zeus Hypsistos, and
with the birth of Heracles ('Nemean' 1.35-72): Teiresias
was a prophet of Zeus Hypsistos, and prophesied about
Heracles' future when the newly born infant killed the
serpents which were threatening him. In spite of the
number of places associated with the story of Teiresias,
there is no evidence of worship (although there is a
shrine of Zeus Hypsistos near the Hypsistan gate, Paus.
9.8.5).

   Other members of the family of Kreon were honored in
Thebes. There were statues of his daughters Henioche
and Pyrrha to the right of the temple of Apollo Ismenios
(Paus. 9.10.3). Henioche appears to have been one of
several incarnations of an original Boeotian goddess of
horsy nature (the name also appears as an epithet of
Hera in Lebadeia, according to Pausanias, 9.39.5, and
as the name of the wife of Kreon in the 'Shield' of
Hesiod, line 83). (36) Pyrrha seems to have been the
Pyrrha named by Moschus (Megara 4, 52) as the wife of
Iphicles. (37)

THE FAMILY OF MELIA: APOLLO

The story of Apollo's intrusion upon the local scene is
expressed in myth in genealogical terms: Apollos carried
away Melia, a local divinity and the daughter of Ocean.
Her brother Kaänthos, unable to retrieve her, set fire to
the sanctuary of Apollo and was shot by the god; his
tomb was shown to Pausanias (9.10.5). Apollo had two
sons by Melia, Ismenos and Teneros. The former gave
his name to the river Ismenos, and became associated with
Apollo in some way in the cult of Apollo Ismenios, while
the latter received the gift of prophecy and became the
prophet of the Ptoion Apollo (Paus. 9.26.1).

   The cult of Apollo Ismenios was one of the most
important Theban cults. The temple of Apollo was located
in the vicinity of the river Ismenos, on a hill outside
the city walls to the southeast. Remains of a peripteral
temple of the classical period on this hill are probably
those of this temple. (38) The precinct contained stone
figures of Hermes and Athena Pronaia carved by the
sculptors Pheidias and Skopas, the stone seat of
Teiresias' mantic daughter Manto, and the images of
Kreon's daughters Henioche and Pyrrha. The large cedar-

wood cult statue of Apollo was compared by Pausanias to
that of Apollo at Branchidai; both were the work of the
sixth-century sculptor Kanachos.

Two passages in Pindar offer clues to the way in which
the fifth-century Thebans viewed the relationship between
Apollo and Ismenos in this sanctuary. In the first only
Ismenos figures, in markedly Theban company:

Shall we sing of Ismenus, or of Melia with her golden
distaff, or of Cadmus, or of the holy race of the
Sparti, or Thebe with her purple snood, or the all-
daring might of Heracles, or the gladsome honour due
to Dionysos, or the bridal of white-armed Harmonia?
(Frag. 9, tr. Sandys)

In the second passage, Semele and Ino are summoned to the
presence of Melia. They are invited to

Come to the inmost treasure-house of the golden-tripods,
the treasure-house which Loxias honored supremely and
named the Ismenian shrine, the seat of truthful
oracles. Come, ye children of Harmonia, where Loxias
biddeth the hosts of heroines assemble to visit the
shrine, that so at nightfull ye may sing the praises
of holy Themis and Pytho and the centre of the world
that judges rightly .... ('Pythian' 11.4-10, tr. Sandys)

The most significant thing about these two passages for
the present discussion is the way in which they treat the
relation between Apollo and Ismenos. It is portrayed as
a sanctioning of a local oracular shrine by Apollo, with
a definite separate existence assumed for Ismenos. The
Theban context is emphasized, both in the mythical
characters named and in the reference to the Theban
custom of having maiden-songs sung at the major festival
held at the Ismenion, the Daphnephoria.

Both Pausanias and Proclus describe the festival of
the Daphnephoria, which seems to have been the principal
patriotic celebration of the city, similar to the
Panathenaic festival in Athens. Its frequency is in
doubt: Proclus says that it was held every nine years,
(39) but the account given by Pausanias suggests that it
was a yearly affair, since the Daphnephoros was chosen
priest for a year (possibly, as in the case of the
Panathenaic procession, greater and lesser forms were
held in various years). Pausanias offers a brief account:
a handsome boy of noble family was chosen priest of
Apollo Ismenios for a year; he wore a wreath of laurel
leaves and was called 'Daphnephoros'; at least some of
the boys dedicated tripods as part of their service to
the god (9.10.4). Proclus gives more details of the
procession and the cult objects. The nearest kinsman of
the Daphnephoros carried a staff of olive wood called the

Kopo, which was wreathed in laurels and flowers. At its
top was a bronze globe signifying the sun, from which hung
smaller globes, representing the stars. In the middle of
the staff was another globe, smaller than the one at the
top, with 365 purple fillets, representing the moon and
the procession of the year. The bottom of the staff was
wreathed with a saffron cloth. The Daphnephoros wore a
golden crown (not a laurel wreath, as Pausanias has it),
a bright-colored garment, and shoes called Iphicratides
(these mark the description as applying to the fourth
century or later). He was followed by a maiden chorus,
carrying branches and singing. Pindar's Fragment 84 is
one of the maiden songs which were sung on the occasion
(see Chapter 6).

DISTANT CULTS

The shrine associated with Ismenos' brother Teneros lay
at some distance from Thebes, in the mountains which
border the plain on the north, about fourteen miles from
the city. (40) It was one of two shrines beyond the
usual range of Theban territory which appear to have been
under some sort of Theban control during much of the fifth
century. The other was also a shrine of Apollo, that at
Delion (Hdt. 6.118), which is about twenty miles from
Thebes, on the coast east of Tanagra, and within the
natural sphere of influence of that city. In both cases,
religious control apparently involved a degree of
political control or involvement as well.
     Theban interest in Delion appears in 470, when the
Thebans took it upon themselves to return to Delion the
cult statue of Apollo which the Persians had taken and
left in Delos. The move on the part of Thebes indicates
that the city had recovered sufficiently from the after-
effects of the Persian Wars to begin to extend its
political concerns into the territory of the rival city
of Tanagra. Similarly, after the defeat of Athens in
the battle of Delion, part of the victory celebration for
the Thebans consisted in the establishment of a special
annual memorial festival, to be held at the shrine of
Apollo in Delion (Diod. 12.70).
     In the case of the shrine of Apollo Ptoios, the
establishment of Theban control occurred much earlier
than the fifth century, perhaps in the period of the
struggle for power with Orchomenos. (41) By the fifth
century, as we have seen, this control was quite
thoroughly grounded in Theban mythology: the prophet of
the shrine was Teneros, the brother of the Theban Ismenos

(Strabo 9.2.34). Not only did these Theban brothers both preside over cults of Apollo, but the cults also bore a close resemblance to each other, in that both were oracular and both had a close association with Athena Pronoia, whose shrine was incorporated in the shrine of Apollo in both cases, rather than being separate, as at Delphi. These resemblances may reflect a Theban reorganization of the cult, as Wilamowitz held, (42) or may simply be the result of parallel development of the two cults from an original common cult-type. (43)

The time of greatest influence and affluence for the shrine of Apollo Ptoion was the archaic period. In the sixth century two Athenians of note, Alkmeonides, one of the Alkmeonid family, and Hipparchos, son of Peisistratos, both made dedications at the sanctuary. (44) This affluent period, and Athenian interest in the shrine, both ended with the Persian Wars; the last notable consultation occurred when Mys, the agent of the Persian Mardonius, consulted the oracle and received an answer remarkable for being in his own Carian tongue (Hdt. 8.135; see Chapter 6). After this, the oracle fell into comparative obscurity: the number of offerings diminished, no building activity took place, and Herodotus even found it necessary to explain to his readers the name of the oracle, its location, and its Theban connections. (45)

CULTS WITHOUT INTERCONNECTIONS

There are a few minor cults (some of them contested) which appear to lack any connection with the mythological history of Thebes, possibly in some cases simply as a result of accidents in the transmission of the tradition. These will be considered in alphabetical order.

Apollo Rescuer (Paus. 9.17.2), located near the temple of
    Artemis Eukleia.

Apollo Spondios (Paus. 9.11.7-8) had an altar made from
    the ashes of victims, which were working oxen (Paus.
    9.12.11); it was the site of an oracle (divination
    by voices). (46)

Hector (Paus. 9.18.5), first attested in about 300 BC by
    Lycophron; the complete silence about its existence
    before this time makes it unlikely that it was an
    ancient cult. It is notable as being the only Greek
    cult of Hector. It has been suggested that after the
    battle of Plataea, the Thebans sought the aid of
    Hector against his ancient foes, (47) but, as Ziehen
    contends, this seems too provocative an act to be
    credible. The most thorough discussion of the cult is

that of Crusius, who thinks the probable time of
introduction was during the struggle for hegemony in
the fourth century, although he does not rule out the
possibility that the cult went back much earlier, even
to the period of greatest interest in heroes, the sixth
century. (48) He definitely rejects an indigenous cult
of Hector, however.

Linos (Paus. 9.29.8-9), whose tomb had disappeared by the
time of Pausanias. The tomb and cult may have existed
in the fifth century, disappearing only after Philip
took the bones of Linos to Macedonia.

The Moirai (Paus. 9.25.4) had a sanctuary, with no temple
or image.

Poseidon: Pausanias does not mention any temple, shrine,
or altar, but Zichen believes that his cult must have
existed in Thebes on the grounds of the evidence of
the 'Shield' of Hesiod and the 'Seven' of Aeschylus
(130). Keramopoullos also argues for his worship. (49)

Themis (Paus. 9.25.4) had a sanctuary with a white marble
image, on the Neistan road near the shrines of the
Moirai and Zeus Agoraios.

Zeus Agoraios (Paus. 9.25.4) had only an image of stone.

Zeus Homoloios, mentioned only by Photius.

CULTS WITH SPECIAL SIGNIFICANCE IN THE FIFTH CENTURY

Some idea of the direction of religious interest in the
fifth century can be inferred from a consideration of
the cults which can be identified as originating in or
having special popularity in this period. These include
the cults whose introduction is attributed to Pindar,
and the cult of the Kabeiroi.

Four cults or dedications were attributed to Pindar
by Pausanias: the Mother of the Gods (9.25.3) who
appears as Pindar's neighbor in 'Pythian' 3.77ff.; (50)
Pan (9.25.3), who is linked with the Mother of the Gods
by Pindar in Fragment 85; Ammon (9.16.1); and Hermes
Agoraios (9.17.2). The dedication of Ammon, an image
carved by the sculptor Calamis, belongs to the context
of Pindar's Cyrenian relationships ('Pythian' 4, 5, and
9, and Fragment 17). Herodotus tells of talking to
Cyrenians who had visited the oracular shrine of Ammon
in Libya (Hdt. 2.32), the Cyrenians had dedicated an
image of Ammon at Delphi (Paus. 10.13.5), and Pindar
connects Cyrene with Ammon in 'Pythian' 4.16. Pausanias
also tells us that he had read a hymn to Ammon sent to
the shrine by Pindar, which was inscribed on a stele
beside the altar (9.16.1); Pindar's Fragment 17 is
perhaps part of this hymn. (51)

It is interesting that the three other cult figures
attributed to Pindar in addition to the cult of Ammon
were each connected in some way with the cult of the
Kabeiroi; this supports other evidence of this cult's
importance in the fifth century. Worship was offered to
the Mother of the Gods, one of Pindar's chosen cults, in
the Kabeirion (Paus. 9.25.5), while Pan is a frequent
participant in the dances and processions portrayed on
the Kabeirion vases. (52) Hermes, known as the father of
Pan, (53) also figured in the cult of the Kabeiroi, (54)
and both Pan and Hermes appear on a Kabeirion cup in a
scene in which Hermes is portrayed as initiating Pan. (55)
      The cult of the Kabeiroi, more than any other Theban
cult, reflects upon the fifth-century religious scene in
the city, for it was during this century that it rose from
its obscure sixth-century beginnings to a flourishing
state. (56) The shrine lies about five kilometers from
Thebes not far from the road to Thespiae. Pausanias
reports something of its origins and early history. A
city had existed on the spot in the dim past, and its
citizens were called Kabeiroi. Demeter gave the cult to
two of these Kabeiroi, Prometheus and his son Aitnaios
(9.25.6-7). The site was abandoned when the Epigoni
attacked Thebes, but the cult was later re-established;
possibly this re-establishment is to be connected with
the otherwise unknown Athenian Methapos, to whom Pausanias
attributes the introduction of rites and mysteries at the
Kabeirion (4.1.7). (57)
      While Pausanias relates something of the history of
the cult, he is careful to reveal nothing significant
about the identity of the Kabeiroi or the ritual
performed in the shrine, and we are still largely in the
dark on both these matters, although the archaeological
evidence for the cult does provide some clues. This
evidence consists mainly in the excavation reports of
the site, the Kabeirion pottery, and the terracotta votive
offerings. The pottery is considered in greater detail
in the chapter on crafts; here the emphasis will be upon
its contribution to an understanding of the cult.
      The cult appears to have been of a chthonic nature,
with a man (the Kabeiros) and a boy (Pais, or Pais
Kabeirou) figuring most prominently in the vase paintings.
(58) The excavations have shown that a major change
occurred at the end of the sixth century: round 'symposium'
buildings were built, and at the same time kantharoi came
into use and metal figures were replaced by clay figurines
as offerings, with a wide range of new types appearing to
supplement the earlier steers: (59) Pan, Silenus, a
standing youth, a reclining man, and grotesque figures now

make their appearance. These changes around the turn of
the century seem to have been the result of a decisive
change in the character of the worship. This might have
been the introduction of new rites by Methapos which
Pausanias mentions, although the excavators suggest that
the change may have been the result of the influence of
the cult of Dionysos. (60) The portrayals of the Kabeiros
on the vases do show a great resemblance to Dionysos
(banquet scenes with kantharoi or horns of plenty,
frequent use of vine-tendril ornamentations), and others
have inferred on evidence aside from the excavation that
Kabeiros assimilated Dionysos in Thebes. (61) The problem
with this theory is the continuing importance of Dionysos
as a major cult god of Thebes. A careful study of the
evidence has led to the cautious assertion of Hemberg:
considered strictly, the evidence shows only that there
was no fixed art type for the portrayal of the Kabeiros
(who appears in many other places in the Greek world
besides Thebes, and in a wide variety of forms and even
numbers), but that his nature was such that the Dionysos
type was suitable for use; the explanation for this is
that both gods developed in rural, wine-producing areas.
(62)
      More votive inscriptions are addressed to the Kabeiros
than to Pais, but terracotta offerings of various boy or
child figures far outnumber those of men, and there are
also numerous dedications of toys, especially tops. (63)
This has led to speculation that the shrine was especially
frequented by children, but the pattern of dedications
could as well be explained by the presence of a significant child in the myth. The combination of a man and a
boy, who is often portrayed holding animals which were a
traditional courtship gift, perhaps should not be overlooked in a city with a strong tradition of homosexual
relationships between men and boys.
      The degree to which female divinities shared in the
worship at the Kabeirion is unclear. Pausanias says
that worship was offered not only to the Kabeiroi but
also to the Mother (9.25.5), and to a certain Pelarge,
a daughter of Potnieas, who with her husband Isthmiades
played some role in re-establishing the rites, and who
was honored by the sacrifice of pregnant victims in
accordance with an oracle of Dodona (9.25.7-8). Female
figures also appear frequently in the vase paintings, but
among the votive offerings, only a few female figurines
or typical female dedications such as spinning whorls
have been found. (64) There was, however, a nearby
shrine of Demeter Kabeira and her daughter Kore (seven
stades from the Kabeirion, but not identified or excavated);

its connection with the Kabeirion is clear not only from
the use of the epithet 'Kabeira', but also from the fact
that the rites of the Kabeiroi were said to have been the
gift of Demeter, and from the similar location of a
Demeter sanctuary at the Kabeirion in Samothrace. The
suggestion has been made that the cult of the Kabeiroi
was mainly oriented to men and boys, while women frequented
the sanctuary of Demeter Kabeira and Kore. (65)
    Some of the vase paintings show processions in which a
sacrificial animal approaches an ithyphallic herm. This
suggests the fertility nature of the cult, as do the
numerous figurines of ithyphallic sileni among the votive
offerings. (66) In the second half of the fifth century
the animal characteristics of these figures decreases,
and the sileni are often portrayed as flute players, but
the coroplasts of the Kabeirion were still far behind
Attic vase painters in shedding the older tradition which
emphasized their animal nature. This is probably a
reflection of the continuing agricultural orientation of
the area, and the more direct interest in fertility which
such an area has. It is interesting that these silenus
figures were dedicated in far greater numbers at the
Kabeirion than at any other Greek sanctuary; in the light
of Socrates' connections with Thebans in the 'Phaedo', one
cannot help but recall Alcibiades' comparison of Socrates
to a silenus figure. (67)
    Probably the most striking feature of the Kabeirion
vase paintings is their evident portrayal of caricatures
of myth. The question raised is, what do these scenes
represent? Are theatrical performances being portrayed,
or do these pictures reflect some form of non-dramatic
epic parody? (68) Comic dances, often involving
imitations and grotesque figures (fat men, ithyphallic
men), were widespread in the Greek world in the archaic
period, as attested by vase paintings: padded dancers
are common on Corinthian vases, (69) not unknown on
Attic pottery, (70) and found in Boeotia as early as the
mid sixth century. (71) Athenaeus gives several local
names which were applied to these dancers, including the
name used by the Thebans, 'ethelontai' (volunteers?
improvisers?). (72) Attic comedy appears to have
developed out of this sort of grotesque dance, and
Webster suggests that the sixth-century Boeotian vases
were inspired by local performances. (73)
    Did a form of drama develop out of the grotesque
dances of the Kabeirion? The apparent story scenes on
the vases suggest this (there is no reason why all the
vases should represent the same aspect of the cult
celebrations: the procession and banquet scenes can

reasonably be taken to illustrate processions and
banquets). More evidence comes from the terracotta
figurines dedicated at the shrine, some of which also
portray parody figures. The appearance of parody in two
forms – the vases and the votive figurines – makes it
seem less likely that the parodies were independently
conceived by craftsmen without the stimulus of actual
performances. (74) The finding of theatrical masks at
the site of the Kabeirion, dating from the end of the
fourth century or the beginning of the third, adds further
weight to the thesis of dramatic performance. The earlier
caricatures of the fifth century can be seen as part of a
continuing tradition of theatrical performances in the
sanctuary, with the local variety having been abandoned
in the fourth century for Attic comedy. (75) Finally,
and perhaps most convincing, is the discovery in the
recent excavations of the Hellenistic theatral area which
is central to the site. An antecedent of this theater
would have provided the context for these fifth-century
performances. (76)

The objection has been raised that theatrical scenes
cannot be intended on the vases since figures are
portrayed which are naked, wear no masks, or appear in
unstageable scenes. (77) This, however, should be
balanced against a consideration of the vase painter's
probable intentions and the conventions within which he
worked (the same considerations hold for the votive
figurines). The suggestion made by Bruns seems
reasonable: many of these paintings were meant to be
souvenir pieces, suggestive of the festival activities
but not 'photographic' representations of specific
scenes. (78) What was portrayed was the act of burlesque
itself, and not the precise instruments whereby it was
carried out (thus masks may be considered as a theatrical
convention to be thought away in appreciating the scene;
as such, they would not be portrayed on a souvenir piece).

Assuming that there were performances, what were these
like? That they must have involved parody of mythological
stories seems to be about the only fairly certain
inference which can be drawn from the evidence. The
combination of the name 'ethelontai', and the lack of any
literary evidence in the form of quotations or fragments,
should probably lead us to assume that the performances
were improvised, perhaps even pantomimes, in a limited
traditional repertoire. Nothing remains to suggest a
chorus (the drama developed in Greek Sicily also lacked
a chorus). If the performances were in fact replaced in
the fourth century by Attic comedies, this could suggest
a similarity of purpose, and adds weight to the theory

ꞏ

that the cult of the Kabeiros was in some way influenced
by that of Dionysos, even if it did not completely
assimilate it.

The Theban cult of the Kabeiroi was a member of a more
extended mystery-cult family, the Kabeiroi cults, which
spread from a Thracian homeland across the Greek world,
giving rise to many local cult variations, the most
famous being that in Samothrace. (79) The original cult
must have been somewhat amorphous, for local traditions
created many variant versions of the same basic material:
the Kabeiroi in different places varied in name, number,
sex, age, size, and sphere of influence from the Kabeiroi
in Thebes, as well as from one another. (80) The Theban
cult of the Kabeiroi should also be viewed within the
even wider context of the phenomenon of the Greek mystery
religions, which manifested itself in other forms in the
worship of Dionysos, the Eleusinian mysteries, Orphism,
Pythagoreanism, and the Sicilian cult espoused by Theron.
The characterization of these various mystery cults by
Burkert as overlapping, 'superimposed circles with some
areas shared, some not', is much more helpful than an
attempt to translate similarities into identities, or to
find influences between one and another of these still
poorly understood cults. (81)

Pausanias attests to the longevity of the cult of the
Kabeiroi; even in his day he was unwilling to reveal its
secrets, and he relates stories of the miserable fates
of those who in one way or another transgressed, including
anonymous victims among the men of Xerxes and Alexander.
Clearly in Thebes it was more than a simple local cult
of rude farmers and shepherd boys (a picture which could
arise only from prejudice, in the face of the evidence).
In the years 440-420 BC it reached an artistic peak with
the production of the Kabeirion vases, which probably
reflected a period of unusual prosperity and creative
vigor in the cult as a whole, and not just among its
vase painters. Plato's 'Phaedo' suggests that, by the
late fifth century, some men of substance in Thebes were
concerning themselves with the fate of the soul after
death. Perhaps it is not simple coincidence that at this
time the Kabeirion potters and painters were producing
their most remarkable product.

CONCLUSION

The impression which results from a survey of Theban cults
in the fifth century is one of a system in which older
religious elements, and even rudiments of a primitive

stage of religion, persisted and predominated. The
Olympian gods played a relatively small role, and when
they did appear they were often merged with, or subordinate to, the local mythical figures. Remnants of
fetish cults appear in the many sacred stones, such as
the stones of Alkmene, Manto, Tydeus, and Heracles, and
in the log image of Dionysos Kadmeios. This primitivism
and conservatism is certainly an important aspect of the
Theban cult system, (82) but it would be a mistake to
overlook the fact that there were also important elements
of change active in that system. The first is the tendency
to synthesize, to draw disparate elements together into
a systematic Theban 'history'. The same intellectual
process is of course to be seen in Hesiod, who lived not
far from the city. Solmsen viewed this as a conservative
method of change; it is interesting that he notes as well
the possibility that this process of synthesis was a
forerunner of philosophical reasoning. (83)
    A second element of change was to be found in Thebes'
receptivity to new cults, especially those of a foreign
or mystery nature. We see this receptivity operating in
the introduction of the cults of the Mother and Pan
(whether they were actually introduced by Pindar or by
someone else is immaterial), and especially in the reorganization and flourishing of the cult of the Kabeiroi
in the fifth century. It is also apparent in Thebes'
reputation for being the earliest home of Dionysos and
his orgiastic worship in Greece. In fact, a strong
interest in other-worldly concerns is the most striking
feature of Theban religious life in the fifth century.
Nor should this be surprising, when we consider the
agricultural orientation of the city and the proliferation
of oracles in Boeotia in general: there were oracles of
Trophonius at Lebadeia, of Amphiaraos at Oropus (after
the late fifth century), and of Apollo at Hysiae, Tegyra,
Ptoion, and Delion. In Thebes itself there were oracles
of Amphiaraos (before the late fifth century), Apollo
Ismenios, and Apollo Spondios.
    Thus at Thebes in the fifth century we find a well-
ordered system of cults with strong ties to the local
landscape and to local history, and relatively little
interest in the panhellenic Olympians. This cult system
evidenced a certain conservatism in the preservation of
primitive elements. On the other hand, it also manifested
a definite receptivity to new elements, especially those
of a mystery nature, which accorded well with the religious
climate of a land populated by oracles from prehistoric
times.

5 Philosophy in Thebes

The receptivity of Thebans to new mystico-religious ideas
manifests itself in a particularly interesting way in
their response to Pythagorean philosophy. Pythagoreanism
in its pre-Platonic form centered upon a belief in the
transmigration of souls, a prescribed Way of Life based
upon reverence for Pythagoras, and a belief that the
cosmos and all things in it are, basically, harmonies of
numbers, a belief which had not yet developed into
scientific mathematics or the derivation of the cosmos
from the One and the Indefinite Dyad, later fruits of
Platonic influence. (1) Having developed in southern
Italy, its teachings were marked by the prominence of
chthonic divinities and eschatological beliefs characteristic of that area, as well as by an unusual degree of
acceptance of women as significant members of the
religious community. (2) The society followed a normal
pattern of Greek culture in which cult-society and
political club were one and the same, and despite its
apparent other-worldly orientation, it was very active
and influential in politics. By mid fifth century its
strong oligarchic character and its involvement in local
politics led to revolts and persecutions against the sect
throughout southern Italy. It was as a result of this
political upheaval that Pythagoreanism reached Thebes,
when Lysis, a Pythagorean refugee from the persecutions,
settled in that city. Lysis, having escaped from the
burning meeting-house in Croton with only one other youth,
made his way first to Achaea in the Peloponnesos, and
then moved on to Thebes, where he stayed to become, at
least in tradition, the teacher of Epaminondas, and to
develop a Pythagorean community, two of whose members were
Simmias and Cebes, Socrates' partners in dialogue in the
'Phaedo'.
    The basic soundness of the tradition of Pythagorean

involvement in Thebes is attested by Plato. The particular
tradition attributing this involvement to Lysis goes back
to Aristoxenos, a disciple of Aristotle. His source may
have been one of the 'last Pythagoreans' mentioned by
Diogenes Laertes (8.46),who were living in Phlious at the
turn of the fifth century and thus would have been in a
position to be well informed. Although Aristoxenos is
notorious for his attempts to discredit Plato, in chronological matters and questions about the involvement of
particular individuals he is considered to be a reliable
authority. (3)

In many ways the choice of Thebes was a logical one
for Lysis, for the city had many characteristics which
suited his Pythagorean background. It was an agricultural
society with strong interests in the early substratum of
mystery religion which underlay the religion of the
Olympians, and it accorded women a relatively important
role in religious observances (important if the Pythagorean
tradition of participation by women was to be maintained).
It was noted for its interest in music, and it was
oligarchic in political orientation and preserved the
aristocratic way of life. All of these would have been
points of attraction to a Pythagorean. But what of it
all might have been known to Lysis?

There were actually several sources of information
available to him which would have suggested the
possibility of a friendly reception for Pythagorean
religious philosophy in Thebes. These could have gone
back to Hesiod's 'Works and Days', which was surely
known to him; its inclusion of number lore and taboos
which were close to if not identical with Pythagorean
traditions would have suggested a receptive environment.
Thebes as a center for the orgiastic worship of Dionysos
was widely known among the Greeks of the fifth century,
and the Theban cult of the Kabeiroi may also have been
known, at least among religious enthusiasts. Knowledge
of Pindar's work, especially those passages which deal
with transmigration and the afterlife (which would be
the most likely passages to attract attention and be
circulated among Pythagoreans) was possible for Lysis.
(Pindar had composed two odes, 'Olympian' 10 and 11, for
Agesidamos of Epizephyrian Locri in southern Italy), and
would have provided more specific and comparatively
recent hints which he might have taken as revealing
tendencies in Pindar's home city. Turning to the
political sphere, we may assume that Lysis was aware of
Thebes' traditional position of leadership in the Boeotian
league, and of its oligarchic and aristocratic political
orientation. It also seems quite likely that he would

have heard of the recent and noted victory of the Boeotians
against Athens at Coronea, which would have been of much
interest to small states, in which the expansionist
tendencies of larger and more powerful neighbors were
closely watched. And the newly regained freedom of
Boeotia would have raised the possibility of the need for
political advice in the mind of a political sophisticate.

Thus, far from being an odd choice for a Pythagorean
refugee, Thebes in fact turns out to have been a quite
logical choice, and one which Lysis conceivably could have
made on the basis of information readily available to him.
It offered him the possibility of successful integration
into a basically sympathetic society, for even though
Thebes was a land-based oligarchy (and therefore, one might
think, unreceptive to landless newcomers), Lysis possessed
a special asset which he had every reason to believe would
open doors for him in Thebes: his identity as a Pythagorean,
and hence as a potential 'wise man', who would surely be
honored in a community with similar religious tendencies
(just as Pythagoras had been honored upon his arrival in
Italy). And if the stories about his being the teacher
of Epaminondas are true, he did in fact settle into Thebes
in the role of honored teacher.

For information about the nature of the Pythagorean
philosophy which developed in Thebes from this beginning,
we have two sources, Plato's 'Phaedo' and the 'De genio
Socratis' of Plutarch. Both have some claim on us as
authorities, Plato because he was present in the last
years of Socrates' life as a follower and must have known
the Thebans in the Socratic circle, and Plutarch because
he was a Boeotian himself, and thus may have had access
to local traditions otherwise unknown to us.

PLATO'S 'PHAEDO'

In the 'Phaedo' Plato portrays two Thebans, Simmias and
Cebes, as among the circle of Socrates' intimate
acquaintances, and the two serve as the chief critics of
Socrates' attempts to prove the immortality of the soul.
Plato makes a point of referring to the pair as having
heard Philolaos at Thebes (61D7). The Theban element in
the dialogue is further underlined by scattered 'Thebisms':
a rare occurrence of the use of a dialect form at 62A8; (4)
the specific mention of Thebes in a form of address at
92A6-B4; Socrates' remark that his bones and sinews, left
to themselves, would long ago have been in Megara (a well-
known center of Eleatic philosophy) or Boeotia (98E5f.);
and possibly the warning against misologia at 89D, a stock
Athenian charge against the Thebans. (5)

When Plato disclaims personal knowledge of the events of
the day of Socrates' death, saying that he was ill (59B),
he is probably claiming a certain degree of creative leeway
in his reconstruction of these events and especially of
the conversation which was held (he may also have been
answering critics of his absence). We are therefore
justified in asking what effect he might have sought to
create by his choice of the two Thebans as Socrates' sole
partners in debate and by his emphasis on their Theban
background and on their study with Philolaos, and why he
might have sought this effect. Surely he has at least
shaped and given form to the historical facts, even if
he has not created them. The answer to the first part of
this question is suggested by the tradition of the
Pythagorean settlement in Thebes: he would have expected
these factors to reinforce the Pythagorean background of
the dialogue which he had already established in the
frame conversation by his use of Echecrates of Phlious
(Phlious was the home of the 'last Pythagoreans' according
to Diogenes Laertes (8.46), and thus a known Pythagorean
center in the fourth century when Plato was writing).
    As Thebans, Simmias and Cebes are men who can be expected
to be acquainted with Pythagorean ideas. Are they also to
be identified as Pythagoreans themselves? Many scholars
do so identify them, (6) but recently there has been a
tendency to be more cautious about assuming this. Plato
never explicitly identifies them as Pythagoreans, and
although they have heard the Pythagorean teacher Philolaos,
Cebes says he has heard 'nothing clear' about his teaching
on suicide (61DE). While this is clearly a literary
device allowing Socrates to offer an explanation to the
reader within the dramatic context, it seems unlikely
that Plato would have used such a device in disregard
of its further implications. It is not so much a
reflection on Cebes' deficiencies as a student, as some
would have it, (7) as it is a characterization of the
teaching of Philolaos and others at Thebes: Philolaos
'provided no clear "rationale" for his teaching'. (8)
Of course, in any case, the passage offers no clue to
the answer to the question whether Simmias and Cebes were
Pythagoreans.
    More important in determining whether to classify
Simmias and Cebes as Pythagoreans is the fact that both
men offer theories as counter-arguments which contradict
the well-known Pythagorean belief in transmigration.
Simmias suggests that the soul is a harmony of bodily
parts (85Eff.). If this is the case, it is not the sort
of thing which could survive to migrate into another
body. Cebes suggests an analogy between soul and body and

a weaver and his work: the soul weaves many bodies which
it outlives, but eventually it dies, just as the weaver
weaves many cloaks which he outlives, but eventually he
dies (86Eff.). Such a soul might be said to transmigrate
for a time, but its eventual death is not consistent with
the Pythagorean theory of transmigration. The idea of
the soul as a harmony, despite its incompatability with
the theory of transmigration, is clearly marked out by
Plato as a theory which was sometimes entertained by
Pythagoreans, for he has Echecrates confess to being
attracted to it (88CD). The attraction was undoubtedly
the superficial resemblance to the theory of the cosmos
as a harmony of numbers. Burkert suggests that Plato
may have been the first to point out the embarrassing
contradiction inherent in these two theories, both of
which were held by Pythagoreans. (9) The analogy of the
weaver, however, is otherwise unknown (at least the idea
of the soul doing its own weaving seems to be an innovation),
(10) and bears no surface marks of Pythagorean origin.
We should probably classify it as a counter-example created
on the spot and attesting to Cebes' philosophical ability,
for it bears exactly upon the weak point in Socrates'
argument.

    The aspect which is most un-Pythagorean about the
arguments of Simmias and Cebes is not so much the exact
content of their objections, but their skeptical spirit
and their refusal to rest content with 'wisdom' unless
that wisdom is accompanied by proof as well. This spirit
is Socratic, and, in fact, far from Simmias and Cebes
being identified as Pythagorean, more is made in the
course of the dialogue of their acquaintance with Socratic
teachings: they are portrayed as thoroughly familiar
with the theory of Forms, (11) and, although Simmias does
have some difficulty recollecting the theory of Recollection
(the point of this may be just the punning self-referential
joke itself, as well as the opening which it gives to
Socrates for an explanation of the theory), it is Cebes
who introduces the theory into the argument (72E).
Elsewhere in the dialogues of Plato their identification
as followers of Socrates is further attested. At 'Crito'
45B Simmias is said to be standing by with money ready
to bribe the jailkeeper and help Socrates to escape, and
Cebes is also said to be ready to help; Simmias is said
to be extremely fond of philosophical discourse at
'Phaedrus' 242B; and Cebes is mentioned by Plato as one
of his own friends in the 13th Epistle (363A). (12)
Xenophon mentions both men as associates of Socrates; (13)
even if he is drawing from the Platonic dialogues, this
serves as a contemporary confirmation of the picture which

the dialogues present. Men who had much opportunity to
become familiar with Pythagorean teachings, but who were
not themselves committed to the sect, and whose wits had
been sharpened for argument by association with Socrates,
would provide the best sparring partners for Socrates in
his attempts to prove the immortality of the soul.
Throughout the dialogue they serve the purpose of raising
sceptical objections and counter-arguments; Simmias says
of Cebes that he is 'the most obstinate person in the
world at resisting an argument' (77A8-9, tr. Tredennick).
      In fact, the Pythagorean elements in the 'Phaedo' are
introduced by Socrates himself, rather than by his two
Theban companions, but these elements have undergone a
Socratic reincarnation: it is the Socratic theory of
Forms which provides the intellectual support for the
doctrine of the transmigration of souls; the highest
stage in the career of the transmigrating soul is reached
by the soul of the philosopher in the Socratic sense of
that word; and the Pythagorean/Orphic myths about the
afterlife are permeated with Ionian science and turned
toward ethical purposes. It seems that Plato had adopted
a Pythagorean setting in order to demonstrate Socrates'
transformation of the material of Pythagorean philosophy
into an integral part of a new Socratic philosophy.
Part of Plato's purpose in writing the 'Phaedo' thus may
have been to clarify the contribution of Pythagoreanism
to Socratic philosophy in general, and to the theory of
Forms in particular. (14) The 'Clouds' of Aristophanes
suggests that on a popular level at least opinion tended
to blur any distinctions between Socratic philosophy and
Pythagoreanism; Taylor has even proposed that the
supposed Pythagoreanism of Socrates may have been the
real grounds of the charges brought against Socrates. (15)
Taylor finds that the 'Phaedo' presents just such a
picture of a Socrates enmeshed in Pythagoreanism; on
the contrary, I would suggest that the 'Phaedo' presents
a defense against such charges, by portraying Socrates
as drawing upon the Pythagorean tradition for his own
purposes, but nevertheless standing essentially
independent of it.
      The question has been raised whether the Pythagorean
elements which are here attributed to the philosophical
environment in which Socrates worked really did belong
to that environment - whether a Pythagoreanizing Socrates
ever really existed to be defended, or whether, as
Hackforth suggests, (16) Plato is adding a Pythagorean
element to his Socrates which was alien to the historical
Socrates. The best evidence for a Pythagoreanizing
Socrates is to be found in the 'Clouds' of Aristophanes.

One may, of course, question the historicity of
Aristophanes' Socrates, (17) but at least the portrait
in the play proves that the Pythagorean/Orphic element
was not a late addition foisted on to Socrates by Plato.
The fact that the 'Clouds' confirms the 'Phaedo' on this
point seems sufficient to rule out the hypothesis of
Hackforth, and to confirm an historical Pythagoreanizing
Socrates, although by no means a truly orthodox Pythagorean
Socrates.

The 'Phaedo' tells us a little about the atmosphere at
Thebes when Simmias remarks that most people think that
philosophers, with their lack of concern for the joys of
everyday life, really want to die, and that death is
therefore quite suitable for them – and that the Thebans
would agree most emphatically with that (64B).   Burnet
aptly remarks that, 'Probably we have here a reflection
of the impression made by the Pythagorean refugees on the
bon vivants of Thebes.   The philosophoi would not appreciate
Copaic eels and ducks'. (18)   The dialogue also tells us
something about the philosophical personalities of Simmias
and Cebes.   We have seen that Simmias could be accused of
being forgetful or inattentive to philosophical issues,
and at one point he is even shown to be guilty of
maintaining two contradictory theories at the same time:
the theory of Recollection and the theory of the soul as
a harmony (92A).   He also once shows an unphilosophic
regard for divine revelation (85D).   Cebes plays the more
active role in the dialogue and is keener in argument:
it is he who insists on the need for more proof of the
soul's immortality (70A), who remembers and introduces
the theory of Recollection and its proofs (72E), and who
brings forward the counter-argument of the analogy of
the weaver and his cloak to the soul and its body (87A).
(19)   On the whole, the two men are presented as
intelligent and devoted to argument, although Cebes is
clearly the more promising thinker; they exhibit a rather
courageous degree of skepticism, given the fact that
they are carrying on the negative side of the argument
about immortality with a man on the brink of death (that
they are not insensitive to this is made clear at 84D).

The thesis that Plato had a specific purpose in mind
(to clarify the relationship between Socrates and
Pythagoreanism) when he chose two Thebans to be the
chief interlocutors of Socrates and in other ways stressed
the Pythagorean element in the dialogue raises the
question, to what extent have these considerations affected
the historicity of the portrait which Plato draws of these
two men?   In arguing for the historical validity of the
portrait, we must in the final analysis depend on an

argument from 'eikos', or probability: in real life we
should expect them to have been somewhat similar to this
Platonic portrait - intelligent, keen on argument,
skeptical yet willing to listen, and ready in the
recognition of a flaw in their opponent's case - or they
would not have found a place among the members of the
Socratic circle.   Certainly, we would say, they could not
have been doctrinaire Pythagoreans.   But in believing
this, are we simply providing living proof of the efficacy
of Plato's art and drawing the conclusion which he intended
his readers to draw?   Perhaps we simply have been led,
step by step, to a position at which we would affirm, 'Of
course Socrates associated with Pythagoreans, in the sense
that he associated with people who came from a Pythagorean
background, but these men were not *real* Pythagoreans.
The picture in the 'Clouds', and the popular notion of
Socrates as a sort of Pythagorean, is quite misleading.
Rather, he transformed Pythagorean ideas into Socratic
philosophy.'

PLUTARCH'S 'DE GENIO SOCRATIS'

The only other large-scale picture of philosophy at Thebes
is contained in the 'De genio Socratis' of Plutarch, a
work of a Boeotian of the first and second centuries AD,
neatly composed to echo and supplement the 'Phaedo'. (20)
In it we re-encounter Simmias twenty years after the time
of the 'Phaedo':   he has followed the advice of Socrates
to travel among the Greeks and barbarians (78A) and has
at length returned to Thebes, a sort of Theban Socrates
who sits, immobilized by a leg wound, while his friends
gather around him to carry on a philosophical discussion
on the brink of a great event.   In the case of the 'De
genio', the event is the liberation of Thebes from
Spartan control, (21) and the subject of the discussion
is the nature of the daimon of Socrates.   Like the
'Phaedo', the work is a narrated dialogue, a dialogue
embedded within a dialogue, and the main speech is
crowned with a myth.   Many small details show the care
with which Plutarch has sought to link this continuation
of the life of Simmias with the earlier work of Plato:
    loosening of bandage/bonds on leg ('De gen.' 586A,
            'Phaedo' 59Ef., 60Bf.)
    reference to daimons at 'Phaedo' 107D parallels
            discussion about the daimon of Socrates in the
            'De genio'
    dream offers material for consideration ('Phaedo' 60E,
        'De gen.' 587A and 588D)

divine command to engage in the art of the Muses
         ('Phaedo' 60E, 'De gen.' 579A, C, D)
   warning about misologia ('Phaedo' 89D, 'De gen.' 575E)
   As the group discusses various subjects in the 'De
genio', we get an idea of the sorts of topics which
Plutarch pictured such philosophical discussions as
including: the discoveries at the tomb of Alkmene, and
the decipherment by Egyptian priests of an inscription
which may have been the one found there (577Df.); the
Delians' request to Plato for aid in doubling the altar
at Delos (579B-D); the search for the tomb of Dirke and
an account of the ancient Theban custom which preserved
its secrecy (578BC). Finally, spurred by the arrival of
a Pythagorean visitor, Theanor, the discussion turns to
the topic of divination, particularly appropriate for
Thebans with their many oracles, and in particular, to
the nature of the sign of Socrates. After others have
made their contributions, Simmias offers the principal
explanation, resorting in Platonic fashion to a myth (the
consultation of the Boeotian oracle of Trophonius by
Timarchus). Theanor's entry also provides an opportunity
to recount the reason for the presence in Thebes of the
Pythagorean Lysis: the story is told of the burning of
the Pythagorean meeting-house at Metapontum (a divergence
from the tradition according to Aristoxenus which will be
discussed below), the escape of Lysis and Philolaos, and
the eventual arrival of Lysis at Thebes. Theanor's
mission is to offer libations at the tomb of Lysis, to
repay Epaminondas' father for his care of Lysis, and,
if the burial has not been carried out properly, to take
the remains back to Italy.   Pythagoreanism has taken
sound root at Thebes, however: the payment is turned
down by Polymnis with a proper philosophic preference for
poverty, and Theanor can report that he need not disturb
the burial, for the Pythagorean rites have been carried
out properly and Lysis' soul has been released to a new
rebirth.
   All of this provides us with a picture of the philosophical scene in Thebes in the period following the
death of Socrates, as portrayed by Plutarch in the first
century AD. This picture shows a group of men who meet
to discuss both political and 'philosophical' topics,
with the philosophical discussions centering upon what
we should perhaps prefer to call religious matters:
Corlu in his edition suggests that 'On doit entendre
"logois kai philosophia" au sens large de controverses
intellectuelles'. (22) Although Simmias' account contains
some elements of a theory of sense perception (588Aff.),
on the whole it is mystical. In this it is not untrue to

the picture of philosophy in the late fifth century as
Plato presents it, or at least to one side of this
picture; however, it lacks the hard-edged, keen intellectual analysis which we also find in Plato's portrait of
Socrates (and in Cebes' persistent questioning of Socrates).
Perhaps the Pythagoreans themselves lacked this intellectual quality, or at least the majority of them did; it may
be that this is exactly what one should have expected of a
satellite group of Pythagoreans in the early fourth
century: political machinations and mystical musings.
Yet it is also possible that this is only the way in which
Plutarch, assisted by his knowledge of Plato's writings
and influenced by the interests of his own day, imagined
the philosophical scene in Thebes in the early fourth
century.

To some extent, the question of Plutarch's purposes in
writing the 'De genio' bears upon this question of
authenticity. Plutarch himself signals at least a part
of his purpose early in the work when he speaks of the
ancient reproach against the Boeotians of misologia, a
reproach which was dying out because of Theban philosophical
activity. (23) Most scholars are agreed that it was at
least in part in order to combat this reproach that the
work was composed in the way in which it was, with
philosophical dialogue interwoven into the story of the
liberation: Plutarch is concerned to show his countrymen
as thoughtful men who combined courage in battle with
interest in and sensitivity to topics of intellectual
interest. (24) Thus we can be fairly sure that he did
not purposely present a false picture in which the
religious element outweighed the intellectual element,
but that he truly believed that these were the sorts of
topics which would have been discussed among philosopher-
statesmen. He could still have been mistaken, and he
could have been misled by the way in which philosophy was
conceived in the first century AD, but it seems likely
that he intended to present an authentic picture.

Is there anything else that the dialogue can contribute
which may provide independent evidence about the Theban
philosophical scene and help in deciding upon the degree
of authenticity which we should accord to Plutarch's
picture? There are three possibilities: the story of
Charillos and the pigs (580D-F); the reports of travels
of Simmias with Plato (578A-579D); and the information
about the history of the Pythagorean presence in Thebes.

The little story about Charillos and the pigs, told by
the mantis Theokritos, (25) is the sort of tale which
might have been passed down in a family tradition.
Theokritos had been visiting Euthyphro (also a mantis) and

was present while Socrates was questioning Euthyphro.
Simmias and Charillos the flute-player, who had accompanied
Theokritos to Athens to visit Cebes, were among the group
as well, walking to the Symbolon. Suddenly Socrates
stopped short in one of his trances; when he recovered, he
said that the sign had come to him, and he turned back.
Most of the group turned back with him, but some, including
Charillos, went on, only to be met by a herd of muddy
swine which knocked down some of the group and muddied
them all. Despite the possible inspiration from the
'Euthyphro', there is nothing inherently implausible in
the story (although a connection with the famous Boeotian
pig might be suspected); neither, however, does the story
offer much in the way of information about philosophical
activities, except to confirm the presence of Thebans in
the Socratic circle, and to widen the circle to include
names otherwise unattested.

The story of the travels of Simmias with Plato is more
ambitious, and also more questionable. That Plato himself
made a trip to Egypt is probable, though not provable. (26)
The presence of Simmias on such a trip is much more
suspicious, however; it is not attested elsewhere, and
such travels were traditionally attributed to philosophers.
Finally, it serves the clear purpose of enhancing the
philosophical status of the Theban Simmias and therefore
of Thebes itself, one of the purposes of the work. Under
these circumstances, we do not seem justified in according
the story much weight.

Finally, there is material in the 'De genio' about the
history of the Pythagorean presence in Thebes. In his
account of the aftermath of the expulsion of the
Pythagoreans from Italy, Plutarch tells us that only
Lysis and Philolaos escaped from the burning meeting-
house at Metapontum, and that Philolaos escaped to
Lucania and from there reached survivors of attacks
against Pythagoreans in other Italian cities, who at
once re-grouped to oppose the attackers. Lysis, however,
escaped to Thebes, and nothing had been known of him
among the Pythagoreans in Italy until the sophist and
rhetorician Gorgias brought back word, probably in 427
(583AB). (27) Lysis died and was buried at Thebes; he
was the teacher of Epaminondas, whose father, Polymnis,
had supported him in his old age and had overseen the
performance of proper Pythagorean burial rites for him
(583C). We can assume that in the first century AD he
was remembered as the focus and source of philosophical
activity and interest in fifth-century Thebes, and
probably that his burial place was known. We need to
ask, to what extent does this tradition agree with other

evidence about the same events, and to what extent does
it agree with the situation in the 'Phaedo'?

The earliest and most reliable account of the events
of the Pythagorean holocaust is that of Aristoxenus,
recounted by Iamblichus. (28) Plutarch deviates from the
account of Aristoxenus in two matters: he gives the
location of the holocaust as Metapontum rather than Croton,
and he says that Lysis and Philolaos survived, while
Aristoxenus says that it was Lysis and Archippos. As
Delatte pointed out, the former variation would have been
a natural one resulting from a confusion caused by reports
of trouble breaking out in several Italian cities, and
from the fact that Metapontum was perhaps the best known
Pythagorean center. (29) The latter difference is also
explained by Delatte as the substitution (probably while
working from memory) of a more celebrated name for one
that was almost unknown; Delatte, however, also suggests
that this was a useful substitution, since Philolaos'
travels in Greece would thereby also be explained. The
problem with that reasoning is that Plutarch seems in fact
to be denying Philolaos any travels in Greece, rather
than wishing to explain them. He makes certain points
very emphatically:

1   Philolaos did not go to Thebes after the holocaust,
    but stayed in Italy, rallying the scattered Pythagorean
    survivors and overseeing a resumption of political
    activity which took place almost immediately.
2   Lysis was responsible for the Pythagorean education
    of Polymnis and his son Epaminondas, and presumably
    of other Thebans as well.
3   Gorgias took word back about Lysis' survival; Aresas
    was concerned but unable to take any immediate action
    in contacting him; eventually an individual named
    Theanor, and not Philolaos, came to pay homage to
    Lysis' grave (Theanor may be fictitious, but the point
    is that for Plutarch the individual is not Philolaos
    but someone else). There is nothing about Philolaos.
In contrast, Plato speaks of Philolaos, but not of Lysis,
when he questions Simmias and Cebes about their philosophical background ('Phaedo' 61DE). Could it be that
Plutarch is correcting Plato, feeling that he did not do
justice to the memory and activity of Lysis as the
teacher of Thebes in philosophy? (30) If this is not the
case, then he has made a very strange error: throughout
the 'De genio' he has carefully followed the 'Phaedo' as
a paradigm, yet he has forgotten the significant point
that Plato never mentions Lysis but does mention Philolaos.
It seems unlikely that Plutarch would have forgotten a
name present in his prototype, especially when he recalls

more insignificant details, and unwittingly transformed
Plato's 'Philolaos' into 'Lysis'. It is more likely that
Plutarch was correcting Plato on the basis of local
tradition, and that he felt that Philolaos was a non-
historical addition of Plato's to the Theban scene.
Whether Plutarch was right or not is a question which will
be considered below.

CONCLUSIONS

Now that we have considered the major sources of information
about the philosophical scene in fifth-century Thebes,
what conclusions can we draw from them?
    First of all, it seems reasonable to accept a Pythag-
orean presence in Thebes, consisting of at least Lysis,
with the pupils he was able to attract, from some time
shortly after mid-century. Aristoxenus bears witness to
this, and he is considered to be a reliable authority for
questions of chronology and the identification of
individual participants in events; moreover, he had access
to good sources of information: his father knew Socrates,
(31) and he himself also claimed to have known Pythagoreans
at Phlious, including Echecrates (DL 8.46). His report
is supported by the statement of Alcidamas that when the
leading men of Thebes became philosophers the city became
prosperous, (32) and by the assumption of Plato's 'Phaedo'
of such a presence as part of the background of the
dialogue.
    As far as the presence of Philolaos is concerned, the
situation is not quite so clear. 'Phaedo' 61DE implies
this, but it could have been a literary fiction which
Plato added to bolster recognition of Thebes as Pythagorean (if any of his readers did not understand that the
general background of Simmias and Cebes was Pythagorean,
a reference to Philolaos would have made this more clear),
and Plutarch's apparently deliberate omission of his name
raises a question. Two points may be made in support of
Plato, however, which appear to turn the balance in his
favor. He seems to have written the 'Phaedo' after
his first trip to Italy, (33) where he saw Philolaos,
according to Diogenes Laertius (DL 3.6); and the 'last of
the Pythagoreans' of Phlious (among them Echecrates)
are named by Aristoxenus as disciples of Philolaos whom
he had himself known. If Philolaos taught in Phlious,
it is likely that he would have made at least a visit to
the Pythagorean community in Thebes, and if Plato visited
Philolaos in Italy, he would have had a first-hand source
for his information. (34) There is always the possibility

that over the centuries a brief visit by Philolaos to
Thebes would have slipped out of Theban tradition, which
had as its main interest the enhancement of Lysis, the
teacher of Epaminondas, and that Plutarch, following a
tradition which no longer remembered Philolaos, would
have felt called upon to correct Plato in order to give
due respect to Lysis.

Another difficulty is an apparent disparity between
the portraits of Simmias which are presented by Plato and
Plutarch. Plato is the earlier and better source, but
his interest in downplaying the extent to which the
Socratic circle was really Pythagorean may have led him
to portray a more secular and skeptical Simmias than was
actually the case; on the other hand, Plutarch also is
concerned to present a certain picture (Simmias as the
Theban Socrates), and he had the additional disability of
having to rely wholly upon tradition, which was unlikely
to have preserved a picture of Simmias as skeptic and
heretic. Perhaps it is unnecessary and unfair to the
genre of these two works to defend the historical accuracy
of their character portrayals; however, it is interesting
that one can reconcile the two portraits by appealing to
the twenty-year difference in their dramatic dates:
Simmias, less intellectually keen than Cebes, may have
become more sympathetic to Pythagoreanism as a faith
once he was separated from the influence of Socrates.
At 'Phaedo' 85D he does refer to a 'logos theios' as a
safer harbor than proof, and perhaps he later felt that
he had found such a harbor; it is also interesting that
it is Cebes who is mentioned in the 13th Epistle as a
member of the Platonic circle. Whatever choice we may
make as to the philosophical personality of Simmias,
however, we are still left with a Theban Pythagoreanism
which is basically mystico-religious in orientation:
this is clear in the choice of subject matter in the
'De genio', and Plato supports it when he mentions the
teaching about suicide of Philolaos and others at Thebes,
but says nothing about mathematical or scientific
teachings or activity. There is perhaps an additional
clue to a mystico-religious bent in Theban Pythagoreanism
when Plato suggests that Philolaos did not provide a
rational foundation for his teaching. All these are
very slight clues to the nature of Theban Pythagoreanism,
but at least they are consistent. They are also consistent
with the reconstruction of pre-Platonic Pythagoreanism
derived by Burkert from sources other than the 'Phaedo'
and the 'De genio'. (35) In the case of the 'Phaedo',
this agreement can be taken as further support for
Burkert's interpretation, while in the case of the 'De

genio' it seems to be more a matter of historical
accident, for the psychological needs of the first century,
leading as they did to a search for a superhuman wisdom,
brought Pythagoreanism full circle back again to its
origins.

6 The Muses

The early Greeks closely connected music and poetry in
the concept of the Muses. The rhythm of music and poetic
meter aided in preserving traditional stories, genealogies,
and other 'historical' materials in memory before writing
came into use. Even after the introduction of writing,
poetry continued to be the predominant form of literary
expression in mainland Greece until the fifth century,
when prose came into more widespread use (in Ionia
experiments with prose began with the philosophers of the
sixth century and the geographer and chronicler Hecataeus,
who died early in the fifth century). The close connection
between music and song remained, however, despite
alterations in traditional forms in some places, such as
Athens. In conservative Thebes, the connection remained
virtually unchallenged. Poetry, especially choral poetry,
continued to be the form for the preservation and
transmission of traditional lore, and provided also, for
some, a vehicle for innovation. The victory odes of the
Theban poet Pindar remain today almost complete as some
of the greatest products of the Greek poetic genius;
these are intricate creations which interweave contemporary
and mythological references and philosophical comment in
a brilliant display of verbal ingenuity. Of Pindar's
many other poetic works - hymns, choral dithyrambs,
processionals, maiden songs, dance songs, encomia, party
songs, and dirges - only fragments remain, but these
fragments attest to the importance of various forms of
poetry and song in the life of Thebes. Fragments of the
work of other poets are also extant, especially of the
works of the woman poet Corinna, a native of Boeotian
Tanagra, but a participant in the Theban poetic scene.
Her poems were composed in the Boeotian dialect, and this,
together with their style and the fragmentary character
of the remains, makes interpretation difficult, but, as we

shall see, they still offer important evidence, especially
about the participation of women in poetic composition.
    Verbal expression was, however, not the only form which
the work of the Muses took in Thebes. While no drama of
the Athenian form developed, we see in the Kabeirion vases
evidence for a probable continuation of traditional
dramatic expression. In addition, a lively tradition of
Theban skill in instrumental music, especially in flute
playing, is reflected in our sources.

THE FLUTE

    Greece judges Thebes to be victor with the flute.
        (Dio Chrysostom, 'Orat.' vii (I.136 ed. Dindorf))
According to Dio Chrysostom, the statue of Hermes bearing
this inscription was the only monument which the Thebans
were concerned about restoring after the destruction of
their city in the fourth century. This story epitomizes
the ancient tradition of Theban musical interest, a
tradition, moreover, which upon closer examination turns
out to have a history of its own and to tell us more
about the fifth century BC than one would at first expect.
    Plutarch explains the Theban esteem for the flute as
a result of a deliberate attempt by the Theban legislators
to temper the manners and character of the youth. (1)
This explanation, however, is suspiciously similar to
theories about the ethical effects of music of the sort
which Plato attributes to Damon. (2) The theories of
Damon, who was a generation younger than Socrates, were
too late to have had the necessary effect on Theban
legislators, whom we should place in the archaic period
with other noted Greek legislators. They did, however,
color the thinking of Plato, and, through him or
independently, could easily have led Plutarch to draw
this conclusion. Flute-playing, moreover, is linked by
Plutarch with a second device also purportedly introduced
to soften the Theban youth, homosexuality, and this
alleged purpose, too, sounds suspiciously late.
Aristocratic homosexuality was traditionally thought to
increase the fighting capabilities of the youth, rather
than to soften him. A shift in the way of thinking about
homosexuality is first evidenced in the late fifth
century in Athens (this will be discussed further below).
In fact, the whole idea of a legislative tempering and
softening makes the passage suspicious. Hardening rather
than softening was likely to have been the aim of an early
legislator (compare this with Herodotus' story of the
deliberate softening of the Lydians by Cyrus, which

1 Theban coin, Heracles with club and bow, British Museum

2 Stele of Pindar, Antikenmuseum und Skulpturhalle Basel

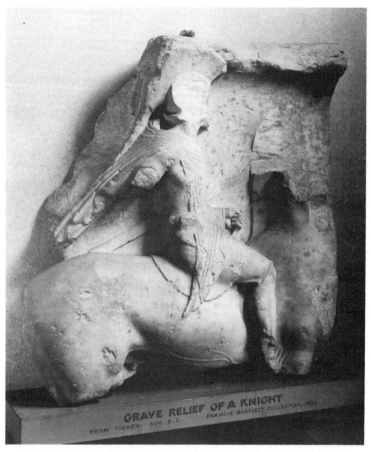

3 Grave relief of knight, courtesy Museum of Fine Arts, Boston. Pierce
Fund, Purchase of E. P. Warren

4 *(left)* Stele of Amphotto, Athens National Museum

5 *(right)* Stele of Polyxena, Staatliche Museen, Berlin

6 Stele of Mnason, Thebes Museum

7 Scene from Judgment of Paris Painter, Berlin, Altes Museum

8 Woman's head vase lid, Bowdoin College Museum

9 Motifs from Kabeirion vases, Wolters-Bruns, Die Kabirenheiligtum bei Theben, pl. 27, courtesy Deutsches Archaeologisches Institut

10 Pig askos, Museo Archeologico, Reggio Calabria

presents such tempering as a useful device for a conqueror
whose aim is to prevent the revolt of a conquered people).
(3)

It is tempting to attribute Theban interests in the
flute to the presence of swamps and reeds suitable for
the construction of the instrument near the city. (4)
This explanation, however, would not account for the fact
that the early musical tradition of Thebes does not
portray the flute as a specially Theban instrument. The
music which is embedded in the foundation legends, and
which attests to an early Theban interest in music,
centers not on the native flute but on the lyre and the
imported Lydian mode. Pausanias records the tradition
that Amphion learned the Lydian mode from the Lydians,
and that he also made an improvement upon the lyre, adding
three strings to the existing four (one was named after
one of the famed Seven Gates of Thebes, the Neistan).
His songs drew beasts and even stones after him, an
ability which he utilized in building the lower walls of
the city. In fact, Pausanias was even shown the stones
which had followed Amphion's singing. (5)

Another legendary musical figure claimed by Thebes who
also had no connection with the flute was Linus. (6)
Nor was the invention of the flute attributed to the
Thebans, at least according to Pindar's account of its
mythological origins in 'Pythian' 12: Athena invented
it, or at least its music and 'techne', although reeds
from the river Cephisus provided its material. (7)
Pindar, a Theban himself, also attributes his own musical
method, the combining of voice and flute in a harmony,
not to the invention of a Theban but of an Epizephyrian
Locrian. (8) He refers to the use of the flute as an
accompaniment for his own songs several times, but
usually in conjunction with the lyre, (9) and nothing
indicates that he saw it as a characteristically Theban
instrument. In fact, it is only in non-Theban sources
of the fifth century or later that we find reflections
of Theban specialization in flute-playing. From earlier
times, and from Thebes itself, we find a tradition and
references which point to Theban interest in music in
general, but not especially in the flute.

The earliest source which connects Thebans with the
flute is Plato, who has Socrates use a Theban, Orthagoras,
as an example of a teacher of flute-playing in the
'Protagoras' (318C). Later sources name earlier flutists,
but the references amount to little. Theophrastus
mentions a Theban named Kleolas who followed the lead of
Andron of Catana in accompanying his flute-playing with
bodily movements, but his achievement was secondary and

imitative and his date is unknown (ap. Athenaeus 1.22C).
A certain Klonas, composer of songs sung to the flute
before the time of Archilochus and claimed by both Tegea
and Thebes, is mentioned by pseudo-Plutarch. (10)
Skopelinus is named as an uncle (or father) and flute-
teacher of Pindar, (11) but the preservation of his name
may owe more to his famous relative Pindar than to his
own outstanding abilities as a flutist.

The first really significant Theban contribution to
the art of flute-playing is attributed to Pronomos, who
lived in the second half of the fifth century and is
also named as a teacher of Alcibiades. (12) He is said
to have enlarged the potential of the instrument by the
invention of a single flute on which Dorian, Lydian and
Phrygian modes could all be played. (13) His success with
his famous pupil Alcibiades was limited, however, as we
shall see below.

The late date of the references to Theban excellence
with the flute and the lack of any mythological reflections
of an early special relationship with the instrument
suggest that the Thebans' reputation as flutists par
excellence may have been developed only in the fifth
century. It may even be significantly correlative with
an Athenian loss of interest in the instrument. (14)
Although the flute had been popular in Athens until about
mid-century, it lost its popularity as an instrument of
the aristocracy there during the second half of the
century. Plutarch attributes this decline in popularity
to Alcibiades, who as a boy set an example for the other
boys by refusing to learn to play the flute. According
to the story, the precocious boy argued that playing the
flute distorted his face and prevented him from talking -
it would be better to leave flute-playing to the Thebans,
who had no talent for conversation anyway. (15) A
similar rationale, but without specific reference to
Thebes, occurs in the story about Athena throwing away
the flute after inventing it, because it distorted her
face. (16) Athena's rejected instrument was picked up
by Marsyas, who challenged Apollo to a musical contest.
Inevitably Marsyas lost, and he was flayed by Apollo as
a punishment for the challenge. (17) Plutarch has
Alcibiades refer to both these stories in support of his
own position: these special patrons of Athens, Athena
and Apollo, set an example justifying his own rejection
of the flute. Pronomos must have been happy to be rid of
such a pupil, but Plato followed his lead in argument
when, in rejecting flute-playing in his ideal city, he
also appealed to the victory of Apollo over Marsyas
('Rep.' 399DE).

As far as we can determine, Athena's negative attitude
first appeared in Athens in the second half of the fifth
century. The version of the story of Athena's invention
of the flute in which she appears with a positive attitude
to the instrument is found much earlier, in Pindar's
'Pythian' 12, composed for Midas of Akragas, winner of the
prize for flute-playing at the Pythian games in 490 and
486 BC. Lest we should think that Pindar was warping
mythology to favor the interests of his client, it must
be pointed out that a similar positive attitude on Athena's
part occurs also in the work of the seventh-century Dorian
poet Alcman and in the fragments of Corinna, (18) where
Athena is credited with teaching Apollo to play the
instrument. These sources appear to involve an earlier,
non-Athenian version of the story, and the conclusion is
tempting that someone in fifth-century Athens made a
conscious decision to de-emphasize the instrument and to
reformulate the mythology of its discovery. Michaelis
has argued persuasively that that person was Euripides.
(19) The motivation of his reformulation was Athenian
rivalry with and jealousy of Thebes. (20)
   It is possible that in a correlative development the
Athenians were also responsible for enlarging on the
Thebans' abilities with the instrument and creating the
Thebans' special reputation as flutists. Several factors,
however, suggest that the Thebans' reputation was in fact
deserved. First in time was, of course, Pindar, whose
songs were performed to the music of flute and lyre,
and whose fame and success must have spurred rivals and
imitators. This increased poetic activity would have
provided increased opportunities for flutists, and in
such a situation one can expect an upsurge in proficiency.
That such was the case is suggested by the appearance of
Pronomos, whose invention greatly extended the capabilities
of the instrument. Finally, there is the arrival in the
city in about mid-century of the refugee Pythagorean
Lysis. The Pythagoreans were noted as flutists, and
Philolaos, the most well-known of the refugees, was named
in the tradition as a flutist. (21) He must have
contributed to the Theban musical scene, along with his
fellow Pythagoreans. Plutarch tells of a flute-player,
Charillos, who was among the philosophical Thebans who
visited Socrates, and so we can see that the tradition
lived on ('De gen. Soc.' 580EF).

PINDAR AND CORINNA

For us, Theban interests in music, in the wider Greek

sense of that word, are most vividly illustrated in the
fifth century by poetry, especially the poetry of Pindar.
We do know of another Theban male poet, Cleon (Athen.
I.19Bf.). None of his works survives, but, unlike Pindar,
he had a bronze statue set up in his honor in Thebes,
probably the one mentioned by Pliny which was made by
Pythagoras of Rhegium ('HN' 34.59). Pythagoras appears
to date to about the third quarter of the fifth century,
(22) so we may infer that this Cleon was a near contemporary
of Pindar, perhaps somewhat younger. It is likely that he
also wrote victory odes: Pythagoras himself was noted for
his statues of Olympic victors, and he might have come to
know Cleon through their mutual interest in these men.

Aside from Pindar and Cleon, our other evidence for
the Theban poetic scene involves women. One of these is
Corinna of Tanagra, who, according to tradition, competed
with Pindar and defeated him. (23) In one of these
fragments she finds fault with another woman poet, Myrtis,
because she entered into competition with Pindar (of this
more later).

Although Pindar had no bronze statue erected in his
honor, the funeral stele of a poet dated to the third
quarter of the fifth century has been identified as the
stele of Pindar (24) (see Plate 3).

Because music and poetry were an intrinsic part of the
life of a Greek city, it is not surprising that we can
find reflections in the work of poets of various aspects
of this life. The poetry of Pindar which was composed
for Thebans reveals a good deal about the religious
beliefs and worship of the city, and the life-style and
values of the wealthy segment of society for which it
was created. Pindar is especially useful in giving us
insight into the ideas and ideals of the Theban male
aristocracy, since he reiterated throughout the odes
composed for his fellow citizens the aristocratic code
of values. He tells us that he himself was a member of
the family of the Aigeidai ('P.' 5), (25) but even
apart from this the identification of the values as
aristocratic would be secure, for they are expressed with
great consistency throughout these odes which were
composed for his aristocratic patrons. Moreover, we can
see a continuity with aristocratic values as these are
presented in Homer, and also with later expressions,
such as that which Thucydides puts into the mouth of
Alcibiades. (26) This code was, of course, not uniquely
Theban; it was subscribed to by Pindar's aristocratic
patrons throughout the Greek world - in Magna Graecia,
mainland Greece, Cyrene - and it formed one of the ties
which bound Thebes to the rest of this world.

The code for which Pindar acts as spokesman is simple
and straightforward. Wealth is not to be kept hidden
within the house but is to be used, lavishly, for a number
of noble purposes: (27) to gain victory in the games,
with all that that involves (horse breeding and training,
training of the man himself for some contests, the support
of trainers, travel to and participation in many contests);
to celebrate and immortalize that victory, (28) preferably
by commissioning a Pindaric ode; to practise hospitality
on as grand a scale as possible; (29) to sacrifice
lavishly to the gods, (30) and to defend one's city in
time of war (31) and support it in time of peach (as all
those do who win victories and adorn public festivals with
poetry). If wealth is obtained justly and used without
hybris in this manner, (32) then a man has done all that
is humanly possible; beyond this lie the incalculable
alterations of fate and the actions of the gods. Yet even
in reverses of fortune there is an aristocratic posture
to be maintained: one carries on. An excellent illustration
of all this is to be found in 'Isthmian' 4, composed for
Melissos of Thebes, whose family was an old and honored
one in the city. By a sudden turn of fortune this family
has been devastated by the loss of four members in a
single day, yet Melissos continued to strive for honor
and was able to gain a victory which brought back the old
fame and revived the house. A similar call to 'carry on',
this time addressed by the poet to himself, is found in
'Isthmian' 8, which we considered earlier for its
expression of Theban reaction to defeat in the Persian
Wars:
  .... and thereto I also, grieved though I be
      at heart, ask leave to call
  the Golden Muse. Slipped free of great sorrows,
  let us not fall into desolation of garlands;
  cherish not your grief.... (lines 5-8, tr. Lattimore)
From the details of the aristocratic ideal which we
gather from Pindar, we can catch a glimpse of the everyday
life of the Theban upper class males, a life which they
shared with aristocrats in many different Greek cities.
Wealth involved large family landholdings, which supplied
the means to feed workers who could free family members
for training and participating in contests, a training
which would at the same time provide preparedness for
war. These contests included not only the four great
Panhellenic games at Delphi, Nemea, the Isthmus and
Olympia, but also lesser games such as those held at
Thebes itself, Athens, and Arcadia. There were also
purely local games in the smaller towns. The victories
of Diagoras of Rhodes give some indication of the time and

travel which could be involved (and these do not include
contests in which he participated but did not win a
victory):

> With flowers from that contest [games of Tlepolemus
> in Rhodes], twice hath Diagoras crowned himself, and
> at the famous Isthmus four times, in his good fortune;
> and again and again, at Nemea and at rocky Athens;
> while he is not unknown to the shield of bronze in
> Argos, and the works of art given as prizes in Arcadia
> and at Thebes, and to the duly ordered contests amid
> the Boeotians, and to Pellana, and to Aegina, where
> he was six times victor, while in Megara the reckoning
> on the tablet of stone telleth no other tale.
> ('Olympian' 7.80-7, tr. Sandys)

With the addition of wild game, which seems to have
been plentiful in Thebes, (33) the estate would also
supply a hospitable table for guests. For some there was
sufficient land to support horses and the expensive
practice of chariot racing: Herodotus son of Asopodoros
had won many chariot victories before the one celebrated
in 'Isthmian' 1; (34) the family of Melissos had a long
history of participation in such contests before he
himself won at Nemea; (35) and a member of the family of
Thrasydaios had been victor in the chariot races. (36)
According to Fragment 95, (37) the Thebans excelled at
chariot-making, which suggests that many Thebans were
wealthy enough to partake of this sport.

The size of the family holding was crucial in
providing the resources necessary for the preservation
of this aristocratic life style which combined the honors
of peacetime games and the glories to be won in war. The
legal framework which maintained these holdings was
provided by some of the laws made for the Thebans by
the Corinthian Philolaos, whose laws of adoption,
according to Aristotle, were intended to preserve
unchanged the number of lots. (38)

The display involved in participation in contests, the
commissioning of victory odes, and the entertainment of
friends (and poets) naturally predominate in the odes of
Pindar, since most of them were composed to celebrate a
victory in the games. We also, however, see another form
of aristocratic expenditure reflected in Pindar's work
in Fragment 84, a 'Daphnephorikon' composed for Aioladas,
the father of Pagondas, victor at Delion. This song was
sung by a young girl in the ceremony in which Agasikles,
Pagondas' son, was installed as Daphnephoros. In singing
it, the girl invited the procession (of which she was a
member) to begin. The song is very much family oriented,
although the ceremony is a public one. It seems that the

procession was made up mainly if not entirely of family
members (much as the 'Partheneion' of Alcman is sung by
a chorus of related girls), (39) and several are mentioned
by name. The emphasis on a single family during a public
ceremony may seem surprising at first, until we recall
the degree to which what we would call the state was
inextricably bound up with the lives of its principal
families, which provided the city with its officials,
military leaders, religious personnel, the wherewithal
for civic celebrations, and even the ties of foreign
relations. These families were often even assimilated
into the mythological history of the city (Melissos claimed
to be akin to the Labdakidai in 'Isthmian' 3.17). Thus
the line between civic and public events and family events
probably was never clearly drawn, at least for the great
families. (40)

Aristotle recognized this situation, in which the state
was in essence no more than a network of family groups, as
a stage in the general development of the Greek state:

But when several families are united, and the
association aims at something more than the supply
of daily needs, the first society to be formed is
the village. And the most natural form of the
village appears to be that of a colony from the
family, composed of the children and grandchildren
who are said to be 'suckled with the same milk.'
And this is the reason why Hellenic states were
originally governed by kings; because the Hellenes
were under royal rule [the family] before they came
together, as the barbarians still are. Every family
is ruled by the eldest, and therefore in the colonies
of the family the kingly form of government prevailed
because they were of the same blood. As Homer says:
'Each one gives law to his children and to his wives.'
('Pol.' 1252b15ff., tr. McKeon)

Aristotle called this early stage the village; it was
followed by the state-proper:

When several villages are united in a single complete
community, large enough to be nearly or quite self-
sufficing, the state comes into existence, originating
in the bare needs of life, and continuing in existence
for the sake of a good life. ('Pol.' 1252b25ff., tr.
McKeon)

Recently this distinction between stages of development
in the community has been revived, with the use of new
terminology borrowed from anthropology: today the tribal
state (or stage of development, or consciousness) is
contrasted with the civic state, and it is recognized that
in Greece the tribal stage was not only monarchical, but

extended also into the period of oligarchical rule. The
oligarchic state was still a tribal state. (41) Thebes
was still a tribal state in the fifth century.

The major co-operative state activity in fifth-century
Thebes, which was the attempt to consolidate and control
a relatively loose confederation of states linked by land
communications rather than by sea, did not require the
sorts of changes which were liable to upset this tribal
orientation. Unlike Athens, whose sea empire created new
requirements which the old system could not provide without
fundamental changes, Thebes' land empire required no large-
scale shipbuilding programs, no fleet to be manned, no new
bureaucracy to be created. Thus in Thebes no vastly
increased urbanization occurred, which would create a
break with the tribal past for the average citizen.
Control of a land confederation required basically only
an army, and the old tribal organization readily supplied
this without a wrenching jolt to traditional values.

An aspect of the male aristocratic way of life which
has recently received considerable attention is the
tradition of homosexual relations between men. (42) Again
Pindar offers evidence, in the fragment for Theoxenos of
Tenedos:

Right it were, fond heart, to cull love's blossom in
due season, in life's prime; but whosoever, when once
he hath seen the rays flashing from the eyes of
Theoxenus, doth not swell with desire, his black
heart, with its frozen flame, hath been forged of
adamant or of iron; and, unhonored of brightly
glancing Aphrodite, he either toileth over hoarded
wealth, or, with a woman's courage, is borne along
enslaved to a path that is utterly cold.

But I, for the sake of that Queen of love, like
the wax of the holy bees that is melted beneath the
heat of the sun, waste away when I look at the young
limbs of blooming boys. Thus I ween that even in
Tenedos Suasion and Charm dwelt in the soul of the
son of Hagesilas. (Fragment 108 (Bowra), tr. Sandys)

The tradition of aristocratic homosexuality was an
old and especially honored one in Thebes. Plutarch,
himself a Boeotian, links Boetians with Spartans and
Cretans as those Greeks who were most susceptible to love,
as well as being most warlike. (43) This link between
homosexuality and military valor is again to be found in
Plutarch when he describes the Theban custom according
to which the lover presented the beloved with a set of
armor upon his official coming-of-age. (44) Heracles
and his friend Iolaos provided powerful role models for
young Thebans, who had a custom of taking lovers' vows on

the tomb of Iolaos. (45)   Xenophon complains about the
physical nature of Theban attachments between men and boys.
(46)   Similarly, Pausanias in Plato's 'Symposium' says
that the Boeotians have a simple law about love: it is
always right for the lover to have his way (182B).

A semi-official stamp seems to have been put upon the
practice of homosexuality in Thebes by the story that
the lovers Diokles and Philolaos the Bacchiad fled to
Thebes to escape the incestuous attentions of Philolaos'
mother.   Not only were they welcomed into the city, but
Philolaos was sufficiently revered to be chosen to serve
as a lawgiver.   Aristotle, who tells this story, also
mentions some of Philolaos' laws dealing with adoption.
(47)   It is possible that some of his other laws encouraged
homosexual relationships, or at least had that practical
effect.   Plutarch says that it was Theban lawgivers who
introduced the practice; (48) as we saw earlier in this
chapter, the rationale which Plutarch gives for this is
suspect, but it may still reflect in a slightly distorted
fashion some aspect of Theban law.

The contrast between fifth-century Athens as a civic
state, and fifth-century Thebes as a tribal state finds
reflections also in the contrasting attitude toward the
aristocratic practice of male homosexuality in these
two cities.   In Athens it appears that an analytical
reassessment of the proper nature of the homosexual
relationship took place late in the century in the
Socratic circle.   Evidence for this reassessment is to
be found in Plato's 'Phaedrus' and 'Symposium', as well
as in Xenophon and Euripides.

In Plato's 'Symposium', Phaedrus (178CD) and
Pausanias (184D) present the traditional view of the
lover as teacher of 'arete', while Socrates offers in
contrast a new, idealistic, 'Platonic' relationship.
In the 'Phaedrus', and in 'Republic' 403A-C, Socrates is
again portrayed speaking for his new interpretation.
We also see the same idea in Xenophon's 'Symposium'
(8.32ff.), where the opinion that homosexuality fosters
courage is again ascribed to Pausanias, while Socrates
rejects the thesis, saying that men display distrust
and not courage when they insist on staying beside their
lovers in battle.   Xenophon's commendation of Spartan
love as fraternal and paternal, in contrast to the sensual
relationships customary in other states, is still another
expression of this reinterpretation of the aristocratic
homosexual relationship. (49)   The idea seems to have
appeared in Euripides' plays as well, for we find in
the 'Dictys' (50) an advocacy of comradeship rather than
sex, while Aelian claimed that Euripides invented the

story of Laios' disgraceful behavior as the origin of
the Theban practice. (51)
     Plato in his latest work rejected homosexuality
altogether, which was perhaps the logical culmination
of the earlier tendencies to idealize it. This rejection
is found at 'Laws' 636Bff. and again at 'Laws' 836Cff.,
where homosexuality is condemned by the standard of nature
(wild beasts do not practise it), and it is said not to
lead to courage or temperance.
     That the reinterpretation of homosexuality within the
Socratic circle did not affect the whole of Athenian
society is clear from the speech of Aeschines, 'Against
Timarchos'. This speech, dated to 345 BC, repeats the
attitudes and even some of the 'topoi' associated with
the traditional aristocratic view (references to Achilles
and Patroclos, and Harmodios and Aristogeiton, as role
models, 135). The speech is especially important because
of the fullness and clarity with which it deals with the
subject. In summary, the relevant points are: that male
prostitution is punishable by law with loss of citizen
rights (18-20 and passim); that Aeschines distinguishes
such prostitution from 'eros', or homosexual love
relationships between free men (137-9); that 'eros'
relationships are fully acceptable (139) and in fact
openly indulged in by both Aeschines himself and a large
number of other older and younger men (whom he even names
at 155-7), and confer status upon the participants (137,
139); and that the charge of effeminacy is attached to
male prostitutes and only to them (185 and passim). It
is claimed that, while ancient law forbade homosexual
relationships to slaves (137), in recent time slaves,
ex-slaves, and other unworthy men have been deeply
involved in such relationships with Timarchos and with
others.
     Aristophanes is sometimes used as evidence for
Athenian attitudes toward homosexuality, especially in
connection with the question of its connection with
effeminacy. The use of charges of effeminacy against
homosexuals was one of the favorite comic themes of
Aristophanes, and it is perhaps not surprising that
these have been seen as evidence of Athenian attitudes
toward all homosexual relations. (52) They cannot,
however, be taken at face value as evidence that all
homosexual behavior was traditionally regarded as
effeminate in Athens, any more than we can accept
Aristophanes' comic statements as evidence that
Euripides' mother was a greengrocer - the aim of this
charge was not to portray Euripides' ancestry accurately,
but to cast a shadow upon it and thereby upon his citizen

status. In a similar way, charges of effeminacy were
meant to cast a shadow upon the status of those so
charged. We see from Aeschines that the laws decreed a
loss of civic rights as a penalty for male prostitution,
and that effeminacy was considered to be a characteristic
of a male prostitute (but was never attributed to the
partners in a love relationship between free men,
according to Aeschines). Since one of the most frequent
comic charges against individuals was to impugn their
citizen status, the motivation for these particular
charges is not far to seek: if a man was found to be
engaged in male prostitution (which is, in effect, what
a charge of effeminacy amounted to), his right to citizen
status was revoked. In short, we should view Aristophanes
not as taking as his theme all types of male homosexuality,
but rather as concentrating on the one form which was
considered disgraceful and which had political ramifica-
tions: the effeminate homosexuality of the male
prostitute.

The evidence suggests that at least a small sub-group
of the Athenian aristocracy found reason in the late fifth
century to redefine and 'refine' the traditional aristocratic custom of homosexuality. Reasons for this
reassessment may perhaps be found in the growing democra-
tization of Athenian life and the shifting patterns of
social and civic status which it entailed. Aristocratic
families had institutionalized the practice as a part of
the initiation of boys into the values of the male
aristocratic culture: the older man was not simply a
lover, but a teacher and guide as well. The boy who
attracted a suitable lover gained status, while the boy
who did not bore a certain stigma. Both success and
failure left lasting marks upon the future status of the
individual. When increasing numbers of citizens were
incorporated into the professional and bureaucratic life
of the city, those who formerly had been insignificant
often found themselves with a new civic significance.
Their response to this particular aristocratic custom,
from which they were excluded by their undistinguished
ancestry, in most cases would have been either to mock
and criticize, or to attempt to adopt it themselves.
We see complaints against just such usurpation of
aristocratic 'rights' by unworthy men in Aeschines'
speech. On the other hand, some at least of the
aristocrats were led by these responses to a reassessment
of their practices. They now tried to distinguish
themselves from those who aped them and to defend
themselves against their critics - by their new 'Platonic'
love they reasserted their own superiority and pointed

out the grossness of the multitude. The debate of the
Two Logoi in Aristophanes' 'Clouds' gives us a glimpse of
all of these responses: those ordinary men who mocked and
criticized old aristocratic ways would be entertained by
the satire on the Old Education, while those who aped
aristocratic ways were themselves mocked (everyone in the
audience is 'euryproktos'). Satire and criticism of the
reassessed aristocratic position is provided by the New
Education: such philosophical sophistication leads to
softness and vice.

In contrast to this situation which arose among the
intellectuals of Athens, in Thebes, which experienced no
significant weakening of aristocratic values during the
fifth century, the ancient tradition linking valor with
homosexual love not only survived intact and in its
original (physical) form, but even underwent a renaissance
in the early fourth century with the accomplishments of
the Sacred Band, a picked military detachment consisting
of pairs of lovers. (53)

Male Theban citizens in the fifth century lived a life
firmly set within the framework of traditional aristocratic values, revealed to us in the poetry of Pindar.
But what of the other half of the picture, what of the
women? Pindar's 'Daphnephorikon' (Frag. 84) offers us
some insight into their world. It shows us that
daughters of noble families took part in important
religious ceremonies, and that that part was important
enough to warrant commissioning Pindar to create the
song (there were at one time three books of maiden songs,
showing that this was a usual occurrence). In the song
itself the girl speaks of the limits of propriety which
restrained her: she is to think and to speak in a
maidenly way (lines 45-7). Her training had been in
handwork, by her mother (if the Andaisistrota of line 53
is to be so identified), and, obviously, in choral
performance (lines 54-5).

We learn from the example of Corinna that women could
be poets as well as participants in choral performances,
but that even here they were expected to keep to their
place. (54) Corinna mentions another Boeotian woman
poet, Myrtis, and there may have been more. (55)
Corinna's Fragment 655 suggests that she may have been a
teacher or trainer of the girls in choral performance;
if so, it seems that a degree of activity and companionship outside the walls of the home was possible for girls
(a Boeotian parallel for Sappho's circle), and that a
real possibility existed for some women to become poets
themselves, as a natural expansion of their role as
choral trainers. A fourth-century Boeotian tombstone

portrays one such woman, part, we may suppose, of an
enduring tradition in this basically conservative
society. (56)

Calame's recent study of female choruses in ancient
Greece (57) appears to offer convincing evidence that
such choruses served an educational and initiatory
function for girls, parallel to the choral training and
participation of boys and young men. Although the use
of maiden choruses seems to have been widespread, if
not universal, in the Greek world, the concentration of
evidence from archaic Lesbos and Sparta, and fifth-
century Thebes, suggests that in these cities its role
was especially important. Calame distinguishes between
the sorts of education provided in Lesbos and in Sparta.
In the latter, emphasis was put upon training as a citizen,
which included firm indoctrination in the peculiar Spartan
way of life and value system; in the former the orientation
was more toward developing feminine charm on an individu-
alistic basis. The direction of the education provided
by participation in Theban maiden choruses is not clear,
but there is no evidence to suggest that a peculiarly
Theban way of life existed for which indoctrination would
be necessary. The surviving fragments and references
suggest that the choral training of Theban girls involved
the learning of local traditions as these were embodied
in the myths of the choral songs, as well as control of
the body and voice ('charm'), and discipline in social
interaction. Thus it paralleled the traditional choric
education of boys. Even in the fourth century, speaking
from a conservative point of view, Plato can equate
choral participation with education: (58)

Athenian: ... No young creature whatsoever, as we may
fairly assert, can keep its body or its voice still;
all are perpetually trying to make movements and
noises. They leap and bound, they dance and frolic,
as it were with glee, and again, they utter cries of
all sorts. Now animals at large have no perception
of the order or disorder in these motions, no sense
of what we call rhythm or melody. But in our own
case, the gods of whom we spoke as given us for
companions in our revels [Apollo and Dionysus] have
likewise given us the power to perceive and enjoy
rhythm and melody. Through this sense they stir us
to movements and become our choir leaders. They
string us together on a thread of song and dance, and
have named our choirs too after the delight they
naturally afford .... May we assume that our earliest
education comes through the Muses and Apollo, or not?

Clinias: We may make that assumption.

Athenian: So by an uneducated man we shall mean one
who has no choric training, and by an educated man one
whose choric training has been thorough?

Clinias: Exactly. ('Laws' 653D-654B, tr. Taylor)
It is important for our understanding of the condition
of women in ancient Greece to realize that such participation allowed girls a degree of activity and companionship
beyond their homes and immediate families. Such social
life would go far in lightening the burden of female
childhood, as would the fact that in a highly traditional
and conservative society, such as fifth-century Thebes,
the education of boys would have been carried out along
somewhat parallel lines. The real problem of 'women's
condition' seems to have risen to consciousness for the
first time when the traditional structuring of society
gave way to new structures and values in the late fifth
century in Athens. At this time and place male roles
were no longer so single-mindedly oriented toward physical
prowess in sports and battle, and citizen activity became
dependent more upon cleverness and the ability to speak
and argue, than upon sheer physical strength. At this
time in Athens the disparity between male and female
education became more marked, as the young upper-class
males flocked to the Sophists for higher education, and
the Sophists brought into question the values of the
traditional choric education. At the same time, the
skills needed of a citizen shifted toward those in which
women too could naturally excel (cleverness, verbal
facility, reasoning). Thus we find Aristophanes'
Lysistrata arguing: (59)
Yes, I'm a woman, but I *am* intelligent,
And my judgment's pretty good;
And after listening to many speeches of
   my father and the older men,
I'm not badly educated. ('Lysistrata' 1123-7)
In considering the nature of the role played by women
in Theban society, it is interesting to note that the
extant material in Pindar which was either performed
during a Theban (or in one case, Boeotian) religious
ceremony, or describes such a ceremony, appears to show
a striking emphasis on women. We must of course allow
for the lacunose nature of the evidence, but the emphasis
is none the less definite enough to occasion thought. The
relevant passages include:
Frag. 84 (the 'Daphnephorikon')
'Pythian' 3, 77-9 (description of nocturnal maiden
   songs)

'Pythian' 11 (sung during a procession to the Ismenion)
'Isthmian' 4.61-8 (description of annual festival of
    the 'Heracleidai')
Frag. 61 (description of celestial festival of Bromius)
Frag. 93 (description of Dionysiac experience, Galaxion
    in Boeotia)
Frag. 85 (from a maiden-song to Pan and the Great Mother)
    Pan is addressed as a guardian of Arkadia, so this
    particular fragment may not have come from a song
    written for Thebans; we may suppose it to be similar
    to the Theban songs mentioned in 'Pythian' 3.77-9,
    as the scholiast thought when he quoted it in
    connection with this passage).
Of these passages, the 'Daphnephorikon' is sung by a girl,
'Pythian' 3 describes maiden-songs sung to the Mother and
Pan, and Fragment 85 seems to be an example of such a
song, though possibly not a Theban song itself. Fragment
93 is classified as a maiden-song, probably because of
the traditional role of women in Dionysiac orgiastic
rites. 'Pythian' 11 begins with an invocation of the
daughters of Kadmos to come into the presence of the
goddess Melia, followed by an invitation to the Theban
women, who are the children of Harmonia, to join the
host of heroines in the night-time ceremony; (60) while
the fragmentary dithyramb for the Thebans (Frag.61)
attributes a similarly woman-centered celebration of the
festival of Dionysos to the gods: in the presence of
the Great Mother, the Naiads, Pallas and Artemis (as well
as the thunderbolt of Zeus and the spear of Enyalios,
of indeterminate sex) participate. The fragment continues
with a woman-centered version of the story of Kadmos
(woman-centered in the sense that it features women
beyond the call of necessity: Harmonia at least is a
gratuitous addition from the usual genealogical stand-
point):
    [Thebes] ... the legend is that there at one time
    Kadmos with lofty mind took as his wife Harmonia.
    and she [he?] heard the voice of Zeus and bore
    [begot?] an offspring famed among men, [Semele].
    O Dionysos .... (lines 21-6)
In these passages women act as participants in most cases.
In a few instances, female divinities are celebrated
(the Great Mother, Melia). Only the festival of the
Heracleidai seems predominantly masculine in orientation
(even in this the sons are identified through their
mother Megara, but this is probably necessary to identify
them as these particular children of Heracles).
    To these passages from Pindar which suggest a feminist
oriented religious atmosphere at Thebes should be added

the maiden-chorus of Corinna (Frag. 655), and Fragment
688 with its reference to the 'partheneia' or maiden
songs, of Corinna. 'Partheneia' made up a good part of
the work of Pindar: the 'Lives' mentions two books,
and a third seems to have been called 'Different
Partheneia' and to have consisted of songs sung by
maidens for festivals other than the Daphnephoria. (61)
Farnell points out that the large number of 'Partheneia'
attributed to Pindar seems to imply that the celebration
of the Daphnephoria was an annual celebration (as
Pausanias has it), and not a nine-year festival (as
Proclus). (62) If he is correct in this calculation of
frequency, we have more reason for stressing the
importance of choral training in the lives of young Theban
girls.

Another important aspect of religious life dealt with by
Pindar is the area of mystery faiths and beliefs about
an afterlife. The relevent passages were composed for
various patrons and only one such passage has even any
likelihood of representing the beliefs of a Theban, yet
they show us the range of beliefs with which Pindar was
familiar, and they demonstrate the widespread dissemina-
tion of such beliefs in the Greek world in the early
fifth century. One should not overlook either the
presence of a mystery cult in Thebes, that practised at
the Kabeirion. Finally, it is important to consider this
material as a background for the later interest shown by
certain Thebans in the afterlife, as witnessed by Plato's
'Phaedo'.
    Two passages describe a life after death. 'Olympian'
2.56-83 reports that immediately after death sinners
suffer punishment, while the good are rewarded by a life
of continual sunlight, without toil, beside the gods.
All who have succeeded in keeping their souls pure from
wrong deeds after three times on either side (in three
lives?) go to the Isles of the Blessed, where Peleus,
Kadmos, and Achilles dwell. Fragment 114 also describes
a place of perfect bliss, with perpetual sunlight. It
adds something about the activities of the inhabitants:
they occupy themselves with the aristocratic pastimes of
horses, wrestling, games, and lyres. It is a land of
light and fragrance, which is contrasted with a land of
unending gloomy night.
    Fragment 116 speaks of the survival of the soul, and
gives arguments for its survival. The body, dying,
leaves behind it an 'eidolon' of itself. It can survive
because of its divine origin. And the evidence for its
existence independent of the body during the lifetime of

the body is found in our experience of dreams. Especially
interesting is the provision of rational foundations for
these beliefs: a reason for the soul's ability to
survive is given, as well as evidence for the theory of
its independent existence. The former argument appears
to be a primitive version of an argument attributed to
Socrates by Plato: in 'Phaedo' 79A-80C the divinity of
the soul is used as a proof of its indestructibility.
   Fragment 127 is the only passage which explicitly
mentions transmigration. It says that souls from whom
Persephone has accepted requital for woe are restored to
life as kings, heroes, and wise men. Rose argued that
the woe was the death of Persephone's son Dionysos, or of
Zagreus at the hands of the Titans, and that this places
the passage in the Orphic sphere. (63) He also identified
a Boeotian element in the eight-year punishment: such
punishments occur in Hesiod ('Theogony' 793ff.), in the
story of Kadmos, (64) and in the story of the Labors of
Heracles (a twelve-year punishment but completed in
eight years, one month). (65) Because of this Boeotian
element, and the lack of any ideas otherwise associated
with Magna Graecia or reflecting Pythagorean views in
the fragment (ideas such as are found in 'Olympian' 2 and
in the fragments of Empedocles), Rose suggested that
Pindar's client was a mainland Greek nobleman. The
reference to Persephone and the inference that the woe
was the death of Dionysos Zagreus led him to identify
this nobleman as an Orphic. The difficulties in the way
of his argument are considerable, since neither the
Orphic nor the Pythagorean can be defined or differentiated
as clearly as his argument assumes. (66) Nevertheless,
his conclusion is not impossible: it may be that the
fragment was composed for a mainland Greek. There is
nothing to rule it out, although the positive argument
is not as strong as Rose would have it. Another
interesting aspect of this fragment is that Plato, in
introducing it in the 'Meno' (81B), says that those who
maintain this belief in transmigration are 'priests and
priestesses who make it their business to be able to
account for the functions which they perform'. This
suggests that the application of rational argument to
such beliefs, which we saw in Fragment 116, was not an
isolated instance or a Pindaric addition.
   Two final fragments include 121, which was composed
for an Eleusinian initiate, (67) possibly for Hippocrates,
brother of Kleisthenes, (68) and Fragment 115, which
appears to be a reference to the efficacy of mystery
rites. (69)
   It would be a mistake to try to reconcile these various

passages or to try to find in them a Pindaric religion. (70)
Pindar wrote to suit his patrons and their beliefs, and it
is their beliefs which we find here: Theron's faith, the
beliefs of an Eleusinian initiate, possibly the faith of
a Boeotian. Some of the passages show strong similarity
with each other ('Olympian' 2 and Fragment 114 for instance),
but important differences also exist, such as those between
fragments which promise bliss from participation in a
mystery rite and fragments which would require a virtuous
life. Reincarnation is suggested in Theon's faith, and
definitely stated in Fragment 127. What is important is
the evidence that these passages provide for a widespread
fifth-century belief in a life of the soul after death in
various local versions, a belief at times even supported
by rational arguments. Pindar may or may not have
entertained such beliefs himself, but they must have been
fairly familiar throughout Greek society in his time. The
existence of a mystery cult at Thebes, that of the Kabeiroi,
suggests that similar beliefs may also have been found in
that city. It may even be that Rose's mainland Greek was
a Theban, although the version of the birth of Dionysos
which seems to be involved does not fit easily into the
Theban mythical picture.

This religiously oriented poetry, which used as raw
material stories about the gods and heroes, and which was
performed during a variety of religious celebrations, was
none the less (like the similarly religiously oriented
Attic tragedy) created and performed under conditions of
spirited competition. 'Pythian' 12 attests directly to
competition in music, for it was composed to celebrate
a Pythian victory in flute-playing. Fragment 40.58-61
speaks of the 'agon' of Loxias:

  for my tongue loveth to pour forth the choicest and
  sweetest bloom of song, when, at the festivals of the
  gods, I have entered the broad lists of Loxias. (tr.
  Sandys)

The last lines of Pindar's 'Daphnephorikon' (80-2) hint
at a competition of choruses, as interpreted in the light
of the clearer agonistic spirit of Alcman's 'Partheneion'.
(71) There are also several passages in which Pindar
refers, or appears to refer, to his poetic rivals in none
too kindly terms as crows or jackdaws, while he is the
noble eagle. (72) In the same critical spirit, Corinna
censures Myrtis because she, being a woman, entered into
competition with Pindar (Frag.664a). If the fragment
refers to a formal contest, it is hard to reconcile with
the tradition that Corinna herself defeated Pindar (once,
or according to another version, five times). If the
competition is taken less literally, it may be more easily

understandable. Possibly what Corinna meant was that
Myrtis abandoned a traditional female poetic format,
perhaps the use of a local dialect such as we observe in
Corinna's work, for a male format. (73)

The tradition which casts Corinna into the role of
victor over Pindar is, if not literally true, at least
true to the agonistic atmosphere in which these poets
worked. Corinna preserves an amusing reflection (could
it be a parody?) of these human contests in the story of
a contest between the mountains Cithaeron and Helicon,
which ended with a display of wounded artistic pride:

> Cithaeron received the greater number of votes,
> And straightaway Hermes proclaimed, shouting,
> That he had won victory dear to the heart.
> With wreaths the blessed gods adorned him,
> And he rejoiced in his mind.
> But Helicon, in the grip of grievous pain,
> Seized a smooth rock; the mountain shuddered;
> Piteously laboring, from the summit he
> Dashed it down into a myriad pieces. (Frag.654.23-4)

Could we perhaps infer that some of the human losers
behaved with a similar lack of self-restraint? It would
be interesting to know if a Theban audience heard this
and went away chuckling over what was to them a transparent
reference to a Great Poet - perhaps even to Pindar himself.
(74)

7 The arts and crafts

Boeotian art of the classical period has received little
attention except in specialized studies, despite the
interesting insights which it can offer into Theban life,
and the increased significance which comparison can
bring to our understanding of Attic work. The fact that
it was 'provincial' has too often been taken to mean that
the works were derivative, or even nothing more than
inept copies, and thus of little interest except to a
few specialists. In fact, however, this is not at all
the case. Closer examination reveals that the copying
and adaptation were done selectively, and in such a way
that they reveal much about the values and interests of
the artist and his public; moreover, even in the provinces,
real originality and first-rate artistic achievements
were sometimes to be found. (1)   Such certainly is the
case in the two areas of Theban art in the fifth century
which have left significant remains: figured funeral
stelai and vase painting. (2)

THE FIGURED FUNERAL STELAI

Funeral monuments, especially stone slabs or stelai
featuring human figures carved in relief, were used from
the mid seventh century in the Cycladic islands, and in
Attica from the end of the seventh century, but the form
underwent intensive development in sixth-century Athens.
When sumptuary legislation prohibiting extravagant
spending was enacted in Athens in about 480, (3) this put
an end for the time being to the Athenian series of
funerary monuments.   Relief carved monuments began to
appear again in Athens after mid-century, but in the
meantime use and development of such stelai continued
elsewhere, especially in Boeotia, which is particularly

rich in funeral monuments from antiquity. (4) The Theban
figured stelai featuring people and scenes from life are
of particular interest. Basically, two types of figured
stelai were produced in Thebes: stelai of light colored
limestone of the type called Thespian marble with bas-
relief scenes, (5) and etched and painted stelai worked
in an especially hard black limestone (painted but
unengraved stelai appear to have preceded and followed
the engraved stelai, but the painting has for the most
part disappeared).

Extant examples of bas-relief Theban stelai of the
fifth century begin with a stele dated to the first
decade of the century. The surviving lower part of this
stele portrays a hoplite warrior in profile facing left.
This work resembles rather closely the Attic stele of
Aristion. (6) Close resemblances are not unusual among
grave stelai. The desires of the families commissioning
these works were generally conservative, as might be
expected when we remember that these were pious memorials
for the dead. Certain popular motifs recur, and it has
even been suggested that some stelai were made up in
advance, with standard scenes which still allowed for
some minor individualization according to the wishes of
the purchaser, or that 'pattern books' existed from which
the family could choose their memorial. (7) Certainly
the local necropolis could serve the same purpose, and
probably helped to determine people's ideas of what was
suitable. Such practices may well explain some of the
later Theban 'copies' of Theban work, but in the case
of this early warrior stele, in which the resemblance
is not to another local stele but to a 'foreign' work,
such an interpretation seems unlikely. In fact, the
opposite of conservatism may be suggested: a Theban
family was so interested in following the latest Athenian
style that they commissioned a work which was unusual
for their area. (8) The sculptor who created this stele
may have migrated from Athens to Thebes when work in
Athens fell off early in the fifth century, possibly as
a result of the sumptuary legislation which outlawed
sculptured stelai. (9)

Another Theban stele which displays foreign stylistic
influences, but this time in the form of combined Attic
and Ionic tendencies deriving from the Ionian islands,
(10) is the mounted warrior in the Boston Museum of Fine
Arts (11) (see Plate 3). In this case, however, the
imported influences were utilized in the creation of a
new type, for the piece has no direct antecedents. It
has been suggested that it is a translation into relief
of an Attic funerary statue in the round, (12) but such

a translation would itself constitute a major innovation.
Again, the motif has been linked to the subsidiary
horsemen which appear on some early Attic stelai, (13)
these, however, do not represent the deceased but rather
his retainers, and so the concept is completely different
from that of the horseman stele with its sole figure
clearly representing the deceased. A comparison appeared
to exist with a relief of a horseman from Chios; however,
a similar piece found in Athens has shown both of these
to be not stelai, but architectural panels probably used
in funerary buildings, representing followers of the
dead man. (14)   Both the Chian and the Athenian reliefs
are attributed to the same Ionian workshop, and possibly
to the same sculptor. (15)   The horseman from Thebes
remains an apparent innovation, in which a sculptor working
under Attic and Ionic influences created a new Boeotian
type of stele representation, which in the future was to
find followers in other Boeotian centers, especially
Thespiae, although not in Thebes. (16)

The work is characteristically Boeotian not only in
its type, but also in its tempering of modern styles of
artistic expression with archaic characteristics. Such
archaizing characteristics can be seen in the stylized
linear patterning of the folds of the clothing, while at
the same time more modern tendencies are evident in the
interest the sculptor displays in natural representation
through the careful modeling of anatomical details in
both the horse and its rider, as well as in the turning
of the horse's head out of the typical archaic profile
position.

We observed above that in the case of the warrior
stele Attic influence was perhaps transmitted in the
person of a sculptor, travelling to Boeotia in search of
work. In a similar way, sculptors from the islands
travelled and worked where the market was good. (17)
Direct evidence of this is to be found in Boeotia in the
stele of Alxenor, from Orchomenos: (18)   Alxenor signed
his work and said that he was from Naxos. We can thus
understand how the mixed Attic-Ionic stylistic tendencies
exhibited in the mounted rider stele came to be combined
in Thebes with locally favored archaizing features. The
work was perhaps created by a local craftsman working
under the influence of a travelling Ionian sculptor.
The aspect of the work which is most surprising is the
creation of a new type; as is often the case, provincial
borrowing turns out to be innovative adaptation instead.

Between 470 and 450 there is an apparent gap not only
in Theban but also in Boeotian stelai from other areas,
probably the result of conditions after the Persian wars.

This gap is not, however, as complete as it seems when
judged by the published evidence, since Schild-Xenidou in
her catalogue of Boeotian grave reliefs identifies two
unpublished stelai as probably belonging to this period.
(19)   Nevertheless, there is a great contrast between
the number of stelai dated before and those dated after
450. (20)   After 450 production became abundant enough in
Boeotia to enable scholars to differentiate the work of
local schools, and we can follow the development of a
truly Theban school. The causes behind this sudden
expansion of interest in what was obviously a luxury
product, the sculptured stele, may probably be found in
the ending of the politically unsettled period in which
control of Boeotia was contested between the Athenians
and the Boeotians. The victory of Coronea settled the
issue of Boeotian independence, while at the same time
internal Boeotian stability was attained through the
regaining by Thebes of a position of relative predominance.
The resulting peace quickly brought prosperity to a
naturally rich land, and we find a blooming not only of
the art of relief sculpture and painting, but also, as
we shall see below, of vase painting as well.

Three works from this period will serve to represent
the work of the Theban school in the later half of the
century. The first example, dated to mid-century, is the
small stele of Amphotto. As is understandable considering
the recent emancipation of Boeotia from Athenian control,
this work follows Ionian rather than Athenian models.
(21)   Even the motif, a standing maiden, appears to have
been Ionian. (22)   In following Ionian models, however,
it also displays the characteristic Theban tendency
toward archaism which was already notable in the stele
of 480/470. In this case, archaism can be seen in the
strong profile position of the figure, the flat plane
surfaces of the face and bodily parts, the frontal view
of the eye, and the stylized patterning of the hair and
drapery. The result is a static and formal figure which
has both great dignity and an indisputable charm about
it (23) (see Plate 4).

The second example which we shall consider is the
stele of Hermophaneia, (24) which is dated to the third
quarter of the century, and for which no more exact
provenance than 'Boeotia' is known. It is interesting
especially because it illustrates a new interest in
multi-figured scenes on the stelai, a characteristic which
first appeared in east Ionia, within the sphere of
influence of Miletus and Ephesus. (25)   Hermophaneia's
figure is worked with relatively successful indications
of its three-dimensional character; in this it stands

in contrast to the figure of the husband, which, by
virtue of its very low relief, seems to fade into the
background. The husband's frontal eye and the poorly
achieved foreshortening of his left arm also contrast
with the treatment of Hermophaneia's figure. The contrast
may be intentional, an effort to concentrate attention on
Hermophaneia or to differentiate the dead from the living,
(26) or it may be simply the result of using a less skilled
assistant for this background figure. (27)

The third example is the stele of Polyxena, which
Schild-Xenidou dates to the last quarter of the fifth
century and considers to be the finest example of the work
of the Theban school. (28) It is very effective in
exhibiting that peculiar conjunction of external aesthetic
influences and local tastes and realities which marks
most 'provincial' work. In particular, it contrasts the
modern fluid treatment of the drapery with the archaizing
use of flat planes to render bodily surfaces. The body
type is also probably determined by Theban aesthetic
ideas: well-fed, sturdy, even heavy-set. It is generally
agreed that the figure represents a priestess, who holds
the attributes of her office: a cult statue and a key
(29) (see Plate 5).

It is odd that not only these three examples, but all
of the confirmed instances of stelai from the Theban
workshop in the second half of the century are memorials
to women or girls, while there are no instances of stelai
commemorating men, or of a theme one might well have
expected in Thebes: the young hunter, with his horse or
dog. The latter theme appears to have been a favorite
one in nearby Thespiae, where women are also portrayed
in fair number. Accidents of survival or discovery may
account for the apparent absence of men on the Theban
bas-relief stelai of this period, but even if several
men's stelai were to be found, the ratio of women to men
would remain unusually high in comparison to Attica. (30)
In contrast, men are almost (but not quite) exclusively
the subjects of the second type of stele, that consisting
of engraved and painted representations. Perhaps these
were thought to be more suitable for men, although if
most of them were created to honor the dead of a single
battle, as has been argued, this explanation loses much
of its cogency.

The engraved stelai represent another aspect of the
creativity of provincial art, for they appear to be a
unique type, displaying both originality and a high degree
of artistic and technical ability on the part of the
artist or artists. (31) The nature of the material
perhaps helped to determine the technique, for the black

limestone is exceptionally hard. The figures are
engraved using lines and lines of dots, and the surface
itself is worked in various ways so as to create a
contrast between smooth and worked areas. When the stones
had been engraved, they were then painted, using a
polychrome technique rather than a four-color method;
whether an encaustic technique was used, as has been
thought, has not been finally determined, but it now seems
doubtful. (32) Because of the loss of most of the paint;
other damage caused by time, re-use, and weather; and
the shallowness of the engraving, the representations are
very difficult to make out today, although variations in
the refraction of light from the varied surfaces help in
some cases, as do the copies made after careful study which
are usually displayed beside the stelai (33) (see Plate 6).

Most of the stelai portray variations on a warrior
theme, but a few fragmentary pieces using the same technique
depict entirely different scenes: a funeral banquet or
symposium (stele of Woikonos); a seated man, possibly with
a horse (stele of Breisada), and a pair of women with a
child. (34) The last stele seems to have the clearest
representation of the three, but only the lower section
is preserved. One woman is seated on a chair, another is
standing in front of her (a favorite scene of seated woman
with standing servant facing her, which is found on bas-
relief stelai from Thespiae and elsewhere), and a child
stands by the back leg of the chair and appears to hold
one of a pair of cocks. The engraving is even shallower
than on the other stelai of this type, and it appears to
be an early example of the technique. (35) It seems to
refute the theory that the form was especially typical of
momuments dedicated to men.

Six other engraved stelai have been found, all of which
portray a version of the warrior theme. (36) The figures
are in battle stance, usually charging to the left,
sometimes uphill. All wear the conical Boeotian helmet,
carry a shield, and are equipped with spears and daggers;
variations occur in type of dress, degree of decoration
(especially on shields, two of which bear a scene depicting
Bellerophon and the Chimaera), presence or absence of
wreaths on the helmets, and footwear (some appear to be
barefooted, but sandals may have been painted on). Some
of the stelai show details of landscape: rocky ground,
trees, flowers. The stele of Saugenes is especially
interesting, since it depicts his last moments in a
dramatic fashion: surrounded by stones which have been
thrown at him, his spear broken and cast aside, armed only
with his shield and dagger, he prepares to ward off an
enemy spear, whose point can already be seen headed toward
him (see Figure 4).

Figure 4   Sketch of stele of Saugenes by P. Saraphianos,
            from Kalogeropoulos, Archaiologika Analekta ex
            Athenon, vol.1, fig.2

The use of perspective devices is especially noteworthy
on these stelai. Round shields are depicted as oval, and
on the stele of Rhynchon a tree in the distance is depicted
as being of nearly the same height as a flower in the
foreground, providing the earliest clear evidence for the
deliberate use of perspective lessening of size to indicate
distance. (37) Another innovation of monumental painting
adopted by the artist is the use of polychromy as opposed
to a four-color scheme, which is found used in a skiagraphic
(impressionistic) fashion on the chiton of Saugenes. The
varied surface treatment also added to the skiagraphic
effects, deflecting light in various ways, even as it does
today.

Ancillary decorations on these warrior stelai also vary.
The pediments of the two more elaborate stones, those of
Rhynchon and Saugenes, bear scenes, the former probably a
family scene of father, mother, and child, (38) the latter
a symposium scene in which are portrayed a set of tools,
apparently those of a smith. Keramopoullos interprets the
presence of these tools as a sign of Saugenes' trade:
he was a well-to-do metal worker, probably the owner of an
armor-making shop. Other stelai indicating occupation are
known from the Boeotian area: the stele of Polyxena the
priestess, of the lyre player, (39) and of the poetess
or teacher Zopyra from Thespiae from the fourth century.
(40) A close parallel known from Attica which also depicts
a trade is the stele of the shoemaker Xanthippos, which
is dated c. 420 BC. (41)

Recent study of the Saugenes stele has confirmed the
earlier suggestion that the second figure on the symposium
couch in the pediment is in fact a woman. (42) This is
an extremely interesting and puzzling discovery. Such
scenes are of course frequent on Greek vases, but these
were presumably intended for use at symposia, and the
identification of the women as hetairai appears both
clear and appropriate. The situation would seem to be
quite different when the scene appears on a funeral stele.
Erotic themes are not entirely unknown in connection with
grave monuments, (43) but it would be surprising to find
one of these rare instances in a conservative Boeotian
city (Saugenes was from Tanagra). It is difficult to
believe that the family would commission a portrayal of
a hetaira, even if it had been the (eccentric) wish of
the deceased. Kontoleon obviously felt the difficulty,
for although he identified the figure as a dancer, he
later added that she was a *free* woman. But nothing in our
experience of fifth-century Greece suggests that free
unmarried girls of good repute were allowed to share
symposium couches and revel with bachelors. Perhaps the

couple should be interpreted as husband and wife, (44)
which might suggest the presence in life, as in death,
of wives at the symposia of their husbands. Unfortunately,
the engraved stele of Woikonos, which appears to have a
symposium scene on its main field, is in too poor
condition to furnish any information on this surprising
development.

Perhaps the explanation of symposium scenes on the
Saugenes and Woikonos stelai is to be sought in another
direction, however. The Saugenes stele is the earliest
known portrayal of a banquet on a funerary monument. The
idea that the dead might enjoy the delights of perpetual
banqueting appears in our written sources first in
Aristophanes (45) and Plato; (46) although the idea fits
well into the picture of the afterlife in Pindar's
'Olympian' 2, banqueting is not specifically mentioned
there. Plato attributes the idea to Mousaios and his
son Orpheus. In mid-fourth century the comic poet
Aristophon connects the idea with the Pythagoreans. (47)
It thus appears to have been an idea which found a ready
reception within the general sphere of the mystery cults.
(48) That its first graphic expression on a funerary
monument was created in a Theban workshop seems appropriate,
for the city was the center both of the mystery cult of
the Kabeiroi (in which symposium scenes involving the
Kabeiros were common on vases), and of the mainland Greek
Pythagorean movement. The artist in looking for a
prototype for this new representation perhaps simply
drew upon a type well known from the symposium scenes on
Attic vases. Later, more sedate representations attest
to the development of a more appropriate type, with the
woman sitting on a stool or on the edge of the couch.
It still seems significant that the woman appears regularly,
and seems to have been a standard element in the type
scene.

Of the warrior stelai, at least those of Mnason, Rhynchon,
Saugenes, and Koiranos, with their close similarity in
technique and, in most details, subject matter, appear to
have come from a single workshop located in Thebes, (49)
although the stelai of Saugenes and Koiranos were found at
Tanagra. The identity of the artist is naturally a matter
of great interest. Keramopoullos has identified him as
Aristeides of Thebes. (50) Pliny mentions this painter
several times, (51) although he confuses him with his
grandson who lived in the fourth century. (52) Aristeides
the painter appears to have been the same man as Aristeides
the bronze sculptor, who made chariots with four horses
and two horses, and who was a pupil of the sculptor
Polykleitos. (53)

Aside from his possible involvement with these stelai,
Aristeides appears to have been connected in another most
interesting way with the intellectual history of Thebes.
In studying the ancient sources in an effort to explain
a procedure used by the Pythagorean Eurytus to ascertain
the 'number' of a living being, the philosopher J.E. Raven
has been led to the conclusion that Eurytus was utilizing
the theory of proportions, or the Canon, of Polykleitos.
(54) He suggests that Eurytus could have learned of the
Canon indirectly through his friend Philolaus, who perhaps
adopted it after reading an exposition written by
Polykleitos.   There was a much more direct way, however,
in which the theory could have been transmitted.   Polykleitos
was the master of Aristeides, and would naturally have
taught him the Canon.   In the 'Phaedo' Plato names Philolaus
as the teacher of the two Thebans, Simmias and Cebes
('Phaedo' 61d), who heard him when he visited them in
Thebes.   While in Thebes, Philolaus could easily have picked
up information about the Canon directly from Aristeides.
To a Pythagorean, whose philosophy centered upon the
concept of proportion, a new theory of proportion would
have been of the greatest interest.
      The Warrior stelai have been attributed by Keramopoullos
to the last quarter of the fifth century, and, in fact, he
believed that they were all created as memorials for men
fallen in the battle of Delion. (55) This suggestion was
based not only upon synchronism between the dates of the
battle and the apparent dates of the stelai, but also upon
the existence of the names 'Saugenes' and 'Koironos' on
a casualty list inscription from Tanagra which Keramopoullos
has identified as listing those fallen at Delion.   The
relative infrequency with which names were duplicated in
the same city and period in Boeotia suggests strongly that
these men were identical with those for whom the stelai
were created, the list belonging to a public memorial,
while the stelai were private memorials commissioned for
use in family burial plots.
      The importance of these stelai as evidence for the
presence in Thebes in the last quarter of the fifth century
of an artist or artists of outstanding artistic and
technical ability is unquestionable, whoever he may have
been.   They offer us a new insight into the potentials of
provincial art.   Just as the bas-relief stelai demonstrate
the selectivity with which themes and techniques were
borrowed and the controlling role which local values played
in the borrowing, adaptation and development of these
themes and techniques, so the engraved and painted stelai
show us a provincial master who was in the forefront in
adapting artistic innovations, and who created a wholly new

genre to suit local materials and requirements. In this
area of artistic endeavor, Thebes was by no means an
isolated backwater.

PAINTED VASES

The products of the vase painters' art differ in obvious
ways from the grave stelai which we have just considered.
Perhaps the most important difference lies in the fact
that the stelai were luxury products, created for a very
few, while painted vases, especially of the less carefully
done variety, must have been fairly inexpensive. Most
Thebans at some time in their lives must have found
occasion to buy a painted vase, if not to adorn their
symposia, at least to mourn a dead relative or to celebrate
some important family event such as a wedding. Thus far
more vases than stelai have survived, in at least fragmentary form, and we have material representing a much wider
range of craftmanship. Price must often have been an
important factor, and not surprisingly, in Thebes as in
many other Greek cities, many pieces offered in the market
were rather sloppily done, and vase painting did not
always attract the best craftsmen. (56) None the less,
the vase painter in his adaptations of external models
displays much the same characteristics of Theban taste
as did the men who created the grave stelai, and on
occasion he also rose to the level of originality and
considerable artistic achievement.
    One of the more important sources of materials for the
study of Boeotian pottery has been not Thebes itself but
the necropolis of Mykelessos (modern Rhitsona), which is
located at some distance from the city. (57) This raises
the question of the possibility of identifying specifically
Theban pottery for consideration: how can we tell if we
are dealing with a Theban vase when it was found in a
distant cemetery? Fortunately, the answer has been
provided by scholars who combined information about local
finds at Thebes with the results of the classification
of the Rhitsona pottery into workshops. A large body of
indisputably Theban pottery does exist, including some
of the best and most original work: the pottery found
in the sanctuary of the Kabeiroi. This pottery has been
analyzed and certain painters identified; (58) works
stylistically close to these painters have then been
found among the vases from the necropolis of Rhitsona,
making possible the identification of these workshops as
Theban. For instance, stylistic links have been recognized
between Kabeiric vases and the black-figure work of the

Thetis painter, (59) which in turn is close to the
Branteghem workshop. (60)   These connections have allowed
scholars to attribute all these workshops to Thebes.   The
Branteghem workshop also produced red-figure ware, and,
in particular, at least some of the series of vases with
a woman's head as decoration; (61) this work is therefore
identifiable as Theban.   Again, there is a close connection
between the Branteghem shop and the shop of the painter
of the Judgment of Paris, (62) and this allows identification of that shop as Theban.   The most prolific red-figure
shop, that of the Argos cup painter, seems also to have
been a Theban establishment (the work on one vase, a
skyphos in Athens, (63) appears to have been the joint work
of the Argos painter and a member of the Thetis workshop).
(64)   Finally, a mid-fifth-century group of vases with
white on black decoration is connected with Thebes by the
inclusion of a vase with a Kabeiric theme. (65)   From such
arguments and interconnections we can see justification
for Cook's opinion that Thebes was the center of production
of Boeotian red-figure vases, and of the better black-
figure ware (he suggests that inferior black-figure work
was the product of northern Boeotia and perhaps Euboea).
(66)
     The background for most Theban pottery is to be found
in the very popular and widely exported black-figure and
red-figure vases of Athens.   The black-figure technique
produced black figures silhouetted against the red background provided by the original color of the clay.   The
black color resulted from the use of a clay mixture painted
on the vase; a complex firing technique resulted in the
contrast of black and red when the different clay mixtures
reacted differently to the reducing and oxidizing effects
of the fire.   Details were engraved in the black figures,
and white and red paint were sometimes also used.   This
technique was at the height of its popularity in Athens
in the sixth century; in c. 530 a reverse technique was
invented, in which the background was black and the figures
were left in the red color of the clay.   This allowed for
details on the figures to be painted on in a thin glaze,
rather than engraved, and thus permitted much more scope
for the representation of expression and for the use on
vases of shading and other innovative techniques for the
representation of perspective developed by the monumental
wall painters.   Red-figure pottery became the most popular
style for Athenian vases in the fifth century, at least in
Athens.   Athenian vases were widely exported, and were
quite popular in Thebes.   Imported vases were relatively
expensive, however, and hostility between Athens and Thebes
also must have put a damper on the import of Athenian

pottery. Local Theban vase painters thus often met the
demands of the market by creating imitations of Athenian
work, and it is these more or less frank copies of Athenian
work which we shall consider first.

In Theban copies of Attic vases (67) we can see the bias
of Theban taste at work, determining how the borrowing
will be done. It is this selectivity which makes a study
of these Atticizing vases most interesting. The most
obvious tendency is one toward conservatism. Thus, although
Theban vase painters took up the red-figure technique
after 480, they continued to prefer the old-fashioned black-
figure; by the end of the fifth century, when the tradition
of Attic black-figure was essentially dead, except for the
production of Panathenaic amphorae, presented as awards at
the traditional cult celebrations of the Panathenaic
procession, the Thebans succeeded in producing fresh and
vigorous examples of the technique in the pottery associated
with the shrine of the Kabeiroi. Preference for black-
figure also reveals itself in the continuing production of
vases in mixed red- and black-figure techniques, (68) as
well as in the production of both red-figure and black-
figure work in the same workshop and even by the same
painter. (69)

Even when red-figure work was produced, a black-figure
approach is evident in the linear tendencies of the work
and in the treatment of bodies as flat surfaces with only
schematized and conventional indications of muscular
structure. Such an approach is similar to the archaizing
tendencies seen in the bas-relief stelai, with their linear
and stylized treatment of drapery and flat rendering of
bodily surfaces. In the light of these archaizing
tendencies, it is not surprising to find that the Boeotian
vase painters rejected the use of such advanced techniques
as perspective foreshortening and impressionistic painting
methods (skiagraphia). (70) While Attic red-figure vase
painters attempted to achieve a more three-dimensional
realism through these methods borrowed from the wall
painters, Thebans stubbornly maintained a basically linear
means of representation. (71) In a somewhat similar way
there was a hesitation among the bas-relief sculptors in
the application of these techniques, and mixed results
when they did adopt them. On the other hand, a strong
contrast exists with the engraved stelai, whose creator
seems to have been in the forefront of experimentation.
This should not be surprising, however, for in the case
of the engraved stelai we are dealing with a master
painter, probably Aristeides, or at least with someone
following closely in the footsteps of the monumental
painters, and working with a surface whose size and flatness

allowed for the use of these techniques. In contrast, the
vase painters were in many cases not the most talented
workmen, and the curved surfaces upon which they worked
offered far more difficulties for the application of the
new techniques than did the flat surfaces of walls. Even
the sculptors of the bas-relief stelai were producing a
basically utilitarian product, and foremost in their minds
must have been the satisfaction of the desires of their
conservative clients, rather than experimentation with the
newest techniques of monumental painting. If Theban tastes
required more avant-garde effects in their vases, they
would have had to turn to the more expensive Attic red-
figure imports. We can assume that usually buyers found
most satisfaction in familiar-looking vases, and that in
their choice they would have been looking mainly for a
clear portrayal of a subject which appealed to them within
their price range. Some careful work is, however, evident,
especially in the elaborate decorative patterning of
clothing in the work of the painter of the Judgment of Paris
(see Plate 7).

A particularly interesting and attractive series of red-
figure vases featuring a large head as the principal
decorative element was produced in Thebes in the last third
of the fifth century and the early fourth century. In
this case, we are not dealing with frank copies of popular
Athenian products, for the woman's head motif never
attained popularity in Athens. The use of a human, or
daimonic, head as a principal decoration on vases first
occurred in mainland Greece near the middle of the seventh
century; the heads appeared independently in Corinth,
Lakonia, Argos, and Attica at this time. Earlier and also
independent appearances occurred in Crete in the second
half of the eighth century and in Pithekussai in the late
eighth century. Most women's heads appeared in this early
period in Corinth, and most of these seem from inscriptions
to have been representations of hetairai. No uniformity
of representation exists within the entire group of early
vases with head motifs, however. Male figures were either
mortals or daimons. Gods began to be recognizable about
the mid sixth century. By the early fifth century still
another change took place: the heads often represented
underworld or fertility deities rising from the underworld.
The earliest Boeotian head vases are four vases dating from
the third quarter of the sixth century; they include one
woman's head, and are considered to be under strong
Athenian influence. (72) The earliest red-figure Theban
woman's head vase dates to early in the third quarter of
the fifth century, and it is significantly different from
the earlier group in that it faces right, has no headdress,
and displays a chiton. (73)

The woman's head motif became quite popular in Thebes in the last third of the fifth century and into the fourth. Ure lists twenty-three extant examples, and Pelagatti adds seven others. (74) The motif provides, according to Ure, 'a not insignificant proportion' of the known Boeotian red-figure vases. (75) Almost all of these heads are women's heads. Usually the decoration appears on the lid of a vase (see Plate 8), or as the main decoration on a krater, with a large palmette on the reverse side. Sometimes the subsidiary decorations vary: pictures of a woman washing and of a hippocamp adorn a krater whose lid features a woman's head, two vases have black-figure animal friezes on the body and a red-figure head on the lid, one has a head of Heracles with club on the reverse, another portrays on the reverse Thetis riding a hippocamp and carrying the shield of Achilles (here the head is unusual in that it is accompanied by a crescent moon and has a star in its head-dress), (76) and one bears a head of a youth (or Amazon) with a horse's head. Heads also appear on two lebetes, a kylix, a lekane, and on plates (one man's head appears on a plate).

One of the woman's head vases cited by Pelagatti was found in the great Etruscan necropolis at Spina in Italy. Copies made locally have also been found in this necropolis, (77) as well as another Theban vase, a skyphos with two male figures by the Painter of the Argos cup. (78) The woman's head motif proved even more popular and long lasting in fourth-century Italy than in Thebes, providing the subject for many Apulian vases, which are perhaps the best known of all the woman's head vases. (79) Given the finds at Spina, it is tempting to see a Theban origin for the Italian style, but any conclusions about possible influences must await further publication of the finds from Spina and a general study of the various other occurrences of the motif in the Greek world in the fifth and fourth centuries. (80) Lacking such a study, we can for the present only try to put these vases into the context of the earlier tradition on the Greek mainland. (81)

In the case of the Theban vases, no uniform identification of the figures represented can be established, because of the variations in the accompanying figures and the appearance of men, and perhaps an Amazon, in the group. It is possible that the women on the Theban vases portray underworld or fertility goddesses, as do earlier women's head vases from other Greek cities. This would be in keeping with the Theban tendency toward mystical religious orientation, and with the apparent emphasis upon feminine divinities in the city's cults.

The most outstanding examples of Theban originality in

vase painting are definitely connected with a religious
cult. These are the figured vases found at the shrine of
the Kabeiroi on the outskirts of Thebes. (82) On these
vases a mostly grotesque series of black-figure characters
appear in a variety of activities: thus there are banquet
scenes in which the Kabeiros and his companion Pais are
sometimes portrayed in normal human fashion but with
grotesque companions, and procession scenes in which
pygmies and satyrs take part, sometimes leading animals
(steers, or in one case, a pregnant sow) toward an
ithyphallic Herm. On other vases the characters are
engaged in caricatures of mythological stories: pygmy
figures portray Penelope at her loom, probably entertaining
Odysseus; the judgment of Paris; Bellerophon and the
Chimaira; and Peleus and Achilles before Chiron (see Plate
9).

The Kabeirion vases appear to be a truly Theban creation,
although earlier models have been suggested. The excavators
of the site even proposed that the originator of the style
may have been an able Athenian craftsman working in the
Boeotian tradition. (83) (This seems to reflect the
ancient Athenian prejudice against Boeotia: nothing of
originality and value can be expected from Thebes; all
such creations must be Athenian.) Others attribute the
inspiration to the padded dancers of Corinthian pottery.
(84) More important, I believe, are the black-figure
Boeotian vases dating before 550 and decorated with
grotesque festival and games scenes, which Ure cites. (85)
She believes that 'curious affinities' between these vases
and the fifth-century Kabeirion vases may be signs of an
unbroken tradition.

In a case such as this, when similar cult activities
took place in various areas of Greece, it would seem to
be a case of parallel development of an early shared
tradition, rather than of a linear series of borrowing,
and Ure's suggestion of local forerunners seems most
convincing. Grotesque dances and proto-dramatic
performances in connection with cult ceremonies were
common to many Greek peoples, who also sometimes shared
the practice of portraying these activities on vases. (86)
In Athens, the fifth-century development of this type of
cult celebration was Attic comedy, brought to an extreme
of sophistication by Aristophanes. In Thebes there appears
to have been less development away from cultic origins,
and 'plots' may not have deviated from simple epic parodies,
perhaps improvised, but some sort of dramatic performances
formed part of the cult activities. (87) In the late
fifth century an inspired Theban vase painter undertook
to represent these performances on a series of vases, and

gained great popularity with his work. It has been called
the only truly comic Greek vase painting style, (88) and
it surely attests to a good sense of humor among the Thebans.
   One of the differences between pots and stelai is the
degree to which pots travel and can thus provide information
about contacts between various areas. It is true that
sculptors also travelled, and that these travels can be
traced through the diffusion of influences; however, pots
can provide a better overall picture, registering trade
contacts, or lack of them, as well as occasional travel
by a wide range of ordinary people (visits to oracles, games
or festivals, travel by exiles, educational travel).
   Theban pottery does not seem to have been exported to
any extent. The large amount of Theban pottery found at
Rhitsona does suggest that Thebes was important in supplying
local Boeotian markets, but beyond this Thebes appears to
have been mainly an importer, bringing in Attic vases when
this was possible (the city would probably have been cut off
from these imports during the Peloponnesian War). The few
Theban vases found elsewhere appear to have been isolated
instances, carried by individual travellers. Thus two
vases of the Argos cup group were found in nearby Lokris,
(89) a faint hint of contact exists as far away as Olbia,
(90) and an interesting imitation of a Fikellura cup was
found in Thebes itself. (91) The woman's head vase found
at Spina, with its Italian copies, and the skyphos of the
Argos workshop found at the same location, do not
necessarily point to trade, even though they do show that
a local potter found the woman's head motif attractive and
found customers for it.
   One interesting woman's head krater perhaps offers
some insight into the type of contact which was possible
between Athens and Thebes in the latter part of the
fifth century, possibly during the Peace of Nicias or
soon after the end of the war. (92) The woman on this
vase wears a head-covering rare on Boeotian vases - a
sakkos with a pompom on top (it is also unusual in having
a crescent moon beside the head and a star on the head-
dress). Ure draws attention to this style as especially
fashionable in Athens in the later years of the fifth
century. Perhaps a Theban customer - or his wife -
ordered this particular style of woman's head-dress after
having been attracted by it on a visit to Athens (perhaps
the man even brought a sakkos home as a gift to wife or
daughter). Ure finds that other elements of the decoration
(the tendrils on the back and the quality of the folds)
suggest that the painter was influenced to an exceptional
degree by Attic masters; a customer interested in the
newest Athenian fashion would probably have picked for his

commission one of the more capable and up-to-date painters.
Perhaps this is too conjectural, but it is equally
conjectural (and perhaps less plausible) to assume that
a Theban vase painter visited Athens and was then
responsible for adding this new Athenian twist to a
popular Theban motif. We do have some evidence that there
were visits to Athens by upper-class Thebans during the
closing years of the century in Plato's 'Phaedo'. In
this context, we should also mention two pieces of
Kabeirion ware found in Athens - a mug and a lekythos -
which show, as Wolters and Bruns suggest, that there were
Athenians who took an interest in Theban affairs, just as
there were Thebans who took an interest in Athenian
affairs. (93)

Another piece of Kabeirion ware is perhaps the most
interesting travelling Theban vase of all. This is a
vase, or askos, in the shape of a pig, found in a tomb
at Epizephyrian Lokri in southern Italy in 1913. (94)
The pig bears a caricatured pygmy scene on each of its
sides: a fox hunt is portrayed on one side and a foot
race on the other (see Plate 10). The work appears to
be that of the Kabeiros painter: (95)   not only the
caricatured scenes, but also the specific details in the
decoration of the vase attest to this: plant types,
rendering of the myrtle garland on the pig's neck, the
type of fox portrayed and his attitude, the heads of the
pygmies and the stick one pygmy is carrying. (96)   Its
date is 440-420 BC. No explanation has been ventured
for the presence of the vase in the tomb; the combination,
however, of a Theban object and an Epizephyrian Lokrian
findspot invites speculation. Could it have been brought
home to Lokri by Plato's Timaeus after a visit to the
Pythagoreans in Thebes?

We have no knowledge about Timaeus aside from Plato's
dialogue, (97) which tells us that he was well born and
wealthy, had held the highest offices and attained the
greatest honors which his country could offer, had
reached the highest eminence in philosophy ('Timaeus' 20A),
was well versed in astronomy, and had made knowledge of
the nature of the cosmos his chief concern ('Timaeus' 27A).
In the dialogue his role is to describe the genesis of
the cosmos, ending with the nature of man; then the account
was to pass to Critias, who would deal with human affairs.
Timaeus is never identified by Plato as a Pythagorean,
and although much of the material in his account is
undoubtedly Pythagorean, he borrows also from other pre-
Socratic philosophers, especially from Empedocles and
Parmenides. (98)   Taylor sees his work as 'exactly what
we should expect in a fifth century Italian Pythagorean

who was also a medical man ... a deliberate attempt to
amalgamate Pythagorean religion and mathematics with
Empedoclean biology'. (99)   The only clue to Timaeus'
age is his record of offices and distinctions. Taylor
infers from this that he must be over seventy at the
dramatic date of the dialogue, which is 421 BC. (100) while
Cornford believes that he was more probably 'a man in
middle life'. (101)

     In speculating upon who was the owner of the pig askos,
other evidence of contact between this Italian city and
Thebes should not be overlooked, however. Pindar composed
two odes for Hagesidamus of Lokri, the winner in the boys'
boxing match in 476. The first of these, a brief ode
composed immediately after the victory, is 'Olympian' 11;
the second 'Olympian' 10 composed for the same victory, was
much later in coming, and Pindar himself apologizes
within the ode for the late repayment of his debt. Pindar's
introduction to the Lokrians probably came about through
his patron, Hieron of Syracuse, who had saved the city
from Anaxilas, tyrant of Rhegium in 477; Pindar refers to
this incident in 'Pythian' 2.18, composed for Hieron.
We can assume that the rulers of the city, after its
rescue by Hieron, would have been favorable to him, and
that Hagesidamus' father Archestratus was among them.
Hagesidamus might have visited the city of Pindar at some
time in his life and brought back the small pig. At any
rate, he and Timaeus must have been near contemporaries.

     The ceramic evidence for contracts between Thebes and
Italy consists in the finds of the vases of Spina, and
the pig at Epizephyrian Lokris. These apparently
isolated finds may reflect, however, a more general level
of contact between Thebes and Italy. A general stylistic
similarity in the vases produced in the two has attracted
notice. (102) Ure mentions the character and prominence
of floral motifs in both areas, the portrayal of human
figures in silhouette without incision, and the use of a
pale clay and a poor glaze, and suggests that these
resemblances cannot be explained adequately by appeal to
the common relations of the two areas to Ionian or Attic
models (as Beazley would have it). Whatever connection
there was does not seem at the present time to have been
of a commercial nature (although additional finds from
Spina may eventually point in this direction), but one
of casual travel by a few people between two areas much
alike in their life style and conservative agricultural
orientation. Such travel, however, may be more significant
in the area of intellectual influences than a strictly
commercial tie.

     Finally, an interesting reflection of Theban interest

in Attic vases is to be found in the 'Acharnians' of
Aristophanes (860-958). Dikaiopolis has opened his
own market after his private declaration of peace, and
one of its visitors is a Boeotian from Thebes who has
arrived with a large selection of Theban delicacies,
greatly tempting Dikaiopolis. A problem arises, however,
over what the Athenian can offer in return, for the
Thebans have no need for Athens' most notable export
product, its pots. These lines should not be taken too
seriously as evidence about the state of the pottery trade
between Boeotia and Athens in the late fifth century. The
very idea of Boeotians being satisfied with their own
pottery was probably a huge joke to an Athenian audience,
aware as it was of Athenian excellence in this field and
possessed of none too high an opinion of Boeotians in the
first place. Moreover, the Boeotian's not wanting Athenian
pots is a necessary prerequisite for the coming joke:
Athenian ingenuity must be allowed the opportunity to
come up with the idea of sending another notable Athenian
product to Thebes, a sycophant, packaged as a pot. On the
other hand, it certainly is the case that Theban pottery
flourished during the years of the war, perhaps partly
because of the enforced abstinence from Athenian pottery
which the war necessitated, so there may be a grain of
truth in Aristophanes' portrayal of the Boeotians' lack of
interest in Athenian pots: the Theban product was now more
acceptable than it had been in the past.

In summing up the information which we can draw from a
consideration of Theban pottery, certain things stand out
as especially significant. First, the Theban adaptation
of Athenian models is marked by the exercise of considerable
selectivity, focusing on older styles, which mirrors
similar preferences in the adaptation of Ionian and Attic
models in bas-relief sculpture. The pottery shows a
preference for black-figure technique and for linear
representation, both archaizing features. Thebans were
slow to pick up new techniques pioneered in Athens, yet
they were not reluctant to move in fresh directions when
it suited their own style and interests, as we can see
by the woman's head vases and the Kabeirion pottery. Here
again we see the same factors at work as we saw in
considering the funeral stelai: outstanding talent found
original outlets for its expression. Finally, in the
matter of foreign contacts, the pottery finds support the
conclusion, suggested by other evidence as well, that
there were insignificant individual contacts between Thebes
and both Italy and Athens in the fifth century: with
imagination we can trace the ceramic footsteps of Simmias
and Cebes in Athens and of Timaeus - or perhaps Hagesidamus -
of Lokri in Thebes.

8 Conclusion

We have now considered a number of individual aspects of
Theban life in the fifth century; it remains to draw them
together and to see what sort of a general picture emerges.
It will be helpful to use the chronological framework
provided by the political and military history of the city
to do this, although, as we shall see, at least one
important aspect of Theban life falls outside its compass.

The overall picture of Theban life in the fifth century
is clear and simple: loss and recovery. The city began
the century as the dominant member of a loose confederation
of Boeotian states, of enough significance in the wider
Greek world to attract the attention of both the Peisistratids
and the Alkmaeonids at the oracular shrine of Apollo Ptoios.
In this period, too, Thebes' own mystery cult, that of the
Kabeiroi, underwent a reorganization and received a new
direction, beginning a course of expansion and development.

Thebes' happy position at the turn of the century was
shattered by the city's medism and the failure of that
cause; the consequent loss of reputation and status made
the material losses of life, leadership potential, and
property all the harder to bear. Despite this, the response
of the city was to take up the Herculean task of re-
establishing both its material prosperity and its political
hegemony. Little record of this effort remains, but we do
have the voice of Pindar which speaks from an otherwise
nearly silent period, mending his poetic ties with friends
in Aegina and building up important relationships in Magna
Graecia with the Sicilian tyrants and their entourage.
Despite a degree of success in Theban efforts (evidenced
by the apparent re-establishment of Theban influence on
the shrine of Apollo in Delion in 470), the city was not
able to prevent the Athenian takeover of Boeotia in 457,
and for ten years Boeotia lay under Athenian control. The
real turning point for Thebes came in 447, when the

Boeotians succeeded in expelling the Athenians and established
Boeotian independence once again. The Thebans then saw to
it that the Boeotian league was reorganized and reconstituted
upon a sophisticated numerical basis which allowed for
flexibility in the number and internal make-up of league
members. The organizational format of the new league gave
Thebes subtle advantages, while on the surface the structure
preserved the appearance of impartiality. At this crucial
point tradition places the arrival of the Pythagorean Lysis,
a refugee from the persecution of the Pythagoreans in
southern Italy, who may have participated in this
restructuring.

The years following 447 witnessed a blossoming of Theban
culture on many fronts. Advances were made in music with
the cultivation of the flute (possibly also under Pythagorean
influence) and the invention of a more versatile form of that
instrument; the vase painters working for the Kabeirion
reached a peak of creative achievement with their amusing
and often grotesque portrayals of cult activities; and the
painter Aristeides with his creation of the engraved and
painted stelai revealed that Theban artists were in the
forefront in the employment of new representational
techniques. Finally, the immigrant Lysis developed a
Pythagorean following which, by the end of the century,
was to provide Socrates with two of his most devoted
followers; Lysis also provided a Pythagorean education
for Epaminondas.

On the military and political front during these years
Thebes was actively involved against Athens in the
Peloponnesian War, to its own considerable profit. After
the defeat of Athens, however, the Thebans moved to help
the Athenian democrats in exile, in an effort to foster
the now-chastened Athens as a counterweight to Sparta's
increased power. The city's ventures beyond Boeotian
borders during the war, and its interest in manipulating
the balance of power after the war, pointed the way toward
the greater role it was soon to play on the Greek scene
under the guidance of Epaminondas.

As we remarked at the beginning of this chronological
review, however, there is one important aspect of Theban
life and thought which slips through the meshes of this
framework. This is the question of the role of women in
the city and the attitude taken toward them. It is not
surprising to find that information about the position of
women is almost entirely missing in a sketch based on
traditional political and military history, since women
played no known political role aside from being transmitters
of citizenship. Nevertheless, they made up perhaps half
the adult population (we cannot be sure of this, since

natural survival rates may have been affected by infant
exposure - for which we have no evidence one way or the
other in Thebes - and women's mortality rates in child-
birth may well have surpassed those of men in battle).
No account of the life of a city can really be adequate
which omits approximately half of its citizens. Numerous
clues about the life of this submerged group are to be
found scattered throughout our material, and it will be
useful to collect these here.

Our first mention of women was to note that we have
no evidence that they partook in the advantages offered
by the agora and gymnasium. This is a salutary place to
start, for it is necessary to keep in mind that Theban
women were, after all, Greek women, and that their position
in Theban society fell within the range of possibility in
that wider culture. The question is, where, within that
relatively limited range, did their situation fall?

Much evidence comes from poetry. We have seen that
women were traditionally held to have been active as poets
in Thebes. This poetic activity probably arose as a
natural consequence of the importance which maiden-choruses
played in Theban cult activity, and the use of women as
trainers for these choruses. Such women might on occasion
overstep the boundaries of coaching and venture to provide
the poetic material themselves, as Sappho did on Lesbos.
This choral training was a form of education for young
girls, parallel to some extent to the traditional choric
education of boys. It provided girls with social contacts
and a life outside the home. Similar choral participation
was to be found in the Sparta of Alcman and in Sappho's
Lesbos; however, it was not really paralleled by the mere
participation of girls in religious processions, as at
Athens, since such participation does not require the
extensive training of choral performance.

The poems and fragments of Pindar also suggest a
'feminist' orientation in Theban religion: those works
which described, or were intended for use in, cult
ceremonies display an apparent emphasis on women, both as
participants in cult activities and as female divinities.
In seeming contrast to this situation, if we consider the
archaeological evidence from the Kabeirion, we find that
women appear to have played little part in that cult. It
seems likely, however, that this is a misleading picture,
the result of the accidents of archaeological discovery.
The role of women in the history and mythology of the
cylt, the report of a nearby shrine of Demeter Kabeira
(not excavated), and the presence at the shrine of the
Kabeiroi in Samothrace of a cult of Demeter, all strongly
suggest that women at Thebes may have had a 'sister cult'
of their own at this important shrine.

In the closely related area of philosophy, the
Pythagorean presence in Thebes might be expected to have
worked toward enhancing the position of women in the city.
Women played an active role in the Pythagorean society,
and were supported in this by some sort of theory. Such
participation, and the theory behind it, would have been
confined to a minority, but the Pythagorean minority
included some well-to-do men (at least Simmias and Cebes).
One would expect some impact on the society as a whole
through them (compare in Athens the philosophically based
questioning of the traditional role of women in the late
fifth century, which surely filtered through to the
society as a whole by such means as Euripidean tragedy
and the comedies of Aristophanes).

The crafts also offer us some evidence about women,
though it is even harder to interpret than that offered
by poetry. We have seen that a preponderance of funerary
stelai were devoted to women in the second half of the
century (in fact, all the known bas-relief stelai). While
it is difficult to draw any conclusions from this, since
it might at any time be changed by new finds, it does at
this time mark a definite contrast with Athens. There
women were in the minority in terms of numbers of stelai,
and girls did not appear. At the least, this shows that
in Thebes women (and even girls) were considered worthy
of relatively extravagant expenditure. Even the
portrayals of women on the bas-relief stelai differ from
those in Athenian sculpture. They depict far sturdier
bodily types, as if the Theban ideal was determined more
by capacity for practical day-to-day living in a basically
agricultural culture, rather than by a slender and
delicate grace more suited to objects of admiration than
to active and useful human beings. Finally, we have
seen that one of the Theban stelai portrayed a priestess.
This illustrates, and perhaps reinforces at least to a
small degree, the picture drawn from Pindar of the
importance of women in Theban religious life.

In vase painting, one of the outstanding developments
of the Theban workshops was the series of woman's head
vases. The motif may have spread from Thebes to southern
Italy, where it had a long history and attained great
popularity among a people whose environment was similar
to that of the Thebans: fertile land which produced an
abundance of food and a basically agricultural orientation.
It is not possible to ascertain the identity of the woman
in every case, since various mythical scenes accompany
the heads; however, at this period in other Greek cities
a connection with mystery cults was developing for similar
motifs.

If the woman on the woman's head vases is a specifically Theban divinity, the possibility is raised that such vases were among the 'works of art' awarded to victors in the Theban games according to Pindar ('O'.7.80ff.), a parallel to the Panathenaic vases with their portrayals of the patron goddess of Athens. Or again, the context may have been nuptial: in Spina the motif appears in one burial in a clear wedding context.

What then can be said in summary about the position of women in Thebes? On the one hand, there is no evidence that Theban girls were given the freedom reputedly allowed to Spartan girls, or that they were allowed to participate in exercise or athletics in a formal way (although Theban sculptural portrayals of women suggest an ideal type well suited to an active life). One the other hand, Theban girls do appear to have received a form of choric education, in preparation for their role in cult activities.

If women did in fact have a certain amount of significance in Thebes, as they appear to have had, all the evidence suggests that it was bound up with their religious role (not surprising in an agricultural society). This, perhaps inadvertently, had, however, the added result of improving the general condition of their lives. Thus in the range of possibilities for women in Greek culture, their cult activities and choric education would place them somewhere mid-way along a continuum which had Spartan women at one extreme and Athenian at the other. That they were not alone among Greek women in holding an in-between position is suggested by hints such as the occurrence of funeral stelai for young girls in Ionia, the activities of Sappho and her friends in Lesbos, and the popularity of the woman's head motif in southern Italy. Much more needs to be done in collecting and analyzing the bits and pieces of evidence about women in the various Greek cities; it appears that the result might be a picture which differs considerably from that provided by the Athenian sources along.

We have traced the steps by which Thebes rose from a position of defeat and disgrace to a triumphant renewal of its hegemony over a league cleverly organized to assure that hegemony, and we have seen it move from subjection to Athens to a major role in Athenian defeat. We have also seen it have the political wisdom to assist Athens to regain its lost independence. We have analyzed Theban cults and the city's involvement with Pythagorean philosophy, examined the achievements of provincial art, and found evidence about the life style of an aristocratic oligarchy in the poetry of Pindar. The picture which has emerged is one of a conservative people, living in a religious atmosphere which centered upon early local heroes and divinities, and emphasized mystery cults and the role of women. Theban conservatism in every field, however, proved itself open to innovation, when that innovation spoke to an interest of its own: witness the late sixth-century reorganization of the cult of the Kabeiroi, the acceptance of Pythagoreanism, the innovations involved in the Kabeirion vases and the engraved stelai, the popularity of the woman's head motif, and the re-organization of the Boeotian league. All this suggests that if Thebes did not always follow exactly the same pattern that Athens did, it was not so much from lack of ability as from an awareness that the pattern itself did not fit its circumstances. For instance, the fact that Thebans did not develop a facility equal to that of the Athenians in debate and oratory, or rival the Athenian expertise in sycophancy, was surely a consequence of their oligarchical form of government, in which there was no need of convincing vast crowds of people from the 'lower classes', rather than a result of a lack of ability with language, as Plutarch's Alcibiades would have it.

Thebes was a city of vast energy and will, coupled with the intelligence to turn these assets to its own purposes, as we can see by its determined recovery and its step-by-step achievement of mastery over its neighbors. Possibly there is a hint of Athenian recognition of this in the portrait of Heracles in Euripides' 'Alcestis'. The hero Admetus *does* behave in a gross and gluttonous manner in his feasting, scandalizing even the servants, and this may well be a slap at Thebes. If so, however, the denouement reveals Heracles to be clever past even our scholarly discerning: despite all our analysis, we still cannot agree whether Heracles truly won his fight with Hades and brought Alcestis back from the dead, or, if he did, whether it was as a reward - or a punishment - for Admetus. Euripides' Heracles is surely a worthy patron for the Thebes which won back its hegemony, and then created the deceptively fair-seeming reorganized Boeotian league.

Appendix:
The position of women
in Pythagoreanism

The evidence about the position of women in early
Pythagoreanism consists of the following: reports about
individual women, including some who are named as pupils
of Pythagoras; the list of Pythagorean women which forms
part of the 'Catalogue of Pythagoreans' of Iamblichus; (1)
and the speeches of Pythagoras. (2) None of this material
goes back beyond the late fifth century, and it is not
all of the same weight; therefore each type must be
examined individually to see what possibility there is
that it may reflect fifth-century conditions.

First, names and accounts of individual Pythagorean
women occur in the tradition. (3) 'Theano' is a name
which recurs, variously identified as the wife of
Pythagoras, (4) or his pupil. (5) Diogenes attributes
to her a version of the teaching about purity after
intercourse which is attributed to Pythagoras himself
in the speeches, as well as advice to women to put aside
shame when they go to their husbands. (6) A daughter
of Pythagoras, Damo, was said in the letter of Lysis to
Hippasos to have been entrusted with his memoirs, (7)
but she is not found in the 'Catalogue' of Iamblichus,
and Burkert suggests that the letter was a third-century
forgery. (8) Other daughters are also named: Aisara, (9)
Arignote, (10) and Myia (who appears in the 'Catalogue'
as the wife of Milon). (11) The survival within the
tradition of these names of women, despite some confusion
about their actual identify, perhaps in itself implies
something about the significance of women in the early
days of the society. That some were named as pupils may
only reflect conditions in the fourth century and
Hellenistic period when the identifications were formulated
(and may also reflect the ingenuity of those seeking to
maintain the celibacy of Pythagoras), but these bits of
tradition are at least suggestive that women may have
played some significant role from an early period.

A catalogue of Pythagoreans, including names of both men and women, occurs at the end of Iamblichus' 'Life of Pythagoras'. (12) Its coincidence with material from Aristoxenus led Burkert to the conclusion that Aristoxenus is the only possible candidate for authorship. (13) The list contains sixteen names of women, including some that go back to the time of Pythagoras himself, such as Theano and Myia the wife of Milon, and some which may date to the fourth century (was Echekrateia the daughter of Echekrates of the 'Phaedo'?) No specific formula seems to have been used to generate the list: six women named are related as wives, sisters, or daughters to men named in the 'Catalogue', and three names are feminine forms of men's names which occur there; however, in three cases a male relative is named in the women's section whose name does not occur in the male section of the 'Catalogue', and four women identified only by city have no other connections at all with the 'Catalogue' beyond their own presence in it. This suggests that the women's section was not created simply by the invention of women's names to correspond with men named in the 'Catalogue'. The discordance between the men's and the women's sections may be due to the fact that the list of women had an independent source; possibly it was drawn from the 'synagoge heroidon etoi Pythagoreion gynaikon' of Philochorus (14) by Aristoxenus (this is just barely possible chronologically: Aristoxenus was born c.375-360, Philochorus held office in 306 and was executed shortly after 261/260). The important point is that there were as many as sixteen names of women preserved in the tradition; this in itself seems to attest to a degree of participation and involvement of women which we, depending mostly on Athenian sources which deal with the Athenian situation, would consider highly unusual in Greek society of the time.

Of the four speeches attributed to Pythagoras in Iamblichus, the speech addressed to the women, (15) and a portion of that addressed to the men, (16) contain material which is helpful in arriving at an understanding of the position of women in Pythagoreanism. The points covered in the speech addressed to the women are as follows:

1 Admonitions about sacrifices: moral excellence is important when sacrificing; sacrifices should be prepared with one's own hands and taken to the altar without the help of servants; bloody sacrifices and large sacrifices are to be avoided.

2 Never oppose your husband; rather, in giving in to him consider yourself the victor.

3 Sexual relations within marriage never render a woman
   unclean, those outside of marriage always do.
4 Speak little and modestly, and give no cause for blame.
   Take care to preserve the reputation for 'dikaiosyne'
   which poets have attributed to women because they lend
   and borrow without witnesses, lawsuits or quarrels –
   this reputation is expressed by poets in the myth of
   the three Graiai who amicably shared one eye among
   themselves.
5 Praise of women's piety: names of divinities are given
   to women at various stages of life: Kore, Nymphe,
   Meter, Maia; the oracles at Dodona and Delphi are
   communicated by women.
6 The example of Odysseus, who refused to forsake
   Penelope even for the immortality promised by Calypso,
   is cited as setting a challenge to women to show
   similar fidelity to their husbands.

In the speech to the men, husbands are urged to practise
fidelity and to treat their wives as supplicants whom
they have brought into their homes in the presence of the
gods ('VP' 48); the use of concubines is also discouraged
('VP' 48); and the separation of children from their
parents is named as the greatest crime ('VP' 49).

It seems to be agreed that the speeches of Pythagoras
were composed in the late fifth or early fourth century,
for they fit the rhetorical and stylistic patterns of
this period. (17) Although on first consideration the
speeches appear to support a traditional view of the
position of women (see especially no.2 above), a more
careful analysis shows several points which seem to be
critical of received traditions about the relationship
between the sexes: a new rule about ritual purity and
sexual relations is proposed, fidelity is required of
husbands as well as wives, husbands are urged to treat
wives as supplicants, separation of children from parents
is named as the greatest crime, and women are praised
for both 'dikaiosyne' and piety. Some of these points
seem to be responses to other ideas which were put
forward in the late fifth century: the passage about the
'dikaiosyne' of women has close parallels with
Aristophanes' 'Ecclesiazusae' 446ff., (18) while the
advice to husbands to treat wives as supplicants addresses
a problem which is recognized in the 'Medea' of Euripides
(230ff.); the praise of women in the speeches also has
a counterpart in the 'Medea', when the chorus says that
such praise will come only when rivers turn back to their
springs (410ff.); while the statement about separating
children from parents may have been aimed at some proposal
advocating such separation, such as we find somewhat later

in Plato's 'Republic' (unless it is to be translated,
'alienation', as in Plato, 'Laws' 875A). Without trying
to trace in detail the various currents of thought on
the subject of the treatment of women in the late fifth
and early fourth centuries, it seems clear that this
Pythagorean pamphlet arises out of a context similar to
that in Athens, and that it makes suggestions which,
though comparatively moderate, are still in the reformist
stream.

The evidence does not allow us to determine the exact
status of a Pythagorean woman (whether it was in all things
exactly that of a man seems unlikely, in the face of the
speech to the women), but it does suggest that women did
play some sort of active role within the Pythagorean cult
and society, and that this participation was supported by
some sort of a theoretical foundation. The tradition can
picture women as pupils and sources of wise advice; not
all Pythagorean women are identified by their male relative,
so we must even allow the possibility of independent
female membership. The evidence is slim, but in the
obscurity which envelops the history of women, it appears
as a comparatively bright spot.

Notes

CHAPTER 1   INTRODUCTION

1   B.V. Head, On the Chronological Sequence of the Coins
     of Boeotia, pp. 30-3 and Pl. 2; Colin M. Kraay,
     Archaic and Classical Greek Coins, p. 111 and #351-4.
     See Plate 1.
2   The Greek recognition of resemblances between deity
     and worshipper, working to the benefit of the latter,
     can be seen in the 'Odyssey', where Athena admits
     that she shows special favor to Odysseus because he
     is like her ('Od.' 13.287-99).
3   Pindar 'O'.6.90, c. 472 BC; Plut. 'De esu carnium' i,
     6.
4   Aristophanes, 'Ach.' 860-958.
5   Plutarch, 'Alcibiades' 2.
6   This interesting suggestion that plays upon the
     special relationship between Thebes and Heracles
     (for which, see Isocrates Philip. 88) was made as
     early as 1792 in Karl Böttiger's 'Pallas Musica und
     Apollo, der Marsyastödter', in Wieland's Attischen
     Museum, 1792, vol.1, pt 2, 279-385, and later
     elaborated by Edmond Pottier, Recueil Edmond Pottier,
     pp. 352-72: the portrait of Heracles as glutton and
     buffoon, which appears in the 'Alcestis' of Euripides
     and the 'Frogs' of Aristophanes, was created as a
     deliberate slur upon Thebes and Boeotia. Coupled
     with the dramatic attacks, Pottier also cites a change
     in the use of mythological imagery on Attic vases in
     the sixth and fifth centuries: the popularity of
     Heracles diminishes and his role is taken over by
     Theseus.
7   Earlier work dealing with Thebes or Boeotia from a
     broader cultural viewpoint goes back to 1895, when the
     Boeotians were defended against the charge of 'Boeotian

pig' by W. Rhys Roberts in The Ancient Boeotians;
again, in 1948 the Thebans found a defender in Pierre
Guillon, who made special reference to the Athenian
transformation of Heracles into a buffoon and the
parallel enhancement of the Athenian national hero
Theseus in La Béotie Antique. Both Roberts and Guillon
went beyond political events to discuss the art, music
and literature of Boeotia as a whole, although without
going into much detail. Other work on Thebes or
Boeotia has concentrated on political history almost
entirely. This includes the 1879 dissertation of
Moritz Müller, Geschichte Thebens von der Einwanderung
der Boioter bis zur Schlacht bei Koroneai, the 1949
Heidelberg dissertation of Heinrich Vogelsang, Theben
und Boiotien, the article, 'Thebai (Boiotien)' by
F. Schober in RE, 1934, vol. 5A, pt 2, cols 1423ff.,
and a book by Paul Cloché, Thèbes de Béotie des
origines à la conquête romaine, which has a brief
excursus on Pindar and a four page treatment of the
arts in the fifth century. The 1975 dissertation of
C.J. Dull, A Study of the Leadership of the Boeotian
League from the Invasion of the Boiotoi to the King's
Peace, and also his article in CP, 1977, vol. 72,
pp. 305-15, have as their aim to reassert the claim
that Thebes was the leader of the league after 447 BC,
in opposition to Larsen's claim of Orchomenian
leadership in CP, 1960, vol. 55, pp. 9-18. Finally,
R.J. Buck's A History of Boeotia contains material
on Thebes and its position within the league at
various periods, as well as detailed analysis of the
mythological traditions.

CHAPTER 2   THE CITY

1 For a recent discussion of Boeotian topography, with
   bibliography, see Robert J. Buck, A History of
   Boeotia. For more detailed treatments of Thebes,
   see J.G. Frazer, Pausanias's Description of Greece,
   vol. 5; Keramopoullos, 'Thebaïka', AD, 1917, vol. 3;
   and Pharaklas' report on the city in AD, 1967, vol. 22,
   pt B-1, p. 247, in which archaeological evidence is
   correlated with literary and mythological references,
   and the most recent opinion on the locations of ancient
   landmarks is given.
2 H.N. Ulrichs, Reisen und Forschungen in Griechenland,
   vol. 2, pp. 4-6.
3 T.G. Tucker, The Seven Against Thebes of Aeschylus,
   p. xxxviii.

4   Keramopoullos, op.cit., pp. 464-78; see map of Boeotia.
5   Ibid., pp. 296-8; Pharaklas, op. cit., pp. 248ff.
6   Hdt. 9.41; see map of Thebes.
7   Keramopoullos, op. cit., p. 288.
8   Hdt. 9.86-8.
9   'Hellenica Oxyrhynchia' 12.3.
10 Thuc. 1.108; Diod. 11.81; Keramopoullos, op. cit.,
    pp. 290f.
11 Thuc. 1.108 on Athenian control of Boeotia; Aristotle
    speaks of a period of democratic government in Thebes
    at 'Pol.' 1302b29; Thuc. 3.62 on Thebes' medism;
    'Hell. Oxy.' 12.1 on pro- and anti-Lacedaemonian
    parties.
12 Aristotle, 'Pol.' 1278a25-6.
13 Athenaeus X, 417-18 collects literary references to
    the gluttony of the Thebans.
14 Aristophanes, 'Ach.' 860ff., 'Peace' 1004f.;
    A. Philippson and H. Lehmann, Die Griechischen
    Landschaften I, part 2, p.520 lists the following
    Boeotian products supplied to Athens in classical
    times: barley, garden vegetables, birds, horses,
    cattle, fish, and wagon seats from Thebes.
15 Pindar, Frag. 95 (Bowra).
16 Aristophanes, 'Ach.' 860ff.; on flutes, see Chapter 6.
17 For a review of the controversy, see Ruth B. Edwards,
    Kadmos the Phoenician, pp. 129ff.
18 See ibid., p. 131, n. 142.
19 Pindar, 'O'.7.80-7 relates the victories of Diagoras
    of Rhodes; see Chapter 6.
20 Hesiod, 'Works and Days', 618-94.
21 Ps.-Xenophon, 'The Old Oligarch'; for a philosophical
    exposition, see Plato, 'Laws' 705-8.
22 This is a point stressed by C.J. Dull, A Study of
    the Leadership of the Boeotian League from the
    Invasion of the Boiotoi to the King's Peace, pp.75,
    83.
23 Xen. 'Hell.' 5.2.29.
24 Keramopoullos, op. cit., p. 288.
25 Pharaklas, op. cit., p. 231 and Pl. 162d; a number
    of burials at Pyri are reported in AD, 1966, vol. 21,
    pt B-1, pp. 197ff.; 1967, vol. 22, pt B-1, pp. 236f.;
    1968, vol. 23, pt B-1, p.221; 1969, vol. 24, pt B-1,
    p. 176; 1971, vol. 26, pt B-1, pp. 211-13.
26 See note 9.
27 All locations are given according to Pharaklas, op. cit.,
    pp. 247ff.
28 For discussions of these elements of the city, see
    R.E. Wycherley, How the Greeks Built Cities; L. Martin,
    Recherches sur l'agora grecque; J. Delorme, Gymnasion.

29   In the time of Pausanias the agora was on the Kadmeia,
     in the place identified as the House of Kadmos
     (9.12.3), but the agora of the classical period stood
     in the lower city, identified by its temple of
     Artemis Eukleia (Plut. 'Arist.' 20); Paus. 9.17.2-3;
     Ulrichs, op. cit., vol. 2, pp. 4-6.
30   On the coffee-house, see The New York Times, August
     10, 1980, section 1, p.9.
31   Plut. 'Pelop.' 18.

CHAPTER 3   THEBAN POLITICAL AND MILITARY HISTORY DURING
            THE FIFTH CENTURY

 1   Histories of Thebes include Moritz Müller, Geschichte
     Thebens von der Einwanderung der Boioter bis zur
     Schlacht bei Koroneia; Heinrich Vogelsang, Theben
     und Boiotien; Paul Cloché, Thèbes de Béotie. The
     unpublished dissertation of C. Dull, A Study of the
     Boeotian League from the Invasion of the Boiotoi to
     the King's Peace, Wisconsin, 1975, treats those
     aspects of Theban history which have to do with the
     League (see especially Chapter IV). The most recent
     history of Boeotia is that of Robert J. Buck,
     A History of Boeotia.
 2   Martin Oswald, Nomos and the Beginnings of the
     Athenian Democracy, chapter 3, especially p. 113.
 3   Ibid., p. 180.
 4   Ibid., p. 118, n. 5.
 5   I.A.F. Bruce, An Historical Commentary on the
     'Hellenica Oxyrhynchia', pp. 160-1.
 6   Hdt. 5.67; 1.52, 61; L. Bizard, 'Inscriptions du
     Ptoion (1903)', BCH, 1920, vol. 44, pp.227-41.
 7   Known to us in its 395 BC form in section 11 of the
     'Hellenica Oxyrhynchia', see B.P. Grenfell and
     A.S. Hunt, Oxyrhynchus Papyri, vol. 5, pp. 110-242;
     V. Bartoletti, Hellenica Oxyrhynchia; Bruce, op.cit.,;
     translation and commentary on section 11 in J.M. Moore,
     Aristotle and Xenophon on Democracy and Oligarchy,
     pp. 125-234.
 8   Bruce, op. cit., pp. 159-60.
 9   Ibid., pp. 106-7.
10   Thus it is unsure whether the two districts allotted
     to Plataea, Scolos, Erythrai, Scaphai, and an
     undetermined number of other towns, under Theban
     control in 395, were part of the original constitution
     or whether they were added in 427 when Thebes destroyed
     Plataea, as Bruce, op. cit., pp. 105-6 suggests.
     Larsen argued that Orchomenos probably controlled three

districts in 447, losing one when Chaeronea was
detached from its sphere of control (Greek Federal
States, p.34), and that Plataea, although an Athenian
ally, originally controlled the two districts in its
area (CP, 1960, vol. 55, p. 12), but this, especially
the latter suggestion, seems highly improbable. The
analysis of the Boeotian districts by Salmon allots
Scolos, Erythrai, Scaphai and Hysiae (but not Plataea)
to Thebes in 447, as ancient possessions regained
(REA, 1956, vol. 69, pp. 52-6).

11 Bruce, op. cit., p. 103.
12 Buck, op. cit., chapter 7.
13 Herodotus 6.108; calculating from Thuc. 3.68, the
date was 519. Grote argued for a date of 509, on the
grounds that Cleomenes was unlikely to have been in
Boeotia in 519 but was there in 509 (History of Greece,
vol. 4, p. 94, no. 1); Grote is followed by G. Busolt,
Griechische Geschichte, vol. 2, p. 399, no.4; and by
M. Amit, AC, 1970, vol. 39, pp. 414-26. Thucydides'
date of 519 is accepted by Hammond, Historia, 1955,
vol 4, p. 389; L. Moretti, Ricerche sulle leghe
greche, pp. 105-8; and Buck, op. cit., chapter 8 and
CP, 1972, vol. 67, p. 98, nn. 27 and 28. I also
prefer Thucydides' date.
14 Dull, op. cit., pp. xii-xiii, 28. Thus Herodotus
speaks of 'Boeotarchs' at 9.15, and uses 'Thebans'
when he clearly means 'Boeotians', at 9.16; 5.81, 89;
6.108.2, 3, 5.
15 The standard work on Boeotian coinage is B.V. Head,
On the Chronological Sequence of the Coins of
Boeotia, see pp. 13-18. The earliest issues (Type I,
660-550, and Type II, 550-480) are probably dated
too early by Head; see W.P. Wallace, 'The early
coinages of Athens and Euboia', NumChron, 1962,
7th series, vol. 2, p. 38, n. 1.
16 Wallace, ibid.
17 Wallace, ibid.
18 There is the probability that the common coinage
could be evidence only of a monetary agreement, as
was the case with the Lesbian coins of Mytilene and
Methymna in approximately the same period (end of the
sixth century to mid fifth century), see E. Babelon,
Traité des Monnaies Grecques et Romaines, vol. 2,
pp. 339ff. For a possible similar agreement on Cos,
see Susan M. Sherwin-White, Ancient Cos, pp. 45f.
19 Buck, op. cit., p. 125.
20 Thus L. Moretti, op. cit., pp. 99f.; P. Guillon, Le
Bouclier d'Héraclès, Annales de la Faculté des Lettres
et Sciences Humaines d'Aix, 1963, vol. 37, p. 66, n.81;

Müller, op. cit., p. 7; J.A.O. Larsen, Representative
Government, 22f., and Greek Federal States, p. 28;
Cloché, op. cit., pp. 17f. But see Buck, op. cit.,
chapter 8, and J. Ducat, BCH, 1973, vol. 97, pp.59-73.

21 Dull, op. cit., p. 129, on the basis of the coinage.

22 Thus M. Amit, RSA, 1971, vol. 1, p. 62; on the
evidence of the coins, see Head, op. cit., pp. 20-3;
B.H. Fowler, Phoenix, 1957, vol. 11, pp. 164-70.

23 Hdt. 7.173; Ephorus ap. Diod. XI,3.2; Plut. 'De Her.
mal.' 864E.

24 de Sanctis, RFIC, 1930, vol. 8, pp. 339ff.; Sordi, Rend.
Ins.Lomb.Sci.Lett., 1953, vol. 86, pp. 305ff.

25 The most thorough recent discussion of this problem,
and, in my view, the most acceptable modern hypothesis
about the content of Alexander's message, is provided
by N. Robertson, JHS, 1976, vol. 96, pp. 100-20.

26 ap. Diod. XI.3.2.

27 G. Hignett, Xerxes' Invasion of Greece, p. 23, objects
that proper names need not guarantee statements, but
his case rests upon the use of a name passed on in
gossip (the Euboean who allegedly bribed Themistokles);
names of officials belong in another class of evidence,
and do carry weight since Greek cities are known to
have kept such records.

28 Hdt. 8.220. The hostage question is treated by
Plutarch, who offers a number of counterarguments
from probability: 'De Her. mal.' 865C-E.

29 Paus. IX.21.2; also II.16.4. Was Pausanias perhaps
led to this view by Diod. XI.65.2, or by Diodorus'
source here, possibly one of the local histories of
Argos to which Pausanias makes frequent reference
(I.13.8; II.19.4, 22.3, 23.8): at Thermopylae the
Mycenaeans alone of those dwelling in the Argolid
fought with the Lacedaemonians? Diodorus is
recounting the background to the war between the
Mycenaeans and the Argives in 468; the reference of
course need not be to the final stand at Thermopylae.

30 Plut. 'De Her. mal.' 867A; see Jacoby, FGrHist.,
vol. 3, B. #379, fr. 6; Müller, op. cit., pp. 42f.;
Buck's theory that Anaxandros was the Theban polemarch
and Leontiades the Boeotarch, op. cit., p. 129; CP,
1974, vol. 69, p. 47, rests upon his thesis that the
League in its early fourth-century form, as described
by P, went back to the late sixth century, as well as
upon his acceptance of Herodotus' anachronistic use
of the term 'Boeotarch' at 9.15; see note 14 above.

31 For a discussion of the problems involved and
references to the considerable previous literature on
Mys, see Georges Daux, 'Mys ai Ptoion', Hommages à

Waldemar Deonna, Collection Latomus, 1957, vol. 28, pp. 157-62.

32   Plut. 'De defectu oraculorum', 5.

33   See W.W. How and J. Wells, A Commentary on Herodotus, vol. 2, p. 287.

34   Heinrich Bischoff, Der Warner bei Herodot, see esp. pp. 72-5.

35   See P.E. Legrand, 'De la malignité d'Hérodote', Mélanges Gustave Glotz, vol. 2, pp. 535-47; Lionel Pearson'sintroduction to Plutarch's 'Moralia', vol. 11, pp. 2ff.; and most recently Alan Wardman, Plutarch's Lives, pp. 189-96.

36   Head, op. cit., p. 23.

37   See ibid., pp. 20-3, and Fowler, op. cit.

38   Plut. 'De Her. mal.' 867A.

39   Text by Bowra; translation by Lattimore.

40   Hdt. 9.69; U. von Wilamowitz, Pindaros, pp. 331.5 accepts the identification, but see E. Thummer, Pindar, Die Isthmischen Gedichte, vol. 2, p.8 and n. 4.

41   Schol. 'I'.1.52 (Drach., vol. 3, p. 205).

42   So Georges Méautis, Pindare le Dorien, p. 256; Schwenn, RE, 1950, vol. 40, col. 1671, 'Pindaros'; L.R. Farnell, A Critical Commentary to the Works of Pindar, vol. 2, p. 347.

43   J.B. Bury, The Isthmian Odes of Pindar, p. 51.

44   Thummer, op. cit., p. 57.

45   Méautis, op. cit., p. 261.

46   Ibid., pp. 307-8.

47   For other hints of a connection between the two, see L.R. Farnell, The Cults of the Greek States, vol. 3, p.52; vol. 4, p. 19.

48   I accept the traditional dates for the battles of Tanagra and Oenophyta, rather than those proposed by B.D. Meritt, H.T. Wade-Gery, and M.F. McGregor, The Athenian Tribute Lists, vol. 3, pp. 158-80. On this question, see R. McNeal, Historia, 1970, vol. 19, pp. 306-25.

49   Keramopoullos interprets this (unfinished) extension of the Theban walls as a counter-action on the part of the Thebans to the building of the long walls by the Athenians, AD, 1917, vol. 3, pp. 291-6.

50   Especially R.J. Buck, CP, 1970, vol. 65, pp. 217-27 and op. cit., 1979, pp. 145-6. Buck rejects Diodorus totally, on the basis of the existence of discrepancies with Thucydides and the existence of internal confusions. I believe that understanding of the probable sources of Diodorus' confusion allows us to use his account selectively, rather than rejecting the good along with the bad.

51 E.M. Walker, CAH, vol. 5, p. 82.
52 D.W. Reece, JHS, 1950, vol. 70, pp. 75f. argues that
    the 10,000 allied troops were not brought by the
    Spartans from the Peloponnesus at the beginning of
    the expedition, but were mainly composed of Boeotians
    who joined the Spartans in Boeotia. He accepts
    Diodorus' statement that Sparta restored Thebes to
    hegemony.
53 See note 22 above.
54 Ephorus is Diodorus' main source here according to
    G.L. Barber, The Historian Ephorus, pp. 89-94.
55 'A strongly biased Athenian source', according to
    ibid., p. 134; see also pp.92ff.
56 A somewhat similar scenario is suggested by G. Busolt,
    Griechische Geschichte, vol. 3, p. 319, n. 2.
57 Thus A.W. Gomme, An Historical Commentary on Thucydides,
    vol. 1, p. 318; Larsen, CP, 1960, vol. 55, p. 9 ends
    Athenian control with the end of the democracy, but
    his view of Thebes as an 'independent island' in a sea
    of Athenian control seems improbable, and he gives
    no reasons for his belief that in citing an Athenian
    affair in Boeotia as an instance of unsuccessful
    Athenian support for aristocrats, pseudo-Xenophon,
    'Ath. Pol.' 3.11 refers to 'some unknown situation ...
    between 479 and 461', rather than to this period.
    G.W. Bowersock, HSCP, 1966, vol. 71, pp. 33-46, does
    offer convincing arguments that pseudo-Xenophon refers
    to conditions in about 446.
58 For a discussion, see Russell Meiggs, The Athenian
    Empire, pp. 158-63.
59 Cloché, op. cit., pp. 69ff. takes this position.
60 Larsen, op. cit., 1960, pp. 9-18.
61 See Larsen, Greek Federal States, p. 34; and Buck,
    op. cit., 1979, pp. 150ff. Dull presents an extensive
    and convincing refutation of the thesis in his
    dissertation, op. cit., chapter 1, and in CP, 1977,
    vol. 72, pp. 305-14.
62 Müller, op. cit., pp. 68-70 and n. 2 on p. 69;
    Arist. 'Pol'.1278a25-26.
63 Amit, op. cit., argued that this reorganization
    occurred under Athenian auspices in 457-447, but it
    seems unlikely that Athens would have strengthened
    Boeotian unity in this way; see Meiggs, op. cit.,
    p. 176.
64 Bruce, op. cit., p. 104.
65 Ibid., p. 108.
66 Head, op. cit., pp. 30-8.
67 'Hell. Ox.' 11.4; see Bruce, op. cit., pp. 109, 163.
68 G. Glotz, BCH. 1908, vol. 32, pp. 271-8.

69 G. Glotz, Histoire grecque, vol. 1, p. 469, refuted
    by Pierre Lévêque and Pierre Vidal-Naquet, Clisthène
    L'Athénien, pp. 91ff.
70 Ibid., pp. 95-9.
71 Larsen, TAPA, 1955, vol. 86, p. 47.
72 Iambl. 'VP' 249f.
73 Polybius 2.39; see K. von Fritz, Pythagorean Politics
    in Southern Italy, pp. 72-4.
74 Arist., 'Ath. Pol.' 30; Bruce, op. cit., p. 160;
    Moore, op. cit., p. 261; Larsen, op. cit., 1955,
    pp. 40-50.
75 In the following summary, some actions are included
    which the sources attribute simply to the Boeotians;
    Theban hegemony in the League makes it reasonable to
    consider these as involving Thebans as well, especially
    since a Theban leader is often mentioned.
76 Thuc. 2.2ff; Diod. 12.41ff.; Hdt. 7.233; Ps.-Demos.
    'Ag. Neaira' 98ff.
77 Dull, op. cit., p. 74.
78 Ibid., p. 75.
79 Thuc. 4.76, 89-101; Diod. 12.69-70.
80 See L.H. Jeffery, The Local Scripts of Archaic Greece,
    19a and b, plate 10.
81 'IG' 1^{2}36.
82 Paul Roesch, Thespies et la Confédération Béotienne,
    p. 41.
83 Thuc. 5.22-25; Diod. 12.75.3-76.1; Dio Chrysostom
    37.17 (Dindorf II.297-8).
84 Thuc. 7.27-8; Diod. 13.9.2; 'Hell. Ox.' 12.3-4.
85 Diod. 13.47.3-8; Strabo 9.2.2.
86 Xen. 'Hell.' 1.3.15, 17, 21-2.
87 Diod. 13.98.4; 13.99.5-6.
88 Xen. 'Hell.' 2.2.19-20; 3.5.8.
89 Xen. 'Hell.' 3.5.5; Plut. 'Lys.' 27.
90 Dull, op. cit., p. 86.
91 Diod. 14.61; 14.32.1-33; Lysias, fr. CXX, p. 373
    (Thalheim); Justin 5.9; Xen. 'Hell.' 2.4.213. See
    Cloché, op. cit., pp. 320-3.
92 Ibid., pp. 95-100.

CHAPTER 4   THE CULTS OF FIFTH-CENTURY THEBES

1 See Figure 3 on page 50. The basic ancient source for
   the cults of Thebes is, of course, Pausanias, but
   other information comes from a wide variety of ancient
   sources, as indicated in the individual notes. For
   the interpretation of this material, I have often
   turned to modern specialists in the area of religious

studies, even though their interests often diverge
from mine. In particular, the Ur cults postulated
by scholars for various cults will not be considered
in most cases; whether a particular god was originally
a chthonic deity, mountain god, or vegetation god in
some primeval day is a question which would probably
never have occurred to a fifth-century Theban. For
similar reasons, other theories about the origins of
myth will not be considered, such as the theory that
myths derive from rites, postulated most recently by
Walter Burkert, Homo Necans.
  The most basic and important modern secondary sources
for the Theban cults are L.R. Farnell, The Cults of
the Greek States, and L. Ziehen, 'Thebai (Boiotien)'
RE, 1934, vol. 5, pt 2, cols 1492-553. Ziehen offers
the most recent comprehensive treatment of Theban
cults; important material, however, has appeared since
1934 which must now be taken into consideration;
moreover, Ziehen limits his insight into one of the
more important aspects of the Theban cult system when
he chooses to deal with each cult in isolation,
adopting an alphabetical principle of organization.
Discussion of the cults within the context of their
own family groups reveals and stresses the inner
logic which the cult system possessed, and which
will, I hope, contribute to a better appreciation of
the significance of these cults within their contemporary historical and cultural context.

2 See Introduction, esp. note 6. Isocrates said that
   the Thebans honored Heracles above all other deities
   ('Philipp.' 88).
3 H.J.Rose, s.v. 'Heracles', OCD.
4 Nicander, ap. Antoninus Liberalis, Metamorph. 29;
   see Manolis Papathomopoulos, ed., Antoninus Liberalis,
   Les Metamorphoses.
5 Aelian 'NA' 12.5; Papathomopoulos, op. cit., notes
   on section 29, pp. 135-8.
6 Paus. 9.16.7; Plut. 'De gen.Soc.' 577Eff.
7 Perhaps the temple occupied the site of the present
   church of Hagios Nikolaos. This was held to be the
   case by H.N. Ulrichs, Reisen und Forschungen in
   Griechenland, vol. 2, p. 12, and Ernst Fabricius,
   Theben, p. 22. Not excavated.
8 On the hypothesis of an earlier Praxiteles, see H.G.
   Frazer, Pausanias's Description of Greece, vol. 5,
   on Paus. 1.2.4.
9 Pindar, 'I'.1.15ff., 5.32f., 7.9; 'P'.2 (games of
   Iolaos), 9.76-88.
10 Plut. 'Pelop.' 18.

11 See Ziehen, op. cit., and Farnell, op. cit., pp. 151-2.
12 Ruth Edwards has discussed the sources, development and
    interpretation of this legend in her book, Kadmos the
    Phoenician, chapter 2.
13 The question is given extensive and careful treatment
    by Edwards, ibid., who finds the Phoenician (or 'Proto-
    Phoenician' Ugaritic) origin most likely, though not
    proved, and an explanation which would identify the
    'Phoenicians' as Cretans the next most likely. The
    most influential skeptic has been A.W. Gomme, JHS,
    1913, vol. 33, pp. 53-72, 223-45, who argued that the
    Phoenician connection was an invention of the
    logographers. He was followed by Ziehen, who then
    viewed Kadmos as only a local mountain god who had
    gradually faded to become only an epithet of Dionysos,
    and by E. Vermeule, 'Kadmos and the Dragon', in Studies
    Presented to George M.A. Hanfmann. Edwards has, I
    believe, effectively refuted Gomme's theory (see
    Chapter 4).
14 The seals were accepted as strong evidence for oriental
    settlement by J. Fontenrose, CP, 1966, vol. 61, p. 189,
    J.M. Sasson, Journal of the American Oriental Society,
    1966, vol. 86, p. 135, n. 53, and N.G.L. Hammond,
    A History of Greece to 322 B.C., p. 654. Edwards,
    op. cit., pp. 133f. points out possible alternative
    explanations as reasons for caution, but finds the
    balance of evidence in favor of some sort of small
    settlement. On the finds from Ugarit, with biblio-
    graphy, see Edwards op. cit., pp. 122-8.
15 Ziehen doubts its existence as a cult in historical
    times, but Farnell sees it only as of lessened
    importance, op. cit., vol. 5, pp. 401f.
16 Line 105; see AD, 1917, vol. 3, pp. 444f.
17 Xen. 'Hell.' 5.2.29; Plut. 'Pelop.' 5.
18 Hesychius, s.v. 'Ongkas Athenas'.
19 H.N. Ulrichs, op.cit., vol.2, p.15; Ernst Fabricius,
    op. cit., p. 28; Wilamowitz, Hermes, 1891, vol. 26,
    p. 217.
20 Ino: Pindar 'P.' 11.2, as interpreted by Ziehen;
    Plut. 'Lacon. Apop. Lyk.' 26; Semele: Paus. 9.12.3-4.
21 Apollod. 3.4.2-3 and 1.9.2.
22 E. Will, Korinthiaka, p. 178 and n. 3.
23 Most of this is inferred for Thebes from other Boeotian
    cities; see Ziehen, op. cit., and Farnell, op. cit.,
    vol. 5, pp. 151ff.
24 Otto Kern, Die Inschriften von Magnesia am Maeander,
    #215.
25 Photius, s.v. 'lusioi teletai'.
26 Farnell, op. cit., vol. 5, p. 120

27 See D.L. Page, Greek Literary Papyri, pp. 60-71.
28 Keramopoullos, AD, 1917, vol. 3, pp. 455 and 303
    maintains that Kadmos built the palace but no other
    walls.
29 Marta Sordi, Atene e Roma, 1966, vol. 11, pp. 15-24,
    interprets otherwise, seeing the Kadmeian legend as
    the product of the propaganda of Delphi against
    Thebes and its league, while Vian looks beyond the
    racial distinction for a deeper significance in terms
    of Dumézil's theory of a universal Indo-European
    tripartite social structure (priest-king, military,
    and demos). In this theoretical interpretation
    Amphion and Zethos fill the role of the second
    function; as such they play a necessary and complemen-
    tary role, and their foundation legend is a complement,
    not a competitor, of the Kadmeian legend (Francis
    Vian, Les Origins de Thèbes, Cadmos et les Spartes,
    especially chapter 11). Although I do not subscribe
    to the tripartite theory as a universal tool of
    analysis, in this case the story that only the
    hipparchs knew the location of Dirke's tomb and that
    the outgoing and incoming hipparchs joined in offering
    secret sacrifice to her suggests that there may have
    been a strong relationship between the Theban military
    organization and the myth of Amphion and Zethos. Were
    the hipparchs propitiating Dirke as the representatives
    of her murderers, Amphion and Zethos?
30 A detailed attempt to analyze and wring history out
    of the various elements of mythical 'history' in
    these foundation stories is made by R.J. Buck,
    A History of Boeotia, chapter 3. His conclusion is
    similar to mine: 'None of the traditions inspires
    any confidence'.
31 See AAA, 1971, vol. 4, pp. 161-4; 1972, vol. 5,
    pp. 16-27.
32 L.R. Farnell, Greek Hero Cults, pp. 332-4.
33 Paus. 9.23.1; Eur. 'Phoen.' 834-1017; Wilamowitz,
    De Euripidis Heraclidis, p. x. accepted by Kroll,
    RE, 1931, vol. 29, col. 918.
34 Paus. 9.8.1; Homer, 'Od.' 15.247; Pindar, 'N.' 9.51ff.;
    'N.' 10.4; 'O.'6.24f.; Aesch. 'Seven Against Thebes',
    570f.; Hdt. 1.46, 49, 52; 8.134; Strabo 9.1.22.
35 Hdt. 8.134; that Herodotus was referring to the
    oracle near Thebes (later moved to Oropus at some
    time between this date and 415/414) is argued by
    Ulrichs, op. cit., vol. 2, pp. 63f., and Basileios
    Petrakos, O Oropos kai to Hieron tou Amphiaraou,
    pp. 66ff.; excavation finds support this, see AD, 1917,
    vol. 3, pp. 261-6.

148   Notes

36   See Weicker, RE, 1912, vol. 15, col. 258.
37   See von Geisau, RE, 1963, vol. 47, col. 78. She
      appears without name in Apollodor. 2.4.11.
38   Pharaklas, AD, 1967, vol. 22, Chron., p. 253.
39   Proclus, ap. Phot. 'Bibl.' 239, p. 321AB (Bekker);
      he says that it was held every ninth year.
40   Hdt. 8.135; Strabo 9.2.34; excavation reports in BCH
      from 1884; see J. Ducat, Les Kouroi du Ptoion, and
      S. Lauffer, RE, 1959, vol. 46, cols 1506-78.
41   The debate over the date of Theban control is an
      involved one; see P. Guillon, Les Trépieds du Ptoion,
      pp. 116-25; Le Bouclier d'Héraclès. Annales de la
      Faculté des Lettres et Sciences Humaines d'Aix, 1963,
      vol. 37, chapter LV; Ducat, op. cit., pp. 246-51.
42   Wilamowitz, Hermes, 1903, vol. 38, pp. 578f.
43   A. Schachter, Proceedings of the 1st International
      Conference on Boiotian Antiquities (Montreal, 1972)
      suppl. 1, Teiresias, 17-30.
44   Ducat, op. cit.; Alkmeonides #141, pp. 242-51, dated
      c. 550/540; Hipparchos #152, pp. 251-8, dated c. 52.
45   Ducat, op. cit., p. 446, n. 1; Lauffer, op. cit.,
      p.1557. The shrine only regained affluence with the
      rebuilding of Thebes and the reorganization of the
      Boeotian League in 316.
46   Keramopoullos, AD, 1917, vol. 3, pp. 443-4.
47   Lycophron 1189-1213 and schol.; Farnell, op. cit.,
      p. 329.
48   O. Crusius, SBAW, 1905, pp. 760ff.
49   Keramopoullos, op. cit., pp. 357f., 437, 443.
50   See schol. on 'P'.9.89. This is also attested by
      the scholiast to 'P'.3.77, Aristodemos, who tells
      an odd story in which an image of the Mother of the
      Gods appeared to fall at the feet of Pindar,
      accompanied by thunder and a lightning blast, while
      he was teaching in the mountains. Ziehen rationalizes
      the story into a report of a comet, but, as he admits,
      the image seen by Pausanias was not a rude rock but
      a finished statue. W.J. Slater, GRBS, 1971, vol. 12,
      pp. 141ff., rejects the story, along with the
      identification of the 'I' in 'P'.3 with Pindar, an
      identification which may have inspired the account of
      Aristodemos (see Lefkowitz, CP, 1975, vol. 70, p. 176,
      on the unreliability of Aristodemos). Slater's
      argument is weakened, however, by his suggestion that
      the shrine in question was in Sicily, an hypothesis
      for which he says it is 'not reasonable' to expect
      evidence; yet an unsupportable hypothesis is even
      less tenable than one supported by vulnerable evidence.
      Slater also argues the weaker case when he claims that

the 'I' of the poem is a choral 'I' rather than the
poet's (see Lefkowitz, HSCP, 1963, vol. 67, pp.177-253).
Finally, even if we reject the story of Aristodemos,
there is no necessity to reject Pausanias as well, as
Slater argues, for it would be amazing if, as he
suggests, all the various sources, including local
tradition and inscriptions, 'found their way along with
Aristodemos into the standard life of Pindar, whether
by Didymus or Plutarch' (p. 149), an hypothetical
source which we have no way to evaluate. For further
criticism of Slater, see A. Henrichs, HSCP, 1976,
vol. 80, p. 256, no. 10.

51 Schol. on 'P'.9.90.
52 See Bruns, AA, 1967, vol. 82, pp. 268-73.
53 See Farnell, op. cit., vol. 5, pp. 4 and 26-7.
54 Bengt Hemberg, Die Kabiren, pp. 39f.
55 Bruns, op. cit., p. 271, fig. 70.
56 Bruns, AA, 1964, vol. 79, pp. 260f.; AA, 1967, vol. 82,
    p. 236; Hemberg, op. cit., pp. 189f.; W. Heyder and
    A. Mallwitz, Die Bauten im Kabirenheiligtum bei Theben,
    pp. 44, 60-72.
57 Heyder and Mallwitz, ibid., p. 72, suggest this as a
    possibility, but leave the question of Methapos' date
    up in the air.
58 Bruns, op. cit., pp. 268-73.
59 Bernhard Schmaltz, Metallfiguren aus dem Kabiren-
    heiligtum bei Theben, vol. I, p. 10: of 562 statuettes,
    534 are steers, 26 are rams or goats, and two are of
    men.
60 Heyder and Mallwitz, op. cit., pp. 69f.
61 Kern, RE, 1905, vol.10, col. 1440.
62 Hemberg, op. cit., p. 194.
63 See Schmaltz, op. cit., vol. I.
64 Ibid., pp. 107f, 114; see also Bruns, AA, 1967,
    vol. 82, p. 241, n. 14.
65 Paul Wolters, AM, 1890, vol. 15, pp. 362ff.; Kern,
    op. cit., p. 1439.
66 Schmaltz, op. cit., pp. 17-32.
67 Plato, 'Symp.' 215B, 216D, 221DE (except that these
    figurines opened in the middle and had images of
    gods in them); Xen. 'Symp.' 4.19, 5.7.
68 L. Breitholtz, Die dorische Farce, pp. 198-201 for a
    review of the history of scholarly debate on this
    question, which is complicated by emotions aroused
    over the question of the origins of Attic comedy.
69 See Sir Arthur Pickard-Cambridge, Dithyramb, Tragedy
    and Comedy, #32-48, pl. XI.
70 An Attic lekythos: Athens #1129, see C.H.C. Haspels,
    Attic Black-figure Lekythoi, pp. 170ff., pls 49-50;

see also Pickard-Cambridge, op. cit., #9, 10, pls 2, 3.

71 Ure, JHS, 1929, vol. 49, pp. 160ff., and JHS, 1935, vol. 55, pp. 227f.; Karl Kilinski II, AJA, 1978, vol. 182, pp. 173-91; 72 Athenaeus XIV.621D.

73 Webster, in Pickard-Cambridge, op. cit., p. 138.

74 Schmaltz, op. cit., pp. 123f.

75 On the masks, see Schmaltz, op. cit., p. 134.

76 Heyder and Mallwitz, op. cit., pp. 25ff., 62, pl.2.

77 Körte, review of Bieber, in Neue Jahrbücher für das Klass. Altertums, 1921, vol. 24, pp. 308-12.

78 Paul Wolters and Gerda Bruns, Das Kabirenheiligtum bei Theban, vol. I, p. 126.

79 Hemberg, op. cit.

80 Ibid., esp. the comparative charts on pp. 328-33 and 270-99.

81 Walter Burkert, Orphism and Bacchic Mysteries: New Evidence and Old Problems of Interpretation, pp. 6f.

82 This is Ziehen's opinion, op. cit.

83 Friedrich Solmsen, Hesiod and Aeschylus, pp. 63, 66-75.

CHAPTER 5   PHILOSOPHY IN THEBES

1 This is in essence the view of pre-Platonic Pythagoreanism espoused by Walter Burkert in his Lore and Science in Ancient Pythagoreanism. For a brief assessment of Burkert's position and of the various other positions taken by modern scholars in their interpretation of Pythagoreanism, see the review of Burkert by Norman Gulley, CR, 1964, vol. 14, pp. 28f., and the review of C.J. de Vogel, Pythagoras and Early Pythagoreanism, by G.B. Kerferd, CR, 1968, vol. 18, pp. 282-4. De Vogel analyzes the non-Aristotelian evidence (Timaeus, Aristoxenus and Dicaearchus) found in Porphyry and Iamblichus, and allows it much greater weight in reconstructing the teaching of Pythagoras and early Pythagoreanism than does Burkert; she thus represents the opposite pole from Burkert in the interpretation of Pythagoreanism.

2 See Appendix.

3 See A. Delatte, Essai sur la Politique Pythagoricienne, pp. 218-37, for a collection of the various versions of the tradition. See also Kurt von Fritz, Pythagorean Politics in Southern Italy, pp. 23-32, who analyzes the various elements in the tradition and evaluates Aristoxenus as a source. The tradition is accepted by Walter Burkert, op. cit., pp. 115f. and n. 43;

J.A. Philip, Pythagoras and Early Pythagoreanism,
pp. 25f.; and E.L. Minar, Early Pythagorean Politics.
Erich Frank, Plato und die sogennanten Pythagoreer,
p. 294, n. 1, rejects it, but see Burkert, op. cit.,
n. 43.

4   S. Levin, Teiresias, 1972, suppl. vol. 1, pp. 51-60.
5   Pindar, 'O', 6.90 and Fragment 72 (Bowra).
6   R.S. Bluck, Plato's Phaedo, pp. 6f., 43, n.2, ii,
ns 1 and 2; W.K.C. Guthrie, A History of Greek
Philosophy, 4th edition, p. 309; Plato's Phaedo,
pp. xix, lv, 59, 72, 85; Burkert, op. cit., p. 78;
A.E. Taylor, Plato, p. 175; on the other hand,
R. Hackforth, Plato's Phaedo, pp. 13f., 63, 102,
avoids the identification, and G.C. Field, Plato and
his Contemporaries, p. 59, is openly skeptical, as is
G.M.A. Grube, Plato's Thought, p. 294. The main
obstacles in the way of the identification (the
skepticism and the 'unPythagorean' theories of the
two) are circumvented by Burnet and Taylor through
the hypothesis that fifth-century Pythagoreans were
pure scientists who had abandoned the religious
doctrine of their founder, but there is no other
evidence for this.

7   Guthrie, op. cit., vol. 1, p. 310.
8   Burkert, Lore, pp. 337-480.
9   Ibid., p. 272.
10 Hackforth, op. cit., p. 104.
11 Grube, op. cit., pp. 291-4, argues that they are not
familiar with the theory of Forms, basing his argument
mainly on the gradual explanation of the theory during
the course of the dialogue; it is reasonable, however,
to assume that Plato offers the gradual explanation
to help the reader, and Grube himself admits that each
step is used as part of the proof of immortality as
it is introduced. Cebes himself introduces the
related theory of Recollection into the argument, so
that we know that the two are meant to be seen as
familiar with Socratic teaching, and this should
enable us to take Simmias' words of emphatic agreement
at 65D and the other uses of the first person plural
in regard to the theory of Forms in a literal sense.
12 The authenticity of this epistle is disputed, see
Burkert, op. cit., 19, n. 20; G.R. Morrow, Plato's
Epistles, pp. 100-9, argues that it is genuine.
13 Xen. 'Mem.' 1.2.48; 3.11.17.
14 By calling the philosophy of the 'Phaedo' and its
theory of Forms 'Socratic', I am not subscribing to
the Taylor-Burnet thesis that the dialogue should be
taken as an exact and accurate presentation of the

philosophical position actually held by the historical
Socrates. What I do mean is that I believe that
Socrates held a theory of Forms, to which Plato has
added elements of his own development (in particular,
the idea that the Forms were separate or transcendent),
and that the philosophy of the dialogue was generally
regarded by Plato as being Socratic - either actually
maintained by Socrates or a natural extension of
positions which he held. A distinction should be
made between the likelihood that Plato would have
attributed such developments of his master's theories
to his master, and the likelihood that he would have
attributed a wholly new characteristic to him which
in real life he did not possess, such as an interest
in Pythagoreanism. The former seems very likely,
while the latter seems very unlikely. On the Taylor-
Burnet thesis, see A.E. Taylor, Varia Socratica, and
Burnet, Early Greek Philosophy and Plato's Phaedo,
op. cit. For discussion, see Guthrie, op. cit.,
vol. 3, pp. 351ff.

15 Taylor, op. cit., p. 30.
16 Hackforth, op. cit., p. 4.
17 See Taylor, op. cit., pp. 129-77; for the skeptical
viewpoint, see K.J. Dover, Aristophanes' Clouds,
pp. xxxii-lvii, and Guthrie, op. cit., vol. 3,
pp. 359-75.
18 Burnet, Plato's Phaedo, comm. on 64B3.
19 For a discussion of Plato's characterization of
Cebes, see R.D. Archer-Hind, The Phaedo of Plato,
pp. 41f. On the spurious writings attributed to
Simmias and Cebes (DL 2.234-5), see Burkert, Lore,
p. 229, n. 56.
20 Although many scholars have seen the closeness of
Plutarch's work to the 'Phaedo', the subject is best
treated by R. Hirzel, Der Dialog, vol. 2, pp. 148-51,
from which the points of comparison noted in the text
were drawn.
21 Plutarch covers the same historical material, in less
detail and without mention of Simmias, in the 'Life
of Pelopidas' 6-13; other ancient accounts, none of
which mentions Simmias, are to be found in Nepos,
'Pelop.' 2.1-4.1; Xen. 'Hell.'5.4.1-13; Diod.
15.25-7.
22 A. Corlu, Plutarque. Le Démon de Socrate, p. 40.
23 575E; the Greek is corrupt, but this is the general
sense.
24 K. Ziegler sees a two-fold patriotic aim: to provide
a memorial for a brilliant moment in Theban history
and a refutation of the bias against Thebes as anti-

intellectual (Plutarchos von Chaironeia, p. 204); thus
too Hirzel, op. cit., pp. 162f., who, however, sees
an emphasis on the Athenian roots of Theban philosophy
and an intention to make the work a monument to Attic-
Boeotian friendship. Corlu thinks that the 'misologia'
theme is overstated, and that the major theme is the
daimon of Socrates and the general topic of demonology,
op. cit., pp. 88f.

25 Compare 'Pelop.' 22.3.

26 See Field, op. cit., 12f.; G.R. Morrow, Plato's
Cretan City, pp. 5f.

27 Xenophon 'Anab.' 2.6.16-20 tells of a Boeotian,
Proxenus, who had studied with Gorgias; since Proxenus
died at 30 on the expedition, he could not have heard
Gorgias in 427. Perhaps he travelled to Sicily, but
it seems as likely that Gorgias made a lecture-tour
including Boeotia, late in the fifth century.

28 On the reliability of Aristoxenus, see above, note 3.

29 Delatte, op. cit., p. 228.

30 P. Corssen, 'Die Sprengung des pythagoreischen
Bundes', Philologus, 1912, vol. 71, p. 346, suggests
that Plutarch has substituted an invented name,
Theanor, for Philolaos, possibly on chronological
grounds. In general, Plato is preferred. The
rejection of the 'De genio' as a serious account is
unanimous, although not always based on adequate
grounds. For example, Delatte did not see that part
of his explanation of Plutarch's 'error' did not
explain the actual situation. Burkert dismisses the
'De genio' as a 'novelistic treatment' with no
value (Lore, p. 228, n. 48); similarly, von Fritz,
op. cit., p. 79, discounts the 'De genio' as a
'fictional embellishment of the original history';
yet the use of a novelistic format does not imply
that all the elements are fictional. On the other
hand, scholars have been almost unanimous in accepting
'Phaedo' 61DE as evidence for Philolaos' presence in
Thebes; the exceptions are G.F. Unger, Sitzungsberichte
der königlichen bayerischen Akademie der Wissenschaften
zu München, phil.-hist. Classe., 1883, p. 190, who,
however, ignores Plato's statement at 61E7; and Frank,
op. cit., p. 294, n. 1.

31 Aristox., frag. 28 (FGH).

32 Ap. Arist. 'Rhet.' 1398b9ff.

33 Hackforth, op. cit., p. 7.

34 The testimony of Olympiodorus, 'In Plato.Phaedon.Comm.',
W. Norvin (ed.), p. 9, is an obvious late attempt to
support Plato and reconcile various traditions and
has no independent value; see Delatte, op. cit., p.235.

35 Burkert, Lore, p. 112, 133-6.

CHAPTER 6 THE MUSES

1 'Pelop.' 19.
2 'Rep.' 400A-C, 424C.
3 Hdt. 1.155; Herodotus portrays Croesus as suggesting
   that Cyrus made the Lydians train their sons in harp
   and lyre playing (in addition to forbidding them
   weapons, changing their mode of dress, and encouraging
   shop-keeping) in order to render them less aggressive
   and prone to revolt. It is interesting that the
   instrument here prescribed is the 'manly' lyre, but
   the basic notion appears to reflect the theory of
   Damon, current in the second half of the fifth
   century.
4 For references to Boeotian reeds see Pindar, frags
   59 (with 'O.'14 and 'P.'12.26f.) and 233, and
   Corinna fragment 684 (Page). For a discussion of
   the preparation of reeds and their use in the
   manufacture of flutes, see Theophrastus, 'Hist. Pl.'
   4.11.4-9.
5 Paus. 9.5.7-9; 9.8.4; 9.17.7.
6 Paus. 9.29.3.
7 'P.'12.25-7; see also Aristotle, 'Pol.' 1341b4.
   According to another tradition, its origins were in
   Phyrgia (Ps.-Plut. 'De mus.' 1132F-1133E).
8 Frag. 125.
9 Frag. 44.36; 'O.'3.8; 7.12; 10.93; 'N.'3.79;
   9.8.
10 'De mus.' 1133A.
11 Eustath. prooemium 25ff., in A.B. Drachmann, Scholia
   vetera in Pindari carmina, vol. 3, pp. 296ff.;
   Suid. s.v. 'Pindaros', vol. 4, p. 384.
12 Athen. 184D.
13 Athen. 631E; Paus. 9.12.5-6; 4.27.7; see A.A. Howard,
   HSCP, 1893, vol. 4, pp. 1-60, esp. 6ff., who suggested
   that he may have increased the number of holes and
   devised some sort of covering, perhaps bands of
   silver, for the holes not in use; see also Kathleen
   Schlesinger, The Greek Aulos, pp. 72-4.
14 See Arist. 'Pol.' 1341a27-35.
15 Plut. 'Alc.' 2.
16 Melanippides, Frag. 758 (Page, PMG).
17 Athen. 616Eff.; Apollod. 1.4.2; Paus. 1.24.1;
   Strabo 13.616; Hyginus #165.
18 Ps.-Plut. 'De mus.' 1136B.
19 A. Michaelis, Annali dell'Istituto di Corrispondenza

Archeologica, 1859, pp. 298ff.; Die Verurteilung des
Marsyas auf einer Vase aus Ruvo, building on the
earlier work of Böttiger, Kleine Schriften, vol. 1,
pp. 3-60, who had suggested that an Athenian satyr
play was the source of the revision of the myth, but
did not identify it as a play of Euripides.

20 Still another possible motivation for the low repute
in which the flute stood is suggested by G. Devereux,
Symbolae Osloenses, 1967, vol. 62, p. 84, n. 2:
'the fact that in modern obscene speech (e.g. French)
flute-playing = fellatio, may explain why flute-
playing was despised by some'.

21 Athen. 184E.

22 See Lippold, RE, 1963, vol. 47, col. 306, 'Pythagoras'
14.

23 Paus. 9.22.2-3. The date of Corinna is one of the
more contested puzzles of contemporary scholarship.
The possibilities range from the fifth century BC
to 200 BC, with most authorities leaning toward a
date at one or the other extreme, but with clear
admission that their arguments can only establish a
probability. For the most recent review of the
question and bibliography, see C.P. Segal, Eranos,
1975, vol. 73, pp. 1-8; and K. Latte, Eranos, 1956,
vol. 54, pp. 57ff., who answers Page's arguments in
favor of the later date which appears in the latter's
Corinna.

24 Karl Schefold, Antike Kunst, 1958, vol. 1, pp. 72ff.
The findspot is unknown, and the work is in the
tradition of the Thespian school, but similar works
are known to have been created in one city for use
in another (the stelai of Saugenes, Koironos, and
Pherenikos), and Thespiae appears to have been the
major Boeotian center for the production of bas-
relief. See Chapter 7.

25 'P.'5.72-6. Whether these lines refer to Pindar is
another of the great debates of modern scholarship;
it seems to me, however, that Lefkowitz has resolved
it affirmatively in her study of first person
statements in Pindar, HSCP, 1963, vol. 67, esp.
pp. 229-32; n. 117 on p. 252 gives a full bibliography
on the question.

26 Thuc. 6.16.

27 'O.'2.53ff.; 'P.'1.90ff.; 'I.'1.67ff., 6.10f.

28 'N.'7.12ff.

29 'N.'1.20, 31ff.

30 'O.'3.39.

31 'I.'1.47ff., 7.27ff.

32 'P.'5.1ff., 8.13ff.; 'N.'8.17.

33 Aristophanes 'Ach.' 860ff., 'Peace' 1004f.
34 'I.'1.59–63.
35 'I.'3.15ff., 4.14f.
36 'P.'11.47.
37 All references to the fragments of Pindar are to the
    2nd edition of C.M. Bowra, Pindari carmina cum
    fragmentis.
38 Arist. 'Pol.' 1274a32–1374b4.
39 Alcman, Frag. 1.50–52 (Page), but see note on line 2
    in D.A. Campbell, Greek Lyric Poetry.
40 Such family ties crossing political boundaries may
    have been involved in some of Pindar's commissions.
    From Laios there had descended a family which at
    some point received the name of Aigeidai. Some of
    the Aigeidai assisted the Herakleidai in the
    subjection of the Peloponnese and then lived on in
    Sparta. One of these, Theras, led the colonization
    of Thera. From Thera a branch of the family went
    to Cyrene, another to Akragas (via Athens and Rhodes,
    or via Gela):

                        Thebes

                        Sparta

                        Thera

        Akragas   Cyrene
    (See Schol. 'O.'2.82d, Drach., vol. 1, p. 182;
    Schol. 'O.'2.15c, Drach., vol. 1, p.64; Cauer, RE,
    1894, vol. 1, cols 949f; Swoboda, RE, 1905, vol. 10,
    cols 2498–500). In 'P.'5.72–6 Pindar speaks of
    himself as an Aigeid, a kinsman of the Cyrenians
    (see above, note 25). Theron was also a member of
    the clan ('O.'2.43–47), and Hieron was allied to him
    by marriage. As early as 490 Pindar was engaged to
    commemorate the Pythian victory of Hieron's brother
    Xenocrates ('P.'6, at the same date he also composed
    'P'.12 for the flute player Midas of Akragas).
    Family connections could have had some bearing on
    these (and subsequent) Akragantine commissions and
    on the choice of poet by Arkesilas; at least Pindar
    felt the connection worthy of mention as an element
    which enhanced his appropriateness as poet for the
    occasion (and perhaps took some of the edge off the
    fact that he was paid as well). That the ties were
    mythical did not detract from their value but rather
    added to it, by investing them with the weight of

great antiquity and the sanction of holy names.   In
Herodotus 5.80 we can see the practical consequences
of such mythical ties in the story of Thebes' choice
of Aigina as ally, where the mythological fact that
Thebe and Aigina were twin sisters was the determining
factor (the oracle said to choose those nearest, and,
reasoned the Thebans, who is nearer than a sister-in-
myth?).

41   Frank J. Frost, American Journal of Ancient History,
1976, vol. 1, pp. 67-73. Earlier recognition of the
significance of the way in which the Greeks conceived
of the state is found in Gernet's review of Riezler,
Finanzen und Monopole in L'Année Sociologique, 1909-6,
vol. 11, p. 562.

42   K.J. Dover, Greek Homosexuality (see review in AJP,
1980, vol. 101, pp. 121ff;   references below in note
52;   and Claude Calame, Les Choeurs de jeunes filles
in Grèce archaïque, vol. 1, pp. 420-7, 454).

43   Plut. 'Erot.' 761CD;   compare with Plato, 'Laws'
636A-D.

44   Plut. 'Erot.' 761B.

45   Plut. 'Pelop.' 18.

46   Xen. 'Lac. Rep.' 2.12.

47   Arist. 'Pol.' 1274a32-1274b4.

48   Plut. 'Pelop.' 19.

49   Xen. 'Lac. Rep.' 2.13.

50   Frag. 8, Dindorf.

51   Aelian 'De anim.' 6.15, p. 324 Gronovius;   Plutarch
attributes the story to poets in 'Pelop.' 19.

52   On stock comic charges, see K.J. Dover, Greek Popular
Morality in the Time of Plato and Aristotle, pp. 30ff.
Dover explained the charge of effeminacy as one
leveled against boys who yield and 'who thereby
detract from their future role as citizen-warriors'
(p. 215, compare Dover, Bull. Inst. Class. Stud.
London, 1964, vol. 11, p. 38: 'Those who hunt as
recreation and not for a living have a poor opinion
of a quarry which waits to be caught' in explaining
the attitude of the lover to the beloved). This
imports modern attitudes, and disregards the clear
evidence for pederasty as an upper class 'rite of
passage' which conferred status upon the boy, as
well as the evidence from Aeschines, which is cited
in the article itself. Despite insistence that he
was dealing with the literary man ('homo Platonicus'
and 'homo Aristophaneus'), and not the real Athenian
aristocrat or farmer, Dover tended to overlook the
literary conventions: Pausanias in the 'Symposium'
is not 'homo Platonicus' but simply one of the

characters in the dialogue (who represents a fairly conventional aristocratic view, according to all the evidence); Aristophanes' world is presented through the rather murky glass of comic distortion and requires interpretation.

Another approach to the explanation of the charge of effeminacy was taken by Devereux, who saw the effeminate as one who failed to complete the evolution to heterosexuality which consisted of being 'eromenos', 'erastes', and husband in turn; this explanation fails to take into account such cases as Socrates, who was both husband and lover but not charged with effeminacy, or Aeschines, who was still a lover at age 45 ('Against Timarchos' 49 and 136), and who names other older men as lovers (ibid., 155-6. Devereux's article appeared in Symbolae Osloenses, 1967, vol. 42, pp. 70-92.

53 Plut. 'Pelop.' 18.

54 Corinna, Frag. 664a (Page).

55 Corinna, Frags 664a, 695a (Page).

56 Wassiliki Schild-Xenidou, Boiotische Grab- und Weihreliefs Archaischer und Klassischer Zeit, #82 and p. 142; this stone from Thespiae is dated to the last quarter of the fourth century, but the conservatism of Boeotian society gives it possible relevance.

57 Calame, op. cit., pp. 26f., 90, and part 4 of vol.I. On the controversy over the educational aspects of Sappho's circle in particular, dated before Calame's extensive treatment of this subject, see Denys Page, Sappho and Alcaeus, pp. 110-12, who is a committed skeptic, vs. R. Merkelbach, Philologus, 1957, vol. 101, pp. 1-29; F. Lasserre, Serta Turyniana, p. 29, n. 41.

58 See also 'Laws' 655A, 672E.

59 Compare Arist., 'Eccl.' 111-20, 243-4.

60 David Young, Three Odes of Pindar, p. 19 and n. 2, questions the significance of the women in this ode, saying, 'Apart from the invocation (where Apollo is present too), 'Py.' 11 "concerns women" only in the myth'. This is a poor argument, given the fact that more than half the ode (37 out of 64 lines) is included in the invocation and myth, so that the use of the word 'only' is scarcely justified.

61 Schol. 'P.'3.139a, Drach., vol. 2, p. 81, and Schol. Theokr, ii, 10a, Wendel, p. 271.

62 L.R. Farnell, A Critical Commentary to the Works of Pindar, vol. 2, p. 425.

63 H.J. Rose, 'The ancient grief', in Greek Poetry and Life. Essays presented to Gilbert Murray, pp. 79-96.

64 Apollod. 3.4.2.

65 Apollod. 2.4.12; compare 2.5.11. On these eight-
or nine-year punishments, see J.G. Frazer's note in
the Loeb edition of Apollodorus, vol. 1, p. 218,
n. 1.
66 Rose, op. cit., pp. 93ff. See I.M. Linforth, The
Arts of Orpheus, pp. 307-64, on the problems of using
the story of the dismemberment of Dionysos as an
identifying mark of Orphism, and on the whole
question of the nature of Orphism; and N. Demand,
GRBS, 1975, vol. 16, pp. 347-57, on the identification
of 'O.'2 and Empedocles as Pythagorean. Despite a
variety of misgivings, Linforth acknowledges 'a high
degree of probability' in Rose's interpretation.
67 Clem. Al. 'Strom.' iii.518.
68 Schol. on 'P.'7.18, Drach., vol. 2, p. 204; see
J. Sandys (ed.), The Odes of Pindar, p. 255.
69 See Otto Schroeder's edition of Bergk, Poet. Lyr.
Graec. vol, 1, p. 444, app. crit., on the various
readings of this fragment.
70 See Erich Thummer, Die Religiosität Pindars, and
reviews by J.A. Davison, JHS, 1960, vol. 80, pp. 203f.,
and Rose, CR, 1959, vol. 9, pp. 231f., for differing
views on this question. Thummer in suggesting that
Pindar made conscious use of traditional religion
to support a failing aristocracy went further than
I should want to go in attributing a religious
position to him on the basis of the odes; I prefer
Davison's position, 'that he was essentially a
"jobbing" poet, and that he was bound to adapt himself
to the wishes of his employers'.
71 The theory that Alcman, Frag. 1, contains an internal
contest, between Hegesichora and Agido or between
their two choruses or semi-choruses, receives a
sufficient refutation in M. Puelma's article in MH,
1977, vol. 34, pp. 1-55; the agonistic spirit is not
thereby excluded, however, for the motifs of
competition clearly present in the poem (lines 63,
65, 77, and 50-9) suggest an external contest, between
those who join together to present this song and at
least one other chorus (the Pleiades?) presenting
another song (see especially p. 28 of Puelma's
article). Alcman, Frag. 3, also contains a suggestion
of competition in the world 'agon'. For discussion
and extensive bibliography on both these theories
(internal and external contests) see Calame, pp. 130f.,
and notes 165 and 166. Calame rejects both theories.
72 'O.'2.86-8 and Scholia; 'N.'3.80-2; see Wilamowitz,
op. cit., pp. 310-18 on 'I.'2; S. Gzella, Eos, 1969,
vol. 58, pp. 175-9.

73 Page thought that the language used precludes the more
    general idea of imitation or a simple claim of
    superiority and requires some sort of formal or
    informal challenge (op.cit., p. 31, n. 1). A
    deliberate switch into a recognizably male genre
    could constitute such a challenge.
74 'Vit. Aes.' 3-5 says that Aeschylus went off to
    Sicily in a sulk after he was defeated by Simonides
    or Sophocles.

CHAPTER 7   THE ARTS AND CRAFTS

1   R. Lullies, JDAI, 1936, vol. 51, pp. 137ff., draws
    attention to these positive aspects of provincial
    Boeotian work, and he is followed by Wassiliki Schild-
    Xenidou in her study of Boeotian figured funeral
    stelai, to which the present work is much indebted,
    Boiotische Grab-und Weihreliefs Archaischer und
    Klassischer Zeit, see especially chapter 4. In
    referring to individual stelai I shall use Schild-
    Xenidou's numbering, in addition to giving information
    about location and reference to a publication
    containing an illustration, where possible.
2   Boeotian art, at least in the two forms which we
    shall be discussing, developed in a recognizably
    different way in the various Boeotian centers in the
    fifth century, although it does possess more general
    Boeotian characteristics as well. Thus Thespian,
    Tanagran, and Theban workshops for the production of
    bas-relief stelai have been identified, as well as
    specifically Theban potters' workshops. The products
    of another craft, the mold-made terracotta figures
    found at the Kabeirion, are primarily of interest
    in connection with the cult and are discussed in
    Chapter 4. See P. Wolters, AM, 1890, vol. 15,
    pp. 355ff.; Bernhard Schmaltz, Terrakotten aus dem
    Kabirenheiligtum bei Theben.
3   Cicero, 'De legibus', II, 26, 64.
4   P.M. Fraser and T. Ronne, Boeotian and West Greek
    Tombstones, p. 36.
5   See Schild-Xenidou, op. cit., p. 84.
6   Schild-Xenidou, K5, Thebes Museum 13; G.M.A. Richter,
    Archaic Gravestones of Attica, p. 47, #67, figs
    155-8; Sheila Adam, The Technique of Greek Sculpture
    in the Archaic and Classical Periods, pp. 108-10
    and pls 54-5.
7   Ibid., p. 6.
8   A suggestion made by B.S. Ridgway.

9 See B.S. Ridgway, The Severe Style in Greek
   Sculpture, pp. 44-5. Hilde Hiller, Ionische
   Grabreliefs der ersten Hälfte des 5. Jahrhunderts v.
   Chr., p. 15, n. 3, discusses this question of
   Athenian emigration at length.

10 Ibid., pp. 72-96.

11 K8 Boston Museum 99.339; C.C. Vermeule, Greek,
   Etruscan and Roman Art. The Classical Collection of
   the Museum of Fine Arts, p. 85, fig. 76; Hiller,
   op. cit., pp. 130, 136, 166-7; Mary B. Comstock
   and Cornelius Vermeule, Sculpture in Stone, pp. 12f.,
   fig. 18; see Plate 3.

12 L.D. Caskey, Catalogue of Greek and Roman Sculpture,
   Museum of Fine Arts, Boston, p. 22; Maxime Collignon,
   Les Statues funéraires dans l'art grec, p. 64,
   fig. 34.

13 Caskey, op. cit., p. 22.

14 Hiller, op. cit., pp. 166-7.

15 F. Willemsen, AM, 1970, vol. 85, pp. 30-4.

16 Riders appear throughout the fifth and fourth
   centuries, mostly from Thespiae, sometimes armed
   (warriors) and sometimes without arms (hunters); on
   some stelai men appear leading their horses. Schild-
   Xenidou interprets these as scenes from daily life,
   op. cit., p. 132.

17 On the peripatetic lives of Greek sculptors, see
   Alison Burford, The Greek Temple Builders at Epidauros,
   pp. 98-206; Craftsmen in Greek and Roman Society,
   pp. 57-67.

18 K7, Athens National Museum #39; F. Gerke, Griechische
   Plastik in archaischer und klassischer Zeit, p. 35,
   pl. 76.

19 See Schild-Xenidou, op. cit., p. 162.

20 Schild-Xenidou lists six stelai dated in the first
   half of the century, in contrast to thirty-nine from
   the second half of the century, twenty-one of which
   are dated to the last quarter of the century, op. cit.,
   pp. 76f.

21 K10, Athens National Museum 739; for a suggested
   Ionian (Parian) model, see C. Blümel, Die klassische-
   griechischen Skulpturen der Staatlichen Museen zu
   Berlin, #2, Stele Giustiniani, pls 2, 4, 6, 9.

22 Hiller, op. cit., pp. 130, 136.

23 A less successful rendering of the same motif is to
   be found in another Theban stele, K15, Thebes Museum
   12; Ch. Karouzos, To Mouseio tes Thebas, p. 17,
   #12, pl. 11.

24 K18, Brussels A 1315; Schild-Xenidou, op. cit.,
   pp. 166f.

25 Hiller, op. cit., p. 140.

26 Ibid., p. 143.

27 Work by more than one craftsman on a particular
    piece was frequent; see Burford, Craftsmen, p. 95.

28 K32, Berlin Museum 1504; Collignon, op. cit., p. 132,
    fig. 71.

29 A badly damaged fragment of a stele in the Thebes
    Museum (K33), unpublished, appears to be another
    example of this same type.

30 Ridgway, The Archaic Style in Greek Sculpture,
    pp. 165f.

31 W. Vollgraff, BCH, 1902, vol. 26, pp. 554-70;
    A. Keramopoullos, AE, 1920, pp. 1-27; Karouzos,
    op. cit.,; J. Threpsiadis, AE, 1963, Beilage,
    pp. 13-15; Schild-Xenidou, op. cit., K43-8, pp. 176-8;
    A.G. Kalogeropoulos, AAA, 1968, vol. 1, pp. 92-6.
    For a discussion of Chian parallels, see N.M.
    Kontoleon, BCH, 1949, vol. 73, pp. 392-7; Ridgway,
    Archaic Style, pp. 164, 170-1; E. Pfühl and
    H. Möbius, Die ostgriechischen Grabreliefs, vol. 2,
    Appendix, 566-8, pls 330f., XX-XXIII. The Chian
    examples are later (early fourth century and on),
    so that Chian priority seems unlikely.

32 Schild-Xenidou, op. cit., p. 177, n. 4.

33 On the difficulties involved in making accurate
    copies of these works, see Kalogeropoulos, op. cit.
    The technique that has been found most accurate is
    that of rubbing with soft graphite, the method used
    on tombstones in New England.

34 K42, Thebes Museum 57; Keramopoullos, op. cit.,
    p. 10, fig. 3; the stele portrays the women and
    child. It is the only one of these fragmentary
    etched stelai included by Schild-Xenidou; for
    sketches and discussion of the other, see
    Keramopoullos, op. cit.

35 Karouzos, op. cit., p. 30; Keramopoullos, op. cit.,
    p. 10, dated after 460 BC.

36 K43   Mnason (Thebes), Thebes Museum 54; E. Pfühl,
          Malerei und Zeichnung der Griechen, vol. 2,
          p. 665, #722, pl. 633.

    K44   Rhynchon (Thebes), Thebes Museum 55; Pfühl 665,
          #722, p. 634.

    K45   Saugenes (Tanagra), Thebes Museum 56.

    K46   Koiranos (Tanagra), Thebes Museum 58.

    K47   Byillos (Thebes), Thebes Museum 43.

    K48   Pherenikos (Asopia), Thebes Museum 240.

37 Keramopoullos, op. cit., pp. 25f.

38 Keramopoullos, op. cit., has suggested that this
    portrays a scene outside the temple of Apollo Ismenios,

with the female figure, perhaps the mother of the boy,
representing Manto sitting on her stone. This ties
in with his identification of Rhynchon as a Daphnophoros
(see Chapter 4); this theory is based on the very
elaborate decorations of the clothing and armor and
especially on the wreath which the figure wears on
his helmet (the Daphnophoros wore a laurel wreath).
Considering the fact that there is a similar wreath
on the helmet of Saugenes, this seems to be an unlikely
interpretation: Keramopoullos does answer this
objection by the claim that the wreath worn by a
Tanagran, Saugenes, would not have the same significance
that it had for the Theban Rhynchon, but given the
close similarity of all the representations, it seems
more likely that similar details bear similar meanings
on them all, and that the wreath is that of a victor,
or funerary.

39 K13, Basle, Kunstmuseum G1957.14; Schefold, Antike
    Kunst, 1958, vol. 1, pp. 69-74, pl. 31.

40 K82, Athens National Museum 817; G. Rodenwaldt, JDAI,
    1913, vol. 38, p. 333, pl. 30.

41 Burford, Craftsmen, pp. 176-9, pl. 6.

42 Suggested by N.M. Kontoleon in Charistirion A.K.
    Orlandos, vol. 1, p. 396, and confirmed in Kalogeropoulos,
    op. cit., p. 96.

43 See E. Pfühl and H. Möbius, Die ostgriechischen
    Grabreliefs, vol. 1, pp. 10f., pl. 3, #7. C. Karouzos,
    AM, 1962, vol. 77, pp. 121-9, discusses the general
    topic of erotic scenes on tombstones, and cites a
    possible parallel to the Saugenes' stele (he does not
    consider this stele, since the identification of the
    figure as a woman was made only in 1968). This is a
    fragment of a relief from Kos, dated to about 510,
    identified as funerary, which portrays an erotic
    scene: a lyre-holding man and an almost naked woman
    share a couch, from which a naked ithyphallic man has
    evidently just fallen. A male flute player entertains
    the party, while a small boy tries to help the fallen
    man. See also Ridgway, Archaic, pp. 175, 273, 279
    note. Ridgway comments on the unusual use of the
    scene on the Kos relief for a grave monument, and
    makes several suggestions: that it might have been
    a votive offering by a professional prostitute, or
    dedicated in return for a miraculous cure (by the
    fallen man probably); or that it is the funeral stele
    of the fallen man and depicts the moment of his
    death. Unfortunately, none of these suggestions helps
    in explaining the representation on the stele of
    Saugenes.

44 As on Etruscan sarcophagi; the common origin for both
    would be east Greece, where symposium scenes in which
    a woman sits on the edge of the couch occur early in
    the fifth century; see Pfühl and Möbius, op. cit.,
    vol. 1, pp. 9f, 30-2, pl. 2, #4 and #6, and pl. 19,
    #73, 74, 76. Stelai with similar scenes (woman
    sitting on edge of couch) are frequent in Boeotia in
    the fourth century: Schild-Xenidou lists five
    examples. Reclining couples have not been found in
    east Greece dating earlier than the third century;
    see Pfühl and Möbius, vol. 2, pp. 443ff., #1844-58.
45 Theodor Kock, Comicorum atticorum fragmenta, vol. 1,
    p. 517, #488.
46 Plato, 'Rep.' 363C.
47 August Meineke, Fragmenta comicorum graecorum, vol. 3,
    p. 362, 4-5.
48 See Rhea N. Thönges-Stringaris, AM, 1965, vol. 80,
    pp. 16-18, 25, 61-6.
49 This judgment has been confirmed by the recent
    redrawing of the Saugenes stele, see Kalogeropoulos,
    op. cit.
50 Keramopoullos, op. cit.
51 Pliny, 'HN' 75, 110, 122.
52 Eugénie Sellers, The Elder Pliny's Chapters on the
    History of Art, note on 'HN' 35.75.13.
53 Pliny, 'HN' 34.72; for a discussion of artists who
    worked in more than one medium, see Burford,
    Craftsmen, pp. 86, 96. Polygnotus was a painter who
    also worked in bronze ('HN' 34.85), as was Euphranor,
    who was a pupil of Aristeides ('HN' 34.50; Paus.
    1.3.4).
54 J.E. Raven, CQ, 1951, n.s. vol. 1, pp. 147-52.
55 Keramopoullos, op. cit., pp. 18ff.
56 See Burford, Craftsmen, pp. 109f. on the subject
    of poor craftsmanship.
57 See P.N. Ure, BSA, 1907-8, vol. 14, pp. 226-318;
    P.N. Ure and R.M. Burrows, JHS, 1909, vol. 29,
    pp. 308-53; P.N. Ure, Sixth and Fifth Century
    Pottery from Rhitsona; Aryballoi and Figurines from
    Rhitsona in Boeotia.
58 See Paul Wolters and Gerda Bruns, Das Kabirenheiligtum
    bei Theben, vol. 1.
59 A.D. Ure, BSA, 1940-5, vol. 41, pp. 24f.
60 Ibid.
61 A.D. Ure, AJA, 1953, vol. 57, p. 249.
62 A.D. Ure, BSA, 1940-5, vol. 41, p. 23; R. Lullies,
    AM, 1940, vol. 65, p. 13.
63 M. Collignon and Louis Couve, Catalogue des vases
    peints due Musée National d'Athènes, #1406.

64   A.D. Ure, BSA, 1940-5, vol. 41, p. 25, and AJA, 1958,
     vol. 62, pp. 390f.
65   A.D. Ure, JHS, 1951, vol. 71, pp. 194-7.
66   R.M. Cook, Greek Painted Pottery, pp. 103, 188;
     the identification and analysis of Theban pottery
     should be greatly assisted by the publication of the
     finds from the necropolis at Pyri, see AD, 1969,
     vol. 24, Chr. 1, pp. 175-7.
67   For the black-figure vases, see L.B. Ghali-Kahil,
     BCH, 1950, vol. 74, pp. 52-61; for red-figure, Lullies,
     AM, 1940, vol. 65, pp. 1-27.
68   B.A. Sparkes, JHS, 1967, vol. 87, p. 124 and pl. xix;
     P. Pelagatti, ArchClass, 1962, vol. 14, pp. 36ff.
69   Sparkes, op. cit., p. 124, and connections between
     the Judgment of Paris, Branteghem and woman's head
     vases; see A.D. Ure, BSA, 1940-5, vol. 41.
70   See A. Rumpf, JHS, 1947, vol. 67, pp. 10-21, for the
     application of shading and perspective techniques
     to Attic vases.
71   See Lullies, AM, 1940, vol. 65, passim.
72   O. von Vacano, Zur Entstehung und Deutung gemalter
     seitansichtiger Kopfbilder auf schwarzfigurigen
     Vasen des griechischen Festlands, pp. 44f.
73   J.-J. Maffre, BCH, 1975, vol. 99, pp. 516-18, fig. 56.
74   A.D. Ure, AJA, 1953, vol. 57, pp. 245-9; JHS, 1957,
     vol. 77, pp. 314f.; with additions by Pelagatti,
     op. cit., pp. 29-41.
75   A.D. Ure, AJA, 1953, vol. 57, p. 249.
76   Miss Gloria Pinney suggests that the figure represents
     Selene; other possibilities, all associated with the
     moon, are Io, Hera, Pasiphae, Artemis, and Hecate.
     Possibly a suggestion of sorcery is present.
77   Mostra dell'Etruria padana e della città di Spina,
     vol. 1, Catalogo, #1063, 1064, 1057, 1073. Salvatore
     Aurigemma, Scavi di Spina, vol. 1, tombs 512 and 271
     each have two plates with heads, one pair male and
     female (but in a three-quarter view), the other pair
     both males; pls 143, 190a, b; vol. 2, tomb #1166
     in which was found an oinochoe with a woman's head,
     thought to be from 'Greece', with hair held as in a
     kerchief-sling, and exposed in a sort of knot in the
     back as well as in the front; this tomb also contained
     two plates with heads, male and female, and a nuptial
     lebete from the workshop of Meidias dated to the first
     decade of the fourth century. This appears to be the
     tomb of a young bride, with the gifts centering around
     the nuptial theme; pp. 109-10 and pls 140-1.
78   Pelagatti, op. cit., pp. 31-33.
79   D.M. Robinson, C.G. Harcum, J.H. Iliffe, Greek Vases

at Toronto, pls LXXI, LXXII, LXXI-LXXV.

80 See R. Hackl, JDAI, 1907, vol. 22, pp. 83ff., for a
    discussion of early instances of the use of human
    heads as independent decorations. More recently
    K. Schauenberg, Jahrbuch des Römisch-Germanischen
    Zentralmuseums Mainz, 1957, vol. 4, pp. 63-72, has
    offered a brief and incomplete survey of later finds
    in various areas, and suggested that a full-scale
    study of the type should be carried out. He cites
    the use of a man's head decoration on sixth-century
    Boeotian vases. Some areas in which the motif was
    popular in the fourth century were Italy (the
    Apulian vases, see above, note 79), Olynthus (see
    D.M. Robinson, Excavations at Olynthus, vol. 5,
    pp. 148-56, pls 117-24; vol. 13, pp. 17, 44, 95,
    97; pls 58, 60), and southern Russia (see K. Shefold,
    'Untersuchungen zu den kertscher Vasen', Archaeo-
    logische Mitteilungen aus russischen Sammlungen,
    vol. 4, p. 148, pls 1, 25).

81 Von Vacano, op. cit.,

82 Wolters and Bruns, op. cit., pp. 95-128, pls 5-17,
    26-33, 37, 44-5, 50-8.

83 Bruns, in Wolters and Bruns, op. cit., p. 126,
    citing as a possible forerunner of the style an
    Attic lekythos: Athens #1129, see C.H.C. Haspels,
    Attic Black-Figure Lekythoi, pp. 180ff., pls 49-50.

84 Sir Arthur Pickard-Cambridge, Dithyramb, Tragedy
    and Comedy, #61, 65, and pl. 138. On these vases,
    see also Alex Seeberg, 'Corinthian Komos Vases',
    University of London Institute of Classical Studies
    Bulletin, 1971, suppl. 27.

85 A.D. Ure, JHS, 1929, vol. 49, pp. 160ff., and JHS,
    vol. 55, pp. 227f. Karl Kilinski II, AJA, 1978,
    vol. 182, pp. 173-91, suggests a Tanagran source
    for this sixth-century komost group. Not quite so
    early are three black-figure vases with grotesque
    figures cited by Maffre, op. cit., pp. 496-504,
    #23-5, which he dates to 470-440.

86 Thus Seeberg sees a reference to drama in the
    Corinthian Komos vases, op. cit., p. 80.

87 For a discussion of the question of dramatic
    performance, see Chapter 6.

88 Cook, Greek Painted Pottery, p. 102.

89 Lullies, op. cit., n. 16, #12, 13.

90 M. Harissiadis, Starinar, 3rd series, vols 10 and 11,
    pp. 95-113.

91 R.M. Cook, BSA, 1933-4, vol. 34, pp. 95f.

92 A.D. Ure, JHS, 1957, vol. 77, pp. 314f.

93 Wolters and Bruns, op. cit., pl. 61, #5-6.

94   'Locri Epizephrii', NSc, 1913, Suppl. Locri Epizephyrii,
     p. 36 and fig. 45; Nicola Bonacasa, ArchClass, 1958,
     vol. 10, pp. 50-4. Sparkes discusses another decorated
     pig askos of Boeotian provenance (op. cit., p. 120 and
     pl. 1, XVab), a member of a group of eight plastic
     vases, all Boeotian, four from Thebes or the Kabeirion
     (see CVA Oxford 2.57); see too Kilinski, op. cit., for
     another Boeotian pig (Paris, Louvre, CA 577, see CVA,
     Louvre vol. 17, pp. 27f.).
95   Compare the chase scene in Wolters and Bruns, op. cit.,
     pl. 10.
96   Bonacasa, op. cit., pp. 51-3.
97   The work which passes for his is late and spurious;
     see A. E. Taylor, A Commentary on Plato's Timaeus,
     Appendix II, pp. 655-64, who dates it to the first
     century AD. See also R. Harder, RE, 1937, vol. 6,
     pt 1, cols 1203-26. Burkert even suggests that
     Plato's Timaeus might be Philistion, a contemporary
     of Plato, but this would be somewhat late for our
     pig, since the other pottery in the tomb also supports
     a date for the group of 440-2, Walter Burkert, Lore
     and Science in Ancient Pythagoreanism, p. 84.
98   F.M. Cornford, Plato's Cosmology, p. 3.
99   Taylor, op. cit., p. 11.
100 Ibid., p. 15.
101 Cornford, op. cit., p. 2.
102 J.D. Beazley, Etruscan Vase Painting, p. 50; A.D. Ure
     in P.N. Ure, Sixth and Fifth Century Pottery from
     Rhitsona, p. 74, n. 3; J.M.T. Charlton, AJA, 1951,
     vol. 55, p. 338; Pelagatti, op. cit., p. 38.

APPENDIX: THE POSITION OF WOMEN IN PYTHAGOREANISM

1   Iamb. 'VP' 267.
2   Ibid., 39-57.
3   By 'Pythagorean woman' I mean a woman who is connected
    with Pythagoreanism either through family ties or
    pupil-teacher relationships, or who is named in the
    'Catalogue' as a Pythagorean; whether these women
    were Pythagoreans in the same sense as the male
    members of the society, or whether they held some
    other status within the group, is what I am trying
    to determine.
4   DL 8.42; Suid., s.v. 'Pythagoras'; Iamb. 'VP' 126,
    265.
5   DL 8.42; Suid., s.v. 'Theano'; see too A. von
    Blumenthal, Glotta, 1928, vol. 17, pp. 152-8.
6   DL 8.43.

7   Ap. DL 8.42.
8   W. Burkert, Philologus, 1961, vol. 105, pp. 17ff.
9   Photius, 'Bibl.', c. 249, 438b.
10 Porph. 'VP' 4 (he says that her writings are extant).
11 Porph. 'VP' 4; also known as daughter of Brontinos
    (Suid., s.v. 'Pythagoras') and as a philosopher
    (Clem. 'Strom.' iv 19, 121, p. 224).
12 Iamb. 'VP' 267 = DK 58A; discussed by Burkert,
    Lore and Science in Ancient Pythagoreanism, p. 105,
    n. 40; E. Rohde, RhMus, 1872, Collectionis Specimen.
13 Burkert, op. cit., p. 105, n. 40.
14 FGrHist 328 T 1.
15 Iamb. 'VP' 54-7.
16 Iamb. 'VP' 48.
17 A. Delatte, Essai sur la Politique Pythagoricienne,
    pp. 39f.; A. Rostagni, Studi Italiani di Filologia
    Classica, 1922, n.s. vol. 2, pp. 180-99; Rohde, op.
    cit., pp. 26-9; C.J. de Vogel, Pythagoras and Early
    Pythagoreanism, pp. 140-7.
18 See ibid., pp. 26f., 135.

Abbreviations

AA	Archäologischer Anzeiger
AAA	Archaiologika Analekta ex Athenon
AC	L'Antiquité Classique
AD	Archaiologikon Deltion
AE	Archaiologika Ephemeris
AJA	American Journal of Archaeology
AJP	American Journal of Philology
AM	Mitteilungen des Kaiserlich Deutschen Archälogischen Institut. Athenische Abteilung
ArchClass	Archeologia Classica
BCH	Bulletin de Correspondence Hellénique
BSA	Annual of the British School at Athens
CAH	The Cambridge Ancient History
CJ	Classical Journal
CP	Classical Philology
CQ	Classical Quarterly
CR	Classical Review
CW	Classical World
GRBS	Greek Roman and Byzantine Studies
HSCP	Harvard Studies in Classical Philology
JDAI	Jahrbuch des Deutschen Archälogischen Instituts
JHS	Journal of Hellenic Studies
MH	Museum Helveticum
NumChron	Numismatic Chronicle
OCD	The Oxford Classical Dictionary, Oxford, 1st ed, 1949; 2nd edn, 1970.
RE	Paulys Real-Encyclopädie der klassischen Altertumswissenschaft. Stuttgart and elsewhere, 1894 onwards.
REA	Revue des Études Anciennes
REG	Revue des Études Grecque
RhM	Rheinisches Museum

RFIC   Rivista di Filologia e di Istruzione
                Classica
RSA   Rivista storica dell'Antichità
TAPA   Transactions and Proceedings of the
                American Philogical Association
Teiresias.   A Review and Continuing Bibliography
                of Boiotian Studies, Montreal.

Bibliography

PRIMARY SOURCES

AELIAN, Claudii Aeliani Opera, Rudolph Hercher (ed.),
2 vols, Leipzig, B.G. Teubner, 1864-6.
AESCHINES, The Speeches of Aeschines, C.D. Adams (tr.),
Cambridge, Mass., Harvard University Press, 1948.
AESCHYLUS, Aeschyli septem quae supersunt tragoediae,
Gilbert Murray (ed.), 2nd edn., Oxford, Clarendon Press,
1955.
ANTONINUS LIBERALIS, Les Métamorphoses, Manolis
Papathomopulos (ed.), Paris, Les Belles Lettres, 1968.
APOLLODOROS, The Library, J.G. Frazer (tr.), Cambridge,
Mass., Harvard University Press, 1921.
ARISTOPHANES, Aristophanis Comoediae, F.W. Hall and
W.M. Geldart (eds), Oxford, Clarendon Press, 1906-7.
ARISTOTLE, Opera, I. Bekker and O. Gigon (eds), Berlin,
De Gruyter, 1960.
ARISTOTLE, Constitution of the Athenians, Hans Oppermann
(ed.), Stuttgart, G.B. Teubner, 1961.
ATHENAEUS, Athenaei Naucratitae Dipnosophistarum, book 5,
G. Kaibel (ed.), Leipzig, B.G. Teubner, 1887-90.
BERGK, THEODOR, Poetae Lyrici Graeci, 5th edn, part 1,
vol. 1, Pindari Carmina, Otto Schroeder (ed.), Leipzig,
B.G. Teubner, 1900.
CICERO, De legibus, G. de Plinval (ed.), Paris, Les
Belles Lettres, 1959.
CLEMENS ALEXANDRINUS, Stromata, O. Staehlin (ed.), 4 vols,
Leipzig, J.C. Hinrichs, 1905-36.
DIODORUS SICULUS, Diodore de Sicile: Bibliothèque
historique, book 12, Michel Casevitz (ed.), Paris, Les
Belles Lettres, 1972.
DIOGENES LAERTIUS, Vitae philosophorum, H.S. Long (ed.),
Oxford, Clarendon Press, 1964.
EURIPIDES, Fabulae, Gilbert Murray (ed.), Oxford,

Clarendon Press, 1966, reprint of vol. 1, 1902; vol. 2,
1913, 3rd edn; vol. 3, 1913, 2nd edn.
Hellenica Oxyrhynchia, Vittorio Bartoletti (ed.), Leipzig,
B.G. Teubner, 1959.
HERODOTUS, Herodoti historiae, C. Hude (ed.), 3rd edn,
Oxford, Clarendon Press, 1927.
HESIOD, Hesiodi Theogonia, Opera et Dies, Scutum, F.
Solmsen (ed.), Oxford, Clarendon Press, 1970.
HESYCHIUS, Lexicon, K. Latte (ed.), Copenhagen, Munksgaard,
1953-66.
HOMER, Homeri opera. Iliadem, D.B. Monroe and T.A. Allen
(eds), 3rd edn, Oxford, Clarendon Press, 1920.
HOMER, Homeri opera. Odysseam, T.W. Allen (ed.), 2nd edn,
Oxford, Clarendon Press, 1917-19.
HYGINUS, Hygini Fabulae, H.J. Rose (ed.), Leiden,
A.W. Sijthoff, 1934.
IAMBLICHUS, De vita Pythagorica, L. Deubner (ed.), Leipzig,
B.G. Teubner, 1937.
JACOBY, FELIX (ed.), Die Fragmente der griechischen
Historiker, Leiden, Brill, 1954-1958.
JUSTIN, M. Iuniani Iustini epitoma historiarum Philippicarum
Pompei Trogi, F. Ruehl and O. Seel (eds), 2nd edn, Leipzig,
B.G. Teubner, 1935.
KOCK, THEODOR, Comicorum atticorum fragmenta, Leipzig,
B.G. Teubner, 1880-8.
LYSIAS, Orationes, T. Thalheim (ed.), Leipzig, B.G. Teubner,
1901.
MEINEKE, AUGUST, Fragmenta comicorum graecorum, Berlin,
G. Reimeri, 1839-57.
MUELLER, KARL (ed.), Geographi Graeci Minores, Paris,
Didot, 1885.
MUELLER, KARL (ed.), Fragmenta Historicorum Graecorum,
Paris, Didot, 1841-1938.
NEPOS, CORNELIUS, Cornelii Nepotis quae extant,
H. Malcovati (ed.), Turin, I.B. Paravia, 1934.
OLYMPIODORUS, In Platonis Phaedonem Commentaria, William
Norvin (ed.), Leipzig, B.G. Teubner, 1913.
Oxyrhynchus Papyri, vol. 5, B.P. Grenfall and A.S. Hunt
(eds), London, Egypt Exploration Fund, 1908.
Oxyrhynchus Papyri, vol. 23, E. Lobel (ed.), London,
Egypt Exploration Society, 1956.
PAGE, D.L., Greek Literary Papyri, 2 vols, Cambridge,
Mass., Harvard University Press, 1942.
PAGE, D.L., Poetae Melici Graeci, Oxford, Clarendon Press,
1962.
PAUSANIAS, Description of Greece, W.H.S. Jones and
H.A. Ormerod (eds and trs), 4 vols, London, Heinemann,
1918-35.
PHOTIUS, Lexicon, S.A. Naber (ed.), Leiden, E.J. Brill,
1864-5.

PHOTIUS, Bibliothèque, R. Henry (ed.), 7 vols, Paris,
Les Belles Lettres, 1959-74.
PINDAR, Scholia vetera in Pindari carmina, A.B. Drachmann
(ed.), 3 vols, Leipzig, B.G. Teubner, 1903-27.
PINDAR, The Odes of Pindar, J. Sandys (ed.), 2nd revised
edn, London, Heinemann, 1919.
PINDAR, Pindari carmina cum fragmentis, C.M. Bowra (ed.),
2nd edn, Oxford, Clarendon Press, 1947.
PLATO, Platonis opera, J. Burnet (ed.), 5 vols, Oxford,
Clarendon Press, 1900-7.
PLINY, Historia Naturalis, C. Mayhoff (ed.), 6 vols,
Leipzig, B.G. Teubner, 1892-1909.
PLUTARCH, Moralia, C. Hubert et al. (eds), 4 vols,
Leipzig, B.G. Teubner, 1952-72.
PLUTARCH, Vitae parallelae, C. Lindskog and K. Ziegler
(eds), 2nd edn, 3 vols in 6, Leipzig, B.J. Teubner,
1957-73.
POLYBIUS, Historiae, L. Dindorf and T. Buettner-Wobst
(eds), 2nd edn, Leipzig, B.G. Teubner, 1924.
PORPHYRY, Porphyrii philosophi Platonici Opuscula selecta,
A. Nauck (ed.), 2nd edn, Leipzig, B.G. Teubner, 1886.
STRABO, Strabonis Geographica, A. Meineke (ed.), 3 vols,
Leipzig, B.G. Teubner, 1877.
SUIDAS, Suidae lexicon, A. Adler (ed.), Stuttgart,
B.G. Teubner, 1828.
THEOCRITUS, Scholia, C. Wendel (ed.), Leipzig, B.G. Teubner,
1914.
THEOPHRASTUS, Enquiry into Plants, Sir Arthur F. Hort
(tr.), 2 vols, London, Heinemann, 1916.
THUCYDIDES, Thucydidis historiae, H.S. Jones and J.E. Powell
(eds), revised end, 2 vols, Oxford, Clarendon Press, 1970.
XENOPHON, Xenophontis opera omnia, E.C. Marchant (ed.),
2 vols, Oxford, Clarendon Press, 1900-21.

SECONDARY SOURCES

ADAM, SHEILA, The Technique of Greek Sculpture in the
Archaic and Classical Periods, London, Thames & Hudson,
1966.
ALLEN, A. and FREL, J., 'A date for Corinna', CJ, 1972,
vol. 68, pp. 26-30.
AMIT, M., 'La date de l'alliance entre Athènes et Platées',
AC, 1970, vol. 39, pp. 414-26.
AMIT, M., 'The Boeotian confederacy during the
Pentekontaetia', RSA, 1971, vol. 1, pp. 49-64.
ARCHER-HIND, R.D., The Phaedo of Plato, 2nd edn, London,
Macmillan, 1894.
AURIGEMMA, SALVATORE, Scavi di Spina, 2 vols, Rome,
Bretschneider, 1960-5.

BABELON, E., Traité des Monnaies Grecques et Romaines,
vol. 2, pt 1, Paris, E. Leroux, 1907.
BARBER, G.L., The Historian Ephorus, Cambridge University
Press, 1935.
BARTOLETTI, V., Hellenica Oxyrhynchia, Leipzig,
B.G. Teubner, 1959.
BEAZLEY, J.D., Etruscan Vase Painting, Oxford, Clarendon
Press, 1947.
BISCHOFF, HEINRICH, Der Warner bei Herodot, Berne-Leipzig,
R. Noske, 1932.
BIZARD, L., 'Inscriptions du Ptoion (1903)', BCH, 1920,
vol. 44, pp. 227-41.
BLUCK, R.S., Plato's Phaedo, London, Routledge & Kegan
Paul, 1955.
BLÜMEL, CARL, Die klassische griechischen Skulpturen der
Staatlichen Museen zu Berlin, Berlin, Akademie-Verlag,
1966.
BLUMENTHAL, ALBRECHT von, 'Messapisches', Glotta, 1928,
vol. 17, pp. 104-6, 152-8.
BÖTTIGER, KARL AUGUST, 'Pallas Musica und Apollo, der
Marsyastödter', Kleine Schriften, vol. 1, Leipzig,
Arnold, 1850, pp. 3-60.   First published in Wieland's
Attischen Museum, 1792, vol. 1, pt 2, pp. 279-385.
BONACASA, NICOLA, 'Askos Locrese nello stile del Kabirion',
ArchClass, 1958, vol. 10, pp. 50-4.
BOWERSOCK, G.W., 'Pseudo-Xenophon', HSCP, 1966, vol. 71,
pp. 33-46.
BOWRA, C.M., 'The daughters of Asopus', Hermes, 1938,
vol. 73, pp. 213-21.
BOWRA, C.M., Pindar, Oxford, Clarendon Press, 1964.
BREITHOLTZ, LENNART, Die dorische Farce, Stockholm,
Almqvist & Wiksell, 1960.
BROWN, HELEN ANN, Philosophorum Pythagoreorum Collectionis
Specimen, dissertation, University of Chicago, 1941.
BROWN, NORMAN O., 'Pindar, Sophocles, and the Thirty
Years' Peace', TAPA, 1951, vol. 82, pp. 1-28.
BRUCE, I.A.F., An Historical Commentary on the 'Hellenica
Oxyrhynchia', Cambridge University Press, 1967.
BRUNO, VINCENT, Form and Color in Greek Painting, New
York, Norton, 1977.
BRUNS, GERDA, 'Das Kabirenheiligtum bei Theben', AA, 1939,
vol. 54, pp. 581-98.
BRUNS, GERDA, 'Das Kabirenheiligtum bei Theben', AA, 1964,
vol. 79, pp. 231-65.
BRUNS, GERDA, 'Kabirenheiligtum bei Theben.   Vorläufiger
Bericht über die Grabungskampagnen 1964-1966', AA, 1967,
vol. 82, pt 2, pp. 228-73.
BUCK, R.J., 'The Athenian domination of Boeotia', CP, 1970,
vol. 65, pp. 217-27.

BUCK, R.J., 'The formation of the Boeotian League', CP, 1972, vol. 67, pp. 94-101.
BUCK, R.J., 'Boeotians at Thermopylae', CP, 1974, vol. 69, pp. 47-8.
BUCK, R.J., A History of Boeotia, Edmonton, University of Alberta Press, 1979.
BURFORD, ALISON, The Greek Temple Builders at Epidauros, Liverpool University Press, 1969.
BURFORD, ALISON, Craftsmen in Greek and Roman Society, London, Thames & Hudson, 1972.
BURKERT, WALTER, 'Hellenistische pseudopythagorica', Philologus, 1961, vol. 105, pp. 16-43.
BURKERT, WALTER, Lore and Science in Ancient Pythagoreanism, tr. E.L. Minar, Jr from the 1962 German edition, Cambridge, Mass., Harvard University Press, 1972.
BURKERT, WALTER, Homo Necans, Berlin, De Gruyter, 1972.
BURKERT, WALTER, Orphism and Bacchic Mysteries: New Evidence and Old Problems of Interpretation, Protocol of the 28th Colloquy of the Center of Hermeneutical Studies, Berkeley, 1977.
BURNET, JOHN, Plato's Phaedo, Oxford, Clarendon Press, 1911.
BURNET, JOHN, Early Greek Philosophy, 4th edn, London, Black, 1958.
BURY, J.B., The Nemean Odes of Pindar, London, J.B.B. Macmillan, 1890.
BURY, J.B., The Isthmian Odes of Pindar, London, J.B.B. Macmillan, 1892.
BUSOLT, GEORG, Griechische Geschichte bis zur Schlacht bei Chaeroneia, Gotha, F.A. Perthes, 1893-1904.
CALAME, CLAUDE, Les Choeurs de jeunes filles en Grèce archaïque, 2 vols, Rome, Edizioni dell'Ateneo & Bizzarri, 1977.
CAMPBELL, D.A., Greek Lyric Poetry, New York, St Martin's Press, 1967.
CASKEY, L.D., Catalogue of Greek and Roman Sculpture, Museum of Fine Arts, Boston, Cambridge, Mass., Harvard University Press, 1925.
CAUER, F., 'Aigeidai', RE, 1894, vol. 1, cols 949-50.
CHAPOUTHIER, FERNAND, 'Kabire béotien et Kabires de Samothrace', REA, 1942, vol. 55, pp. 329-30.
CHARLTON, J.M.T., 'A Boeotian bell-krater in Rochdale', AJA, 1951, vol. 55, pp. 336-8.
CLOCHE, PAUL, Thèbes de Béotie des origines à la conquête romaine, Namur, Secrétariat des publications Facultès universitaires, 1952.
COLLIGNON, MAXIME and COUVE, LOUIS, Catalogue des vases peints du Musée National d'Athènes, Paris, A. Fontemoing, 1902-4.

COLLIGNON, MAXIME, Les Statues funéraires dans l'art grec, Paris, E. Leroux, 1911.
COMSTOCK, MARY B. and VERMEULE, C., Sculpture in Stone, Boston, Museum of Fine Arts, 1976.
COOK, R.M., 'Fikellura pottery', BSA, 1933-4, vol. 34, pp. 1-98.
COOK, R.M., Greek Painted Pottery, 2nd edn, London, Methuen, 1972.
CORLU, ANDRÉ, Plutarque. Le Démon de Socrate, Paris, Klincksieck, 1970.
CORNFORD, FRANCIS M., Plato's Cosmology, New York, Liberal Arts Press, 1957.
CORSSEN, P., 'Die Sprengung des pythagoreischen Bundes', Philologus, 1912, vol. 71, pp. 332-52.
CRUSIUS, O., 'Sagenverschiebungen', Sitzungsberichte der Bayerischer Akad. der Wissenshaft, 1905, pp. 749-802.
DAKYNS, H.C., Works of Xenophon, vol. I, London, Macmillan, 1890.
DAUX, GEORGES, 'Mys ai Ptôion', Hommages à Waldemar Deonna, Collection Latomus, 1957, vol. 28, pp. 157-62.
DAVISON, J.A., review of Thummer, Die Religiosität Pindars, in JHS, 1960, vol. 80, pp. 203-4.
DELATTE, A., Essai sur la Politique Pythagoricienne, Paris, E. Champion, 1922.
DELORME, J., Gymnasion, Paris, Boccard, 1960.
DEMAND, N., 'Pindar's "Olympian 2", Theron's Faith, and Empedocles' "Katharmoi"', GRBS, 1975, vol. 16, pp. 347-57.
DEMAND, N., 'Plato and the Painters', Phoenix, 1975, vol. 29, pp. 1-20.
DEMAND, N., review of Dover, Greek Homosexuality, in AJP, 1980, vol. 101, pp. 121ff.
DEVEREUX, G., 'Greek pseudo-homosexuality and the "Greek Miracle"', Symbolae Osloenses, 1967, vol. 42, pp. 70-92.
DOVER, K.J., 'Eros and nomos (Plato, "Symposium" 182A-185C)', Bulletin of the Institute of Classical Studies, London, 1964, vol. 11, pp. 31-42.
DOVER, K.J., Aristophanes' Clouds, Oxford, Clarendon Press, 1968.
DOVER, K.J., Greek Popular Morality in the Time of Plato and Aristotle, Berkeley, University of California Press, 1974.
DOVER, K.J., Greek Homosexuality, Cambridge, Mass., Harvard University Press, 1978.
DUCAT, JEAN, 'Le Ptoion et l'histoire de la Béotie à l'époque archaïque', REG, 1964, vol. 77, pp. 283-90.
DUCAT, JEAN, Les Kouroi du Ptoion, Paris, Boccard, 1971.
DUCAT, JEAN, 'La confédération béotienne et l'expansion thébaine a l'époque archaïque', BCH, 1973, vol. 97, pp. 59-73.

DULL, CLIFFORD, A Study of the Leadership of the Boeotian
League from the Invasion of the Boiotoi to the King's
Peace, dissertation, University of Wisconsin, 1975.
DULL, CLIFFORD, 'Thucydides 1.113 and the leadership of
Orchomenus', CP, 1977, vol. 72, pp. 305-14.
EDWARDS, RUTH B., Kadmos the Phoenician, Amsterdam,
Adolf M. Hakkert, 1979.
FABRICIUS, ERNST, Theben, Freiburg, J.C.B. Mohr, 1890.
FARNELL, LEWIS R., The Cults of the Greek States, 5 vols,
Oxford, Clarendon Press, 1896-1907.
FARNELL, LEWIS R., Greek Hero Cults, Oxford, Clarendon
Press, 1921.
FARNELL, LEWIS R., A Critical Commentary to the Works
of Pindar, 3 vols, London, Macmillan, 1930-2.
FEHR, BURKHARD, Orientalische und griechische Gelage,
Bonn, Bouvier, 1971.
FIELD, G.C., Plato and his Contemporaries, 3rd edn,
London, Methuen, 1967.
FLACELIÈRE, R., 'Plutarque et les oracles béotiens', BCH,
1946, vol. 70, pp. 199-207.
FONTENROSE, J., review of Francis Vian, Les Origines de
Thèbes, in CP, 1966, vol. 61, pp. 189-92.
FOWLER, B.H., 'Thuc. 1.107-108 and the Tanagran federal
issue', Phoenix, 1957, vol. 11, pp. 164-70.
FRANK, ERICH, Plato und die sogenannten Pythagoreer,
Halle, M. Niemeyer, 1923.
FRASER, P.M. and RÖNNE, T., Boeotian and West Greek
Tombstones, Lund, G.W.K. Gleerup, 1957.
FRAZER, J.G., Pausanias's Description of Greece, vol. 5,
London, Macmillan, 1898.
FRAZER, J.G. and VAN BUREN, A.W., Graecia Antiqua, London,
Macmillan, 1930.
FRITZ, KURT VON, Pythagorean Politics in Southern Italy,
New York, Columbia University Press, 1940.
FRITZ, KURT VON, 'Pythagoras', RE, 1963, vol. 47, cols
172-209.
FROST, FRANK J., 'Tribal politics and the civic state',
American Journal of Ancient History, 1976, vol. 1,
pp. 66-73.
FURLEY, DAVID J., review of Burkert, Lore and Science...
in CW, 1975, vol. 68, pp. 403-4.
GEISAU, HANS VON, 'Pyrrha', RE, 1963, vol. 47, col. 78.
GERKE, F., Griechische Plastik in archaischer und
klassischer Zeit, Berlin, Atlantis, 1938.
GERNET, L., review of Riezler, Finanzen und Monopole, in
L'Année Sociologique, 1906-9, vol. 11, pp. 559-62.
GHALI-KAHIL, LILLY B., 'Coupes à figures noires du Musée
d'Athènes', BCH, 1950, vol. 74, pp. 54-61.
GILDERSLEEVE, BASIL L., Pindar. The Olympian and Pythian

Odes, New York, Harper, 1885.

GLOTZ, GUSTAVE, 'Le conseil fédéral des Béotiens', BCH, 1908, vol. 32, pp. 271-8.

GLOTZ, GUSTAVE and COHEN, ROBERT, Histoire grecque, Paris, Les Presses Universitaires de France, 1925-38.

GOMME, A.W., 'The literary evidence for the topography of Thebes', BSA, 1910-11, vol. 17, pp. 29-53.

GOMME, A.W., 'The topography of Boeotia and the theories of M. Bérard', BSA, 1911-12, vol. 18, pp. 202-10.

GOMME, A.W., 'The legend of Cadmus and the Logographi', JHS, 1913, vol. 33, pp. 53-72, 223-45.

GOMME, A.W., ANDREWES, A. and DOVER, K.J., An Historical Commentary on Thucydides, Oxford, Clarendon Press, 1945-80.

GRENFELL, B.P. and HUNT, A.S., Oxyrhynchus Papyri, vol. 5, London, Egypt Exploration Fund, 1908.

GROTE, GEORGE, History of Greece, London, John Murray, 1869.

GRUBE, G.M.A., Plato's Thought, London, Methuen, 1935.

GUILLON, PIERRE, Les Trépieds du Ptoion, Paris, Boccard, 1943.

GUILLON, PIERRE, La Béotie Antique, Paris, Les Belles Lettres, 1948.

GUILLON, PIERRE, 'Corinne et les oracles béotiens', BCH, 1958, vol. 82, pp. 47-60.

GUILLON, PIERRE, Le Bouclier d'Héraclès. Annales de la Faculté des Lettres et Sciences Humaines d'Aix, 1963, vol. 37, pp. 1-101.

GULLEY, NORMAN, review of Burkert, Weisheit und Wissenschaft in CR, 1964, vol. 14, pp. 28-9.

GUNDERT, H., 'Der alte Pindar', Mnemosynon Theodor Wiegand, Munich, F. Bruckmann, 1938.

GUTHRIE, W.K.C., A History of Greek Philosophy, vol. 3, Cambridge University Press, 1969.

GZELLA, S., 'Self-publicity and polemics in Greek choral lyrics', Eos, 1969, vol. 58, pp. 175-9.

HACKFORTH, R., Plato's Phaedo, Cambridge University Press, 1955.

HACKL, R., 'Zwei frühattische Gefässe der Münchner Vasen-sammlung', JDAI, 1907, vol. 22, pp. 83-105.

HAMILTON, W., 'The myth in Plutarch's de genio (589F-592E)', CQ, 1934, vol. 28, pp. 175-82.

HAMMOND, N.G.L., 'Studies in Greek chronology of the sixth and fifth centuries B.C.', Historia, 1955, vol. 4, pp. 371-411.

HAMMOND, N.G.L., 'The main road from Boeotia to the Peloponnese', Studies in Greek History, Oxford, Clarendon Press, 1973, pp. 417-46.

HAMMOND, N.G.L., A History of Greece to 322 B.C., 2nd edn, Oxford, Clarendon Press, 1967.

HAMPE, RONALD, 'Zur Eschatologie in Pindars zweiter
Olympischer Ode', Ermeneia, Festschrift Otto Regenbogen,
Heidelberg, C. Winter, 1952, pp. 46-65.
HARDER, R., 'Timaios', RE, 1937, vol. 6, pt 1, cols
1203-26.
HARISSIADIS, MARA, 'Les vases grecs', Starinar, 3rd series,
vols 10 and 11, pp. 95-113.
HASPELS, C.H.C., Attic Black-Figure Lekythoi, Paris,
Boccard, 1936.
HEAD, B.V., On the Chronological Sequence of the Coins
of Boeotia, London, Rollin & Feuardent, 1881.
HEMBERG, BENGT, Die Kabiren, Uppsala, Almqvist & Wiksell,
1950.
HENRICHS, A., 'Despoina Kybele', HSCP, 1976, vol. 80,
pp. 253-86.
HEURTLEY, W.A., 'Notes on the harbours of s. Boeotia,
and sea-trade between Boeotia and Corinth in prehistoric
times', BSA, 1923-5, vol. 26, pp. 38-45.
HEYDER, W. and MALLWITZ, A., Die Bauten im Kabiren-
heiligtum bei Theben, Berlin, De Gruyter, 1978.
HIGNETT, C., Xerxes' Invasion of Greece, Oxford, Clarendon
Press, 1963.
HILLER, HILDE, Ionische Grabreliefs der ersten Hälfte
des 5. Jahrhunderts v. Chr., Tübingen, Wasmuth, 1975.
HIRZEL, RUDOLF, Der Dialog, 2 vols, Leipzig, S. Hirzel,
1895.
HOW, W.W. and WELLS, J., A Commentary on Herodotus,
Oxford, Clarendon Press, 1936.
HOWARD, A.A., 'The aulos or tibia', HSCP, 1893, vol. 4,
pp. 1-60.
HUMPHREYS, S.C., 'Economy and society in classical Athens',
Annali della Scuola Normale Superiore di Pisa, 1970,
vol. 39, pp. 1-26.
JEFFERY, L.H., The Local Scripts of Archaic Greece,
Oxford, Clarendon Press, 1961.
JEFFERY, L.H., 'Eight tombstones from Thebes', AD, 1967,
vol. 22, pt I, pp. 2-5.
KALOGEROPOULOS, A.C., 'Nuovo aspetto della stele di
Saugenes', AAA, 1968, vol. 1, pp. 92-6.
KAROUZOS, CH., To Mouseio tes Thebas, Athens, Karouzos,
Museum of Thebes, 1934.
KAROUZOS, CH., 'Aspil' en Neoisin', AM, 1962, vol. 77,
pp. 121-9.
KERAMOPOULLOS, ANTONIOS, 'Thebaïka', AD, 1917, vol. 3.
KERAMOPOULLOS, ANTONIOS, 'Eikones polemiston tes en
Delio maches (424 p. Ch.)', AE, 1920, pp. 1-36.
KERFERD, G.B., review of de Vogel in CR, 1968, vol. 18,
pp. 282-84.
KERN, OTTO, 'Die boiotischen Kabiren', Hermes, 1890,
vol.25, pp. 1-16.

180   Bibliography

KERN, OTTO, 'Kabeiros und Kabeiroi', RE, 1905, vol. 10, col. 1440.
KERN, OTTO, Die Inschriften von Magnesia am Maeander, Berlin, W. Spemann, 1900.
KILINSKY, K., II, 'The Boeotian dancers group', AJA, 1978, vol. 82, pp. 173-91.
KÖRTE, A., review of Bieber, History of the Greek and Roman Theater, in Neue Jahrbücher für das Klass. Altertums, 1921, vol. 24, pp. 308-12.
KONTOLEON, N.M., 'Monuments a décoration gravée de Musée de Chios', BCH, 1949, vol. 73, pp. 392-7.
KONTOLEON, N.M. 'Archaike Zophoros ek Parou', Charistirion A.K. Orlandos, Athens, Biblioteke tes en Athenais Archaiologikes Hetaireias, 1965.
KRAAY, COLIN M., Archaic and Classical Greek Coins, Berkeley, University of California Press, 1976.
KROLL, W., 'Menoikeus (2)', RE, 1931, vol. 29, col. 918.
LARSEN, J.A.O., Representative Government, Berkeley, University of California Press, 1955.
LARSEN, J.A.O., 'The Boeotian confederacy and fifth century oligarchic theory', TAPA, 1955, vol. 86, pp. 40-50.
LARSEN, J.A.O., 'Orchomenos and the formation of the Boeotian confederation in 447 B.C.', CP, 1960, vol. 55, pp. 9-18.
LARSEN, J.A.O., Greek Federal States, Oxford, Clarendon Press, 1968.
LASSERRE, F., 'Ornaments érotiques dans la poésie lyrique archaïque', Serta Turyniana, Urbana, University of Illinois Press, 1974.
LATTE, KURT, 'Die Lebenzeit der Korinna', Eranos, 1956, vol. 54, pp. 57-67.
LATTIMORE, RICHARD, The Odes of Pindar, University of Chicago Press, 1947.
LAUFFER, S., 'Ptoion', RE, 1959, vol. 46, cols 1506-78.
LEAKE, W.M., Travels in Northern Greece, vol. 2, London, J. Rodwell, 1835.
LEFKOWITZ, MARY, 'TO KAI EGO: The first person in Pindar', HSCP, 1963, vol. 67, pp. 177-253.
LEFKOWITZ, MARY, 'The influential fictions in the scholia to Pindar's "Pythian 8"', CP, 1975, vol. 70, pp. 173-85.
LEGRAND, P.E., 'De la malignité d'Hérodote', Mélanges Gustave Glotz, Paris, Les Presses Universitaires de France.
LÉVÊQUE, PIERRE, and VIDAL-NAQUET, PIERRE, Clisthène L'Athénien, Paris, Les Belles Lettres, 1964.
LEVIN, S., 'Itto Zeus: Boeotians using their dialect or conforming to the national koine', Proceedings of the First International Conference on Boiotian Antiquities, Teiresias, suppl. vol. 1, pp. 51-60.

LINFORTH, IVAN M., The Arts of Orpheus, Berkeley,
University of California Press, 1941.
'Locri Epizephyrii', Notizie degli Scavi, 1913, pp. 1-54.
LULLIES, REINHARD, 'Zur frühen boiotischen Plastik',
JDAI, 1936, vol. 51, pp. 137-53.
LULLIES, REINHARD, 'Zur Boiotisch rotfigurigen Vasenmalerei',
AM, 1940, vol. 65, pp. 1-27.
McNEAL, R., 'Historical methods and Thuc. 1.103.1',
Historia, 1970, vol. 19, pp. 306-25.
MAFFRE, JEAN-JACQUES, 'Collection Paul Cannellopoulos:
Vases Béotiens', BCH, 1975, vol. 99, pp. 409-520.
MARTIN, ROLAND, Recherches sur l'agora grecque, Paris,
Boccard, 1951.
MÉAUTIS, GEORGES, Pindare le Dorien, Neuchâtel, La
Baconnière, 1962.
MEIGGS, RUSSELL, The Athenian Empire, Oxford, Clarendon
Press, 1972.
MERITT, B.D., WADE-GERY, H.T. and McGREGOR, M.F.,
The Athenian Tribute Lists, vol. 3, Cambridge, Mass.,
Harvard University Press, 1950.
MERKELBACH, R., 'Sappho und ihr kreis', Philologus, 1957,
vol. 101, pp. 1-29.
MICHAELIS, ADOLF, 'Apoline e Marsia', Annali dell'
Instituto di Corrispondenza Archeologica, 1859, pp. 298ff.
MICHAELIS, ADOLF, Die Verurteilung des Marsyas auf einer
Vase aus Ruvo, Greifswald, F.W. Kunike, 1864.
MINAR, EDWIN L., Early Pythagorean Politics, Baltimore,
Waverly Press, 1942.
MOORE, J.M. Aristotle and Xenophon on Democracy and
Oligarchy, Berkeley, University of California Press,
1975.
MORETTI, LUIGI, Ricerche sulle leghe greche, Rome,
L'Erma di Bretschneider, 1962.
MORROW, GLENN R., Plato's Cretan City, Princeton
University Press, 1960.
MORROW, GLENN R., Plato's Epistles, Indianapolis, Bobbs-
Merrill, 1962.
Mostra dell' Etruria Padana e della Città di Spina,
vol. 1, Catalogo, Bologna, Alfa, 1960.
MÜLLER, MORITZ, Geschichte Thebens von der Einwanderung
der Boioter bis zur Schlacht bei Koroneia, Leipzig,
Pöschel & Trepte, 1879.
NILSSON, MARTIN, 'Das Ei im Totenkult der Alten', Archiv
für Religionswissenschaft, 1908, vol. 11, pp. 530-46.
OSTWALD, MARTIN, Nomos and the Beginnings of the Athenian
Democracy, Oxford, Clarendon Press, 1969.
PAGE, D.L., Corinna, London, Society for the Promotion
of Hellenic Studies, 1953.
PAGE, DENYS, Sappho and Alcaeus, Oxford, Clarendon Press,
1965.

PATRONI, G., review of Robinson, Olynthus, vol. 5,
Athenaeum, 1934, vol. 12, p. 167.
PEARSON, LIONEL, Plutarch's Moralia, vol. 11, London,
Heinemann, 1965.
PEDLEY, J.G., review of Ducat, Les Kouroi, in AJA, 1973,
vol. 77, pp. 238-40.
PELAGATTI, PAOLA, 'Vasi di fabbriche della Beozia',
ArchClass, 1959, vol. 11, pp. 70-6.
PELAGATTI, PAOLA, 'Nuovi vasi di fabbriche della Beozia',
ArchClass, 1962, vol. 14, pp. 29-41.
PETRAKOS, BASILEIOS, O Oropos kai to Hieron tou Amphiaraou,
Athens, Hellenike Archaioligike Hetaireia, 1968.
PFUHL, ERNST, Malerei und Zeichnung der Griechen, Munich,
F. Bruckmann, 1923.
PFUHL, ERNST, and MÖBIUS, H., Die ostgriechichen
Grabreliefs, Mainz, Von Zabern, 1977-9.
PHARAKLAS, N., review of needed archaeological work at
Thebes, AD, 1967, vol. 22, pt B-1, pp. 247ff.
PHILIP, J.A., Pythagoras and Early Pythagoreanism,
University of Toronto Press, 1966.
PHILIPPSON, A. and LEHMANN, H., Die Griechischen
Landschaften, vols 1 and 2, Frankfurt, Klostermann,
1950-9.
PICKARD-CAMBRIDGE, SIR ARTHUR, Dithyramb, Tragedy and
Comedy, 2nd edn revised by T.B.L. Webster, Oxford,
Clarendon Press, 1962.
POTTIER, EDMOND, 'Pourquoi Thésée fut l'ami d'Hercule',
Revue de l'Art ancien et modern, 1901, vol. 1, pp. 1-18.
POTTIER, EDMOND, Recueil Edmond Pottier, Paris, Boccard,
1937.
PUELMA, VON MARIO, 'Die Selbstbeschreibung des Chores
in Alkmans grossem Partheneion-Fragment', MH, 1977,
vol. 34, pp. 1-55.
RAUBITSCHEK, ISABELLE K., 'Early Boeotian potters',
Hesperia, 1966, vol. 35, pp. 154-65.
RAVEN, J.E., 'Polyclitus and Pythagoreanism', CQ, 1951,
n.s. vol. 1, pp. 147-52.
REECE, D.W., 'The battle of Tanagra', JHS, 1950, vol. 70,
pp. 75f.
ROHDE, ERWIN, 'Die Quellen des Jamblichus in seiner
Biographie des Pythagoras', RhM, 1872, vol. 27, pp. 23-61.
RICHTER, G.M.A. Archaic Gravestones of Attica, London,
Phaidon, 1961.
RIDGWAY, B.S., The Severe Style in Greek Sculpture,
Princeton University Press, 1970.
RIDGWAY, B.S., The Archaic Style in Greek Sculpture,
Princeton University Press, 1977.
ROBERTS, W. RHYS, The Ancient Boeotians, Cambridge
University Press, 1895.

ROBERTSON, N., 'The Thessalian expedition of 480 B.C.',
JHS, 1976, vol. 96, pp. 100-20.
ROBINSON, D.M., Excavations at Olynthus, vol. 5,
Baltimore, The Johns Hopkins Press, 1933; vol. 13,
Baltimore, The Johns Hopkins Press, 1950.
ROBINSON, D.M., HARCUM, C.G. and ILIFFE, J.H., Greek
Vases at Toronto, University of Toronto Press, 1930.
RODENWALDT, G., 'Thespische reliefs', JDAI, 1913, vol. 38,
pp. 309-39.
ROESCH, PAUL, Thespies et la Confédération Béotienne,
Paris, Boccard, 1965.
ROSE, H.J., 'The ancient grief', Greek Poetry and Life.
Essays presented to Gilbert Murray, Oxford, Clarendon
Press, 1936.
ROSE, H.J., review of Thummer, Die Religiosität Pindars,
in CR, 1959, vol. 9, pp. 321f.
ROSE, H.J., 'Heracles', OCD, 1970.
ROSTAGNI, A., 'Un nuovo capitolo della retorica e della
sofistica', Studi Italiani di Filologia Classica, 1922,
n.s. vol. 2, pp. 148-201.
RUMPF, A., 'Classical and post-classical Greek painting',
JHS, 1947, vol. 67, pp. 10-21.
SALMON, PIERRE, 'Les districts Béotiens', REA, 1956,
vol. 69, pp. 51-70.
SANCTIS, G. DE, 'La spedizione ellenica in Tessaglia
del 480 a.C.', RFIC, 1930, vol. 8, pp. 339-42.
SANDYS, J., ed., The Odes of Pindar, 2nd edn, London,
Heinemann, 1919.
SASSON, J.M., 'Canaanite maritime involvement in the
second millenium', Journal of the American Oriental
Society, 1966, vol. 86, pp. 126-38.
SCHACHTER, A., 'Some underlying cult patterns in Boeotia',
Proceedings of the First International Conference on
Boiotian Antiquities, Teiresias, 1972, suppl. 1, pp. 17-30.
SCHAUENBURG, K., 'Zu einigen böotischen Vasen des
sechsten Jahrhunderts', Jahrbuch des Römisch-Germanischen
Zentralmuseums Mainz, 1957, vol. 4, pp. 63-72.
SCHEFOLD, KARL, 'Untersuchungen zu den kertscher Vasen',
Archaeologische Mitteilungen aus russischen Sammlungen,
1934, vol. 4.
SCHEFOLD, KARL, 'Grabrelief eines Dichters', Antike
Kunst, 1958, vol. 1, pp. 69-74.
SCHEURLEER, C.W.L., 'Beiträge zur tarentinischen
Kunstgeschichte', Critica d'Arte, 1937, vol. 2, pp. 209-15.
SCHILD-XENIDOU, WASSILIKI, Boiotische Grab- und
Weihreliefs Archaischer und Klassischer Zeit, dissertation,
Munich University, 1972.
SCHLESINGER, KATHLEEN, The Greek Aulos, London, Methuen,
1939.

SCHMALTZ, BERNHARD, Terrakotten aus dem Kabirenheiligtum
bei Theben, Part 1, Berlin, de Gruyter, 1974.
SCHMALTZ, BERNHARD, Metallfiguren aus dem Kabirenheiligtum
bei Theben, Berlin, de Gruyter, 1980.
SCHOBER, F., 'Thebai (Boiotien)', RE, 1934, vol. 5A,
pt 2, cols 1423-92.
SCHWENN, 'Pindaros', RE, 1950, vol. 40, col. 1671.
SEEBERG, ALEX, Corinthian Komos Vases, University of
London Institute of Classical Studies Bulletin, 1971,
suppl. 27.
SEGAL, C.P., 'Pebbles in Golden Urns', Eranos, 1975,
pp. 1-8.
SELLERS, EUGÉNIE, The Elder Pliny's Chapters on the
History of Art, tr. Jex-Blake, London, Macmillan, 1896.
SHERWIN-WHITE, SUSAN M., Ancient Cos, Göttingen,
Vandenhoeck & Ruprecht, 1978.
SLATER, W.J., 'Pindar's House', GRBS, 1971, vol. 12,
pp. 141-52.
SOLMSEN, FRIEDRICH, Hesiod and Aeschylus, Ithaca, Cornell
University Press, 1949.
SORDI, MARTA, 'La Tessaglia dalle Guerre Persiane alla
Spedizione di Leotichida', Rendiconti Instituto Lombardo
di Scienze e Lettere, Classe di Lettere e Scienze Morale,
1953, vol. 86, pp. 305-11.
SORDI, MARTA, 'Mitologia e propaganda nella Beozia
arcaica', Atene e Roma, 1966, vol. 11, pp. 15-24.
SPARKES, B.A., 'The taste of a Boeotian pig', JHS, 1967,
vol. 87, pp. 116-30.
SWOBODA, HEINRICH, 'Emmenidai', RE, 1905, vol. 10,
cols 2498-500.
TAYLOR, A.E., Varia Socratica, Oxford, J. Parker, 1911.
TAYLOR, A.E., A Commentary on Plato's Timaeus, Oxford,
Clarendon Press, 1928.
TAYLOR, A.E., Plato, 6th edn, London, Methuen, 1963.
THÖNGES-STRINGARIS, RHEA, N., 'Das griechische Totenmahl',
AM, 1965, vol. 80, pp. 1-99.
THOMPSON, DOROTHY, review of Schmaltz, Die Terrakotten ...
in AJA, 1975, vol. 79, pp. 382-4.
THREPSIADIS, J., 'E epanekthesis tou Mouseiou Thebon',
AE, 1963, pp. 13-15.
THUMMER, ERICH, Die Religiosität Pindars, Innsbruck,
Wagner, 1957.
THUMMER, ERICH, Pindar. Die Isthmischen Gedichte, vol. 2,
Heidelberg, C. Winter, 1968-9.
TOD, M.N., Greek Historical Inscriptions, 2 vols, Oxford,
Clarendon Press, 1933-48.
TUCKER, T.C., The Seven Against Thebes of Aeschylus,
Cambridge University Press, 1908.
ULRICHS, H.N., Reisen und Forschungen in Griechenland,
2 vols, Bremen, J.G. Heyse, 1848-63.

UNGER, G.F., 'Zur Geschichte der Pythagoreier',
Sitzungberichte der königlichen bayerischen Akademie der
Wissenschaften zu München, phil.-hist. Classe, 1883,
pp. 140-92.
URE, ANNIE D., 'Boeotian geometricising vases', JHS,
1929, vol. 49, pp. 160-71.
URE, ANNIE D., 'More Boeotian geometricising vases', JHS,
1935, vol. 55, pp. 227-8.
URE, ANNIE D., 'Some provincial black-figure workshops',
BSA, 1940-5, vol. 41, pp. 22-8.
URE, ANNIE D., 'Koes', JHS, 1951, vol. 71, pp. 194-7.
URE, ANNIE D., 'Boeotian vases with women's heads', AJA,
1953, vol. 57, pp. 245-9.
URE, ANNIE D., 'A Boeotian krater in Trinity College,
Cambridge', JHS, 1957, vol. 77, pp. 314-15.
URE, ANNIE D., 'The Argos Painter and the Painter of the
Dancing Pan', AJA, 1958, vol. 62, pp. 389-95.
URE, ANNIE, D., 'Two groups of floral black-figure',
Bulletin of the Institute of Classical Studies, London,
1961, vol. 8, pp. 1-6.
URE, ANNIE D., 'Boeotian pottery from the Athenian Agora',
Hesperia, 1962, vol. 31, pp. 369-77.
URE, PERCY NEVILLE, 'Excavations at Rhitsona in Boeotia',
BSA, 1907-8, vol. 14, pp. 266-318.
URE, PERCY NEVILLE, Sixth and Fifth Century Pottery from
Rhitsona, London, Oxford University Press, 1927.
URE, PERCY NEVILLE, Aryballoi and Figurines from Rhitsona
in Boeotia, Cambridge University Press, 1934.
URE, PERCY NEVILLE, and BURROWS, R.M., 'Excavations at
Rhitsona in Boeotia', JHS, 1909, vol. 29, pp. 308-53.
URE, PERCY NEVILLE and URE, A.D., Corpus Vasorum
Antiquorum, Great Britain #12, London, Oxford University
Press, 1954.
VACANO, OTFRIED VON, Zur Entstehung und Deutung gemalter
seitenansichtiger Kopfbilder auf schwarzfigurigen Vasen
des griechischen Festlandes, Bonn, R. Habelt, 1973.
VERMEULE, C.C., Greek, Etruscan and Roman Art. The
Classical Collection of the Museum of Fine Arts, Boston,
Museum of Fine Arts, 1963.
VERMEULE, E., 'Kadmos and the Dragon', Studies Presented
to George M.A. Hanfmann, Mainz, Ph. von Zabern, 1971.
VIAN, FRANCIS, Les Origins de Thèbes. Cadmos et les
Spartes, Paris, Klincksieck, 1963.
VOGEL, C.J. DE, Pythagoras and Early Pythagoreanism,
Assen, Van Gorcum, 1966.
VOGELSANG, HEINRICH, Theben und Boiotien, dissertation,
Heidelberg University, 1949.
VOLLGRAFF, W., 'Deux stèles de Thèbes', BCH, 1902, vol. 26,
pp. 554-70.

WALKER, E.M., 'Athens and the Greek powers, 462-445 B.C.',
CAH, Cambridge University Press, 1927, vol. 5, pp. 68-95.
WALLACE, W.P., 'The early coinages of Athens and Euboia',
NumChron, 1962, 7th series, vol. 2, pp. 23-42.
WALTERS, H.B., 'Odysseus and Kirke on a Boeotian vase',
JHS, 1892-93, vol. 13, pp. 77-87.
WARDMAN, ALAN, Plutarch's Lives, Berkeley, University of
California Press, 1974.
WEICKER, G., 'Henioche', RE, 1912, vol. 15, col. 258.
WEST, M.L., 'Corinna', CQ, 1970, vol. 20, pp. 277-87.
WILAMOWITZ-MOELLENDORFF, ULRICH VON, De Euripidis
Heraclidis, Greifswald, F.G. Kunike, 1882.
WILAMOWITZ-MOELLENDORFF, ULRICH VON, 'Die sieben Thore
Thebens', Hermes, 1891, vol. 26, pp. 191-242.
WILAMOWITZ-MOELLENDORFF, ULRICH VON, 'Apollon', Hermes,
1903, vol. 38, pp. 575-80.
WILAMOWITZ-MOELLENDORFF, ULRICH VON, Pindaros, Berlin,
Weidmann, 1922.
WILL, ÉDOUARD, Korinthiaka, Paris, Boccard, 1955.
WILLEMSEN, FRANZ, 'Stelen', AM, 1970, vol. 85, pp.30-4.
WINTER, FRANZ, Die Typen der Figürlichen Terrakotten,
vol. 1, Berlin, W. Spemann, 1903.
WOLOCH, M., 'Athenian trainers in the Aeginetan odes of
Pindar and Bacchylides', CW, 1963, vol. 56, pp. 102-4.
WOLTERS, PAUL, 'Das Kabirenheiligtum bei Theben', AM,
1890, vol. 15, pp. 355-67.
WOLTERS, PAUL and BRUNS, GERDA, Das Kabirenheiligtum
bei Theben, vol. 1, Berlin, de Gruyter, 1940.
WYCHERLEY, R.E., How the Greeks Built Cities, London,
Macmillan, 1962.
YOUNG, DAVID C., Three Odes of Pindar, Leiden, E.J.
Brill, 1968.
YOUNG, DAVID C., Pindar's Isthmian 7, Myth and Exempla,
Leiden, E.J. Brill, 1971.
ZIEGLER, KONRAT, Plutarchos von Chaironeia, Stuttgart,
J.B. Metzler, 1949.
ZIEHEN, L., 'Thebai (Boiotien)', RE, 1934, vol. 5, pt 2,
cols 1492-553.

General Index

Achaea, 39
Aegina, 29, 30, 126
agora, 12-15, 42, 128, 139
Akragas, 29f., 30f., 89, 156
Alcibiades, 3, 65, 88
Alcman, 89, 93, 128
Alkmene, 12, 51, 55, 69, 78
Alkmeonides, 62, 126
Alxenor, stele of, 108
Amphiarios, 23, 58
Amphion and Zethus, 13, 55-7, 87, 147
Amphitryon, 48, 51
Amphotto, stele of, 109
Anaxandros, 22
Aphrodite, 12, 48, 53f.
Apollo, 59-61, 88f.; Delios, 61, 126; Ismenios, 23, 48, 54, 59f., 162f.; Ptoios, 23, 59, 61f., 126; Rescuer, 13, 62; Spondios, 62
archaism, 108, 109, 110, 118, 125
Argos cup painter, 117, 120; workshop, 122
Arignote, 132
Aristeides, 42, 114f., 118, 127, 164
Aristion, stele of, 107
aristocracy, 90-8
Aristophanes comicus, 96f., 129

Aristophanes of Boeotia, 21, 22
Aristoxenos, 70, 81, 82, 150f., 153 n. 28
Artemis, 51; Eukleia, 13, 139
Asopodoros, 28
Asphodikos, 12, 58
Athena, 89; Girder, 13; Onca, 48, 54; Pronoia, 59, 62; Zosterias, 48, 51
Athens, 44; bias against Thebes, 3, 89; confederacy, 37; control over Boeotia, 10, 35, 126; funerary stelai, 106-10; and the flute, 88f.; Kabeirion vases at, 123; literary forms, 85; oligarchy of 411, 39; reassessment of homosexuality, 95-8; relations with Thebes during Peloponnesian war, 122f.; and Speeches of Pythagoras, 135; women in, 100, 128, 129
Attic vases, 117-19, 121, 125, 136
Attiginos, 25f.

Boeotian league, 15, 17, 35, 37f., 40, 42f., 71, 126, 127, 131

Ugarit, 52f., 146

walls, 12, 15, 142; of
    Kadmeia, 8; lower walls,
    8, 12, 31f., 87; of
    Thespiae dismantled by
    Thebes, 42

Warrior stele, 107f.
woman's head vases, 119f.,
    122f., 129f., 131, 165,
    166
women, 15, 54, 98-102, 110,
    113, 127-9, 131;
    Pythagoreanism and women,
    129, 132-5
Woikonos, stele of, 111,
    114

Index of Ancient Authors

Aelian: NA 6.15, 95i., 157;
NA 12.5, 145
Aeschines, Ag. Timarchos,
96
Aschylus: Seven Against
Thebes, 63; Seven 105,
54, 146; Seven 570, 147
Alcman: Frag. 1, 50-2, 159;
Frag. 3, 159
Antonius Liberalis,
Metamorphoses 29, 145
Apollodorus: 1.4.2, 154;
1.9.2, 146; 2.4.11, 148;
2.5.5, 57; 2.4.12, 159;
2.5.11, 159; 3.4.2,
158; 3.4.2-3, 146
Aristophanes: Ach., 3;
Ach. 860ff., 125, 136,
138, 156; Clouds, 75-7,
98; Eccl. 111-20, 158;
Eccl. 243-4, 158;
Eccl. 446ff., 134;
Frogs, 136; Lys.1123-7,
100; Peace 1004f, 138,
156; Frag.488, 114, 164
Aristophon, Frags 4-5, 114,
164
Aristotle: Ath. Pol., 30;
Pol.1252b15ff., 93;
Pol.1252b25ff., 93;
Pol.1274a32-1274b4, 92,
95, 156, 157; Pol.1278a25-
6, 10, 138, 143;
Pol.1302b29, 34;

Pol.1321a9-12, 9;
Pol.1341a27-35, 154;
Pol.1341b4, 154;
Rhet.1398b9ff., 153
Aristoxenus: Frag.28(FGH),
153
Athenaeus: I.19Bf., 90;
II.22C, 87f.; V.184D,
154; V.184E, 155;
X.417B-428B, 138;
XIV.616Eff., 154;
XIV.621D, 66, 150;
XIV.631E, 154

Cicero: De leg. II,26,64,
160; De leg. II,26,64,
160
Corinna: Frag. 654.23-4,
105; Frag. 655, 98;
Frag. 664a, 104, 158;
Frag. 684, 154;
Frag. 695a, 158

Dio Chrysostom: Orat.7
(I.136 Dindorf), 86;
Orat.37(II.297-8 Dindorf),
114
Diodorus Siculus: 11.3.2,
141; 11.4.7, 21;
11.9.1, 22; 11.9.2, 22;
11.28, 24; 11.79, 31;
11.79.4-83.4, 32;